3

Fusilier Geordie

Fusilier Geordie

Tales from The Fifth,
(Royal Northumberland) Fusiliers 1944 to 1968

Based on stories and suggestions by
Colonel Paddy Baxter
and contributions from Fifth Fusiliers

Compiled, edited and written by
Captain John Masters

With cartoons from
Fusilier Reg Smyth
and Fusilier Preston Little

The Pentland Press
Edinburgh – Cambridge – Durham – USA

First published in 1997 by
The Pentland Press Ltd
1 Hutton Close
South Church
Bishop Auckland
Durham

Typeset by Carnegie Publishing, 18 Maynard St, Preston
Printed and bound by Bookcraft, Bath

Contents

Appendices

Illustrations

Acknowledgements

This book was started to give Lieutenant Colonel Paddy Baxter an occupation after his accident. Much of what is written is set round the time from when he joined the First Battalion, at Warminster, to the time he left in Aden, where he was Second in Command of the Battalion.

Most contributors only sent their efforts because it was to be 'Paddy's book'. Many incidents revolve round 'the officer with the big black moustache'. Whilst there is no chapter devoted solely to Paddy there would have been no book without him. Although he was unable to type, and therefore could not take the book through its early stages, it was, nevertheless, through his leadership, his help and his unfailing good humour that this book was finished. He was able to dictate his contributions both to his daughter-in-law, Georgia, and on tape to me. These have been more than a valuable part of the book, and have made it what it is. It started as 'Paddy's book' and it is still 'Paddy's book'.

I owe much to the contributors who are listed at the back of the book and to many others who suggested pieces. I must pay thanks to my wife who corrected, when she could, my poor English and punctuation. She also typed and retyped many pages, did all the initial work on the index and much of the initial proof reading. Paddy too did much of the proof reading and has been responsible with Captain Peter Marr and Major Alan Hill for getting the book published and printed.

The book is dedicated to those who served with the Royal Northumberland Fusiliers, otherwise known as 'the Fifth Fusiliers', 'the Old and Bold', 'the Shiners' or 'the Fighting and Never Failing Fifth'. To the crude, it was also known as 'the Fighting and F——ing Fifth'.

Any profits from the book will be paid into Fifth Fusilier Charities.

John Walton Masters
Ex-Fifth Fusiliers
Editor, Joint Author and Compiler
1 March 1997

Foreword

by
General Sir John Akehurst KCB CBE
(Formerly Northamptonshire Regiment)

'Paddy's Book', as one joint author chooses to call it, is fun; but it's more than that. It is a tribute to Paddy Baxter's own spirit and courage in maintaining a sense of humour and of the ridiculous despite his forced immobility. It is also an expression of what a Regiment means to those who have had the honour to belong to and serve in one, a source of wonder and perhaps envy to those who have not.

The British Army is famous for its resilience in the face of adversity, its capacity to recover from disaster and its ability to draw entertainment from calamity and fiasco. Anyone who has not served may be forgiven for wondering how the catalogue of cock-ups in the Royal Northumberland Fusiliers, here faithfully recorded by loyal members of varying ranks, can yet allow them to take fierce pride in every aspect of the Regiment. Equally, much of the humour and the stories will be incomprehensible to soldiers of another era who might indeed find some of it hard to believe. Those, like me, who served in the National Service army of the 1950s will believe every word – well, nearly every word.

The real tragedy behind this regimental anthology is that the Regiment no longer exists. It was an early casualty of the continous and continuing reduction of the infantry over fifty years and is but one example of the lobbying and vacillation which has created the present hotch-potch of 'large' and 'small' regiments. Happily the same spirit of pride and professionalism that also springs from these pages has somehow brought today's infantry through its travails to continuing excellence and professionalism despite the depredations and ingratitude of successive governments.

The hero, throughout, is the Geordie, a mystery to most of us, even, it seems, to some of his officers, but mostly a fine, loyal and brave soldier, bemused though he may have been by some of his officers, and sometimes the worse (or better) for copious consumption of Newcastle Brown Ale.

Paddy's Book is a greatly entertaining medley from the closing years of a famous Regiment. It wasn't then the best in the world – mine was! – but it is perfectly summed up by ex-Fusilier Reg Smythe's Andy Capp cartoon on page 2. We can say what we like about the Regiment, but you knock it at your peril. That's what it's all about.

J. B. A.
Warminster
March 1997

Introduction

This is the story of the last twenty-four years of the Royal Northumberland Fusiliers, a regiment that joined the British Army in 1674 at the Restoration. It is told, 'warts and all', in a series of anecdotes. It has been difficult to thread them together into a coherent narrative except that the stories are, in the main, in chronological order. Everyone who served with the Fifth Fusiliers considered that they were in the best regiment in the British Army and, therefore, the world. The few stories that do not show the Regiment in the best of light are the exceptions that proved the rule.

It is hoped that this book gives a small insight into the life of an extraordinary infantry regiment. The loyalty of the Fusiliers to their fellows, their non-commissioned officers, their officers, their section, their platoon, their company and their regiment was astonishing. The many good officers returned this loyalty in full. They knew that loyalty went both ways. Fortunately, in the Fifth Fusiliers, only a few bad officers took this loyalty for granted. Loud calls or references to loyalty, like calls and references to patriotism, got Fusiliers checking their kit for missing items. If loyalty was deserved, it was given without asking.

The years 1944 to 1968 were a time of great political and social change. Changes in the social structure, the loss of an empire, the lowering of Britain's status to that of a second league power and economic problems had their effect on the Army. Limitations in the quality and quantity of the British Army's equipment in Korea and the time taken to get our forces to assemble for Suez showed the Army, Britain and the world that things had to change. This meant that a 'Wind of Change' had to sweep through the Army but, being a conservative organisation, change came slowly and there was resistance in the middle-aged middle ranks. The Fifth was not immune from this and the first manifestation was the merging of the First and Second Battalions, whom some thought came from different armies, and finally, the emergence of the Royal Regiment of Fusiliers.

The mental resistance to change showed itself in little ways. There were those who preferred to wear the distinctive side hat in preference to the dull service dress hat or, horror of horrors, a beret even if it did have a red and white hackle. The saga of the officers' regimental shirt was another illustration. From 1952 to 1962 new colonels, seconds in command, returning pear-shaped majors and adjutants all had their views on the 'correct regimental shirt'. Majors would suffer from extreme apoplexy if they saw a young officer wearing what he considered to be the 'wrong shirt' and impecunious subalterns would be instructed to obtain the correct apparel, which happened

Reproduced with the kind permission of (4270927) Ex-Fusilier Reg Smyth and Mirror Group Newspapers.

to be the same as that worn by the now purple-faced major. Regimental tailors could have bought Jaguars on the profits of producing the 'right shirt', the pattern and colour of which would change in direct proportion to the faulty memory of incoherent majors, depending on whether these officers originated from the First or Second Battalion. When Colonel Robert ended the battle, some officers had no fewer than five versions of the 'correct Fifth Fusilier Officer's shirt' in their military chests waiting, in vain, for the resurrection of patterns 1, 2, 3, or 4.

The Regiment, like the rest of the Army, was involved in the question of whether it was to be run in three different ways. Was it to be on pre-war lines, with officers spending most of their non-combat postings in the pursuit of country sports, along the lines of the First Battalion's 'wealthy, brilliant and gifted' approach? Was it to be run like a perpetual Territorial Army two-week camp? Or was it to be really professional, as 'the Second Battalion was run'? A typical Fifth Fusilier fudge was the answer – it was to be really professional in the run-up to or in times of combat, and muddle through at other times.

However, young single officers, who were living in the Mess, were expected by married majors to live a 'proper Mess life' even though the latter only lived in when they were waiting for an absent wife. These married officers waxed lyrical on the benefits of mess life as they vaguely remembered it, safe in the knowledge they would not have to enjoy it for any extended period. This was not appreciated by living-in officers who looked on the Mess as their home and there was the occasional 'mutiny'.

Throughout these goings on, Fusilier Geordie watched with an air of stoic tolerance and a feeling of slight bemusement. What his mad officers did was quite inexplicable and part of the great army chocolate box of life. What did it matter if the outer trappings were peculiar, provided he got his Newcastle Brown Ale at reasonable intervals and the Sergeant Major did not know him too well?

This book is not a Regimental History in the accepted sense. We are sure that others will write of the great campaigns, and use John Winn's wonderful account of the Battle of the Imjin and other historical documents. We hope the reader may enjoy this series of what we see as amusing anecdotes of an era, written by those who suffered, enjoyed, were exasperated by, and lived the period of comradeship we called 'service with the Fifth Fusiliers'.

Chapter I

Joining the Regiment

After the war, when regiments were reducing to their peacetime establishment, Gerald Style had to look for employment in another regiment. He therefore asked Lord Stratheden of the Coldstream Guards for advice on where he should go. Lord Stratheden suggested the Oxford and Buckinghamshire Light Infantry, the Fifth Fusiliers or the Royal Norfolks, all of which had been in Guards Brigades either in the Eighth Army or in North-West Europe. Not being too keen on the physical exertion of the Light Infantry march, he decided to try the Fifth Fusiliers and wrote to General Herbert, the Colonel of the Regiment. General Herbert asked Major Ben Van der Gucht, who commanded the Fifth Machine-Gun Company in the Guards Armoured Division, if he knew of this Gerald Style. He was told, 'Oh I know him, he plays the piano'. This was, apparently, good enough for the General.

So Gerald Style found himself with the need to change uniform, and went to see Major Derek Lloyd, who was his senior officer at the liaison section at RAF West Raynham. Derek Lloyd was of little help, saying that the Fifth wore anything. After some research, the problem resolved itself into acquiring the NF title, the small-sized pips and the highly distinctive red V worn on the sleeve of one's battledress, although the tendency was for officers to wear their own variations on an original theme.

When Gerald Style first joined the Second Battalion in Gibraltar in 1947, Reggie Pratt used to wear the most superior cavalry twill service dress in a sort of a light buff colour, while Robert Ferguson was not far behind with a magnificent collection of plain clothes which were made for his father some 40 years earlier. These he wore with immaculate 'grace and favour'.

Paddy Baxter was commissioned in 1945 into the Argyll and Sutherland Highlanders, but was immediately attached to the Rajput Regiment for two years. When the Raj came to an end in India he received a regular commission in the Fifth Fusiliers, but under the then rules of the Yorkshire and Northumbrian Brigade, was posted to the Duke of Wellington's Regiment in the Sudan, and then York, until March 1950.

In April 1950, he joined the First Battalion, Fifth Fusiliers in Warminster and was posted to Z Company, where to his delight he discovered Sergeant Clarke who had been his platoon sergeant in the Sudan. Prior to the first morning's muster parade, Sergeant Clarke gave advice to Paddy on exactly what his duties to the platoon would be, whereupon the young officer replied, 'Whose platoon is this anyway?' and received the answer, 'It is mine, sir,' and the situation returned very much to exactly how it had been in the Sudan.

4

Paddy had forgotten, that is, if at that stage he ever knew, that senior NCOs and warrant officers have the same responsibility for bringing up young officers as royal nannies do to bring up princes and princesses. They have no desire to join the almighty, but they are going to be perfectly certain that the almighty know how to behave themselves.

Unfortunately, Paddy had not hoisted in the full message when, one lovely summer's morning, he and the Company Sergeant Major took the company for a beautiful day's work on the ranges at Mere. There was the usual 40 minutes' fight with the range telephone, an instrument of communication last used by Noah when talking to the dove. When this had been made to work properly, the Sergeant Major took over the firing point, organized the men into details and in the view of Baxter, removed all sense of command from him. At that point an altercation took place between the Sergeant Major and Baxter as to who was responsible for what on the range. This finished with the Sergeant Major saying, 'In that case, I might as well go home,' and he was cordially invited by Baxter to do whatever he wished, providing he did not get under Baxter's feet on the range. The Sergeant Major saluted and returned in anger to Knook Camp.

The day continued beautifully for the young Baxter, high scores were made, the men on duty in the butts sang little songs to show their pleasure at being so involved in such interesting work, while the blackbirds sang in the hedgerows. The young master returned to barracks full of high spirits and in the certain knowledge that he would be met by a delighted Company Commander for such a useful day. In fact, he was met by Major John Winn who appeared to be half a degree from apoplectic. He ordered Baxter into his office and slammed the door behind him. It is as well that what was said from the senior to the junior has never been fully recorded, but it boiled down to the fact that Baxter was a bloody young stuck-up snob without the like of whom Winn could easily do, and the company would be run much better by a good Sergeant Major than by condescending upstarts.

Again, Baxter had run across that narrow boundary between who is in charge and who should carry out his responsibilities correctly. Some do not believe that the hole in Z Company roof has been properly repaired since that day, and Baxter feels about half an inch high every time he passes the camp on the way to Salisbury, even now.

St George's Gazette does not record Ronnie Cowe's arrival in the First Battalion from Sandhurst in 1950, such was the confusion and uncertainty of the time, as the Battalion absorbed its contingents of Reservists and 'K' Volunteers to bring it up to strength for Korea. He arrived at Bury St Edmunds where all this was happening and made his way to the Officers' Mess at Blenheim Barracks at about teatime. There were few people about as he found his way around, but he was soon joined by a distinguished looking officer dressed, like him, in civilian clothes. Ronnie Cowe took him to be very senior and kept his peace as did the other officer for a while.

Having finished his cup of tea, the distinguished officer glanced at Ronnie Cowe and asked, 'Just joined?'

'Yes, sir,' Ronnie Cowe replied.

'So have I. You and I have lots of people to get to know.' And with that the distinguished officer rose and left. As Ronnie Cowe was soon to learn, this was Lieutenant Colonel Kingsley Foster, the new Commanding Officer, and he was to meet him again rather sooner than he expected.

Ronnie Cowe's stay at Bury St Edmunds was a brief interlude before attending young officers' courses at Hythe and Warminster, and he was posted to X Company, under Major Reggie Pratt, where he was to be available for odd jobs. One assignment was to be in charge of 20 drivers detailed to travel down to an Ordnance Depot in Middlesex to collect the Battalion's allocation of jeeps for Korea. They travelled by 3-tonner, 20 drivers for the jeeps and a REME Staff Sergeant in case of breakdown and as adviser on the takeover of the vehicles. This aspect of military knowledge had not been covered at Sandhurst. They were to return that day in convoy.

The vehicles were duly taken over but it turned out that the assignment also included the CO's Humber staff car, a great lumbering machine. The Staff Sergeant wisely suggested that they should winch one of the jeeps into the 3-tonner and then he would drive Ronnie Cowe in the staff car.

'No need,' said Ronnie Cowe, making his first command decision. 'I shall drive the staff car myself.' After what he thought was a very adequate drivers' briefing, they set off in convoy.

There were far too many vehicles but the intrepid Ronnie Cowe led off the column which soon got split up at traffic lights and in general congestion, finally breaking up into small groups. Ronnie Cowe's leading role came to an end in Oxford where he ran into the back of a bus. Amazingly, all the other vehicles straggled back to the barracks by about 2 a.m. where the MTO, an irate Captain Jumbo Wilson, was waiting to give Ronnie Cowe a rocket with the promise that Ronnie Cowe would be asked to explain to the CO how it had come about that his new staff car had buckled mudguards.

Thus it was that Ronnie Cowe was formally introduced to Colonel Kingsley Foster in his office – an inauspicious start! Colonel Foster enquired how fast he had been going at the time of the collision.

'Oh, not more than twenty m.p.h., sir.'

'Well, whatever speed it was, it was evidently too fast. Fortunately, I have no intention of using a Humber staff car in Korea.'

The incident passed off to Ronnie Cowe's relief. He had learned some useful lessons – always listen to advice from senior NCOs, how to fill in an accident report and the major elements of road convoy procedure.

Ronnie Cowe saw Colonel Kingsley Foster only once again. Not long before the Imjin battle the Colonel visited X Company's position.

'Well, my boy, how are you enjoying your first war?' he asked.

'It is very interesting, sir.'

'After a while, the interest value fades,' he was told.

Nearly 40 years later, Colonel Ronnie Cowe was enjoying seasonal mince pies and mulled wine with the congregation of the Chapel Royal at Hampton Court when he got into conversation with a young man and talk turned to Army connections. He learnt that the young man was Colonel Foster's grandson and he was reminded of these brief encounters.

Most new recruits joined at Fenham Barracks in Newcastle-upon-Tyne. Here Geordies realized with a shock that their officers spoke a different language and often did not understand what the new recruit was saying. The recruit training period was a time of adjustment where new officers tuned in to the local dialect and Geordie moderated his speech so that officers could understand him.

Corporal Mills, when he joined in 1952, first went into a recruiting office on Sandyford Road, Barras Bridge, Newcastle. Being a pitman he did not have to join up, but he felt that Korea was safer than his pit, and he was persuaded by his mate, Harry Heron, to join. Having passed his medical, he was asked which Corps he wished to join and said the RNFs. Much to his astonishment, the Recruiting Officer tried to dissuade him but, because he was a pitman, he did not have to join and it was the Fusiliers or nothing, besides his grandfather was in the Fusiliers in the First World War. The manager at the pit blew a gasket when he was told.

The big day was 17 November 1952. His mother gave him a good breakfast and he said his goodbyes. His father said little except, 'Just wait until you've got to get up in the morning.'

An hour later he was in Fenham Barracks being issued sheets and blankets. He was then taken to the top floor of one of the blocks where he met six others waiting for the next intake. The first morning was a shock. Mills was never one for getting up early, and he discovered that if you did not get up early the water was cold. From then on he got up at 0530 Army-time, middle of the night civilian time, just to get hot water. The next day he was issued with his webbing, denim fatigues and his boots. By this time he had got to know the other lads who helped to sort out his kit, although he had some idea as he had been an army cadet. Even though they had not been issued with their battledress, they still had to muster behind the rest of the Depot under the eagle eye of RSM Jock Snell.

After getting up early with nothing to do, Fusilier Mills decided that a visit to the cookhouse in Sandhurst Block was in order. He made his presence known to the two cooks preparing breakfast and was given a couple of jobs to do. As a reward, the cooks told him to help himself to half a dozen sausages, bacon and egg sandwiches and waterbottles full of hot tea. These he took to his mates back in the barrack room which made him very popular. He did this during the whole of his stay at Fenham Barracks and it was made easier as his squad was billeted in Sandhurst Block above the dining room.

Once the new intake was assembled, the next two months were hectic. They were getting fit doing weapon training, drill, marching and generally run off their feet by the training company staff, all of which was in the middle of winter. However, they made the Depot staff suffer later. On New Year's Eve, they drank the NAAFI dry and drove a baby Austin round and round the square with 50 of the new recruits trying to get into it. The guard was called out, the Sergeants' Mess was called out, even the Officers' Mess was called out. The next morning, at 0530, the recruits were called out in PT kit and sent on a run, but they laughed it off. It was great, they knew they had become a fighting unit, one for all and all for one in the true spirit of the Royal Northumberland Fusiliers.

The day of the passing-out parade came, and for the recruits this was the moment of truth after all those hours on the parade ground. They mustered in the gymnasium and were brought to attention for the inspection. They were then given a lecture on how well they had done and told that they were the best intake ever to set foot in Fenham Barracks. The inspecting officer was right because they knew they were the best. To remember the occasion they had their photographs taken and were sent away on a week's leave prior to being sent to the First Battalion.

NCOs explained to recruits that officers were a little odd and it was no use trying to understand them. During a period of flu, most of the Depot Mess Staff were laid low and a recruit was persuaded to act as a mess waiter for one night. John Webb, the Depot Commander, was the only officer in that evening and the new mess waiter served him dinner. This started with pudding, followed by soup, followed by cheese and then roast beef. John ate this stoically, but at the end of the meal asked the mess waiter why he served the meal in this order. He said he thought it was the right order for officers. When John asked him how he would serve it at home, he said, 'Soup, beef, pudding and then cheese.' John did not pursue the matter; perhaps the waiter had heard that the Queen eats fish with two forks.

Joining from Sandhurst in the 1950s, involved a visit in Camberley to the Regimental tailor. This was a battle between what the tailor said you needed, some out-of-date information from the Regimental representative, what you really did need and the meagre clothing allowance the Army gave you. Often parents had to stump up for the extras and the author certainly had one or two articles he never wore.

One officer, with perhaps more money than sense (George Connolly said of him that he had to pick him up after he had tripped over his wallet), told the tailor when asked what he needed, 'Everything, like everyone else'. This was too good to be true for the Regimental tailor. The officer was supplied with dress coats, dress swords, cocked hat, two forms of overcoat, 16 shirts (of varying patterns – the one wise purchase), tropical uniforms, ski uniforms, puttees and everything one could think of.

Danny Seidl and John Masters joined the Fifth in February 1954. An astute clerk had discovered that they had both been born in Egypt. They were from then on called the 'Egyptian Officers' by the soldiers, although not to their faces, of course. Both had somewhat tenuous connections with the Fifth Fusiliers. Danny Seidl was related by marriage to some serving officers as a result of the First Battalion's time in Egypt before the war. The First Battalion was sent to Egypt as a punishment for nearly burning down Barbados in the mid-1930s and were only allowed twenty-four hours in Southampton to change ships before going on to Alexandria. However, they certainly made the best of their posting as Alexandria was a delightful cosmopolitan community, with plenty of very good-looking girls. John Masters's connection was through his father who had been a wartime soldier with the Fifth in the First World War before going to Alexandria as a lawyer in the mixed courts. After the war John Masters's father had stayed in the Army, on the legal side, before being invalided out as a major/acting brigadier, but still on the books of the Fifth. Brigadier is a funny rank which used to be Brigadier General (one-star general in the US Army), one of the peculiar hierarchy of general officer ranks. Why a Major General is junior to a Lieutenant General goes back to the time when the former was a Sergeant Major General.

Before Danny Seidl and John Masters were sent on their Young Officer courses at Hythe and Warminster they were posted to the Depot. Danny, having parents and other interests of a more personal kind in the Camberley area, was sent on leave. John Masters, without a base, with his parents in Singapore, and seventeen shillings and sixpence a day being insufficient to give much scope for expensive hotels and holidays, stayed at the Depot. He was given some duties that the other more senior officers thought would suit a callow young officer of no experience. In view of his plump appearance it was thought he would have an interest in food, and so he was made Depot Messing Officer. Full of the need to carry out his duties to the best of his limited abilities, he went to inspect the kitchens. He asked the Cook Sergeant what the soldiers were having for lunch that day. One of the items on the menu was soup. John Masters thought that this would be a good start for his investigations and enquired how the Cook Sergeant proposed to prepare this delicacy. He was led to some very large boxes and the Cook Sergeant indicated that he proposed to make the soup from the powder that was contained in the boxes. When the Cook Sergeant was asked what the powder was he looked at John Masters as if he must be some sort of idiot.

'It's soup, sir.' Like many sergeants of long standing, the emphasis on the 'Sir' left little doubt of the sergeant's thoughts as to the mental capacity of the very junior officer he was addressing.

'Soup, eh, but what sort of soup?'

'Soup, sir.' The 'Sir' was now verging on the insolent and John Masters's dignity demanded more explanation.

'Perhaps, Sergeant, you did not hear me correctly. I asked what sort of soup.'

'Sir, I am not inflicted with a hearing defect. I did hear you correctly. This is just soup.'

John Masters was then shown three very small containers. One had a green powder, the second a red powder and the third a brown powder. If one wanted to make pea soup, green powder was added. For tomato soup the red powder was added and the brown was for the Brown Windsor Soup. This was 1954, army food and mass catering have improved considerably since then, one hopes, although a visit to a motorway service station sometimes leaves doubts.

John Masters learned a valuable lesson one day at the hands of Dick Blenkinsop when he took a phone call at Recruit Company Office sometime after 9 a.m. It was the Adjutant, Tony Perrins, who wanted to speak to Dick Blenkinsop, the Recruit Company Commander. 'He is not in yet,' John Masters informed the Adjutant and thought no more of it. Tony Perrins told Dick Blenkinsop what John Masters had said sometime later, and John was duly carpeted by the irate Company Commander. 'Never say that someone is not in yet to Headquarters or indeed anyone, even, or perhaps particularly, that someone's wife. Just, "he is not here just now. Can I take a message?"' The lesson – no Fusilier officer must ever go even near to dropping another 'brother' Fusilier officer in the mire.

In early 1955, after their post-Sandhurst Hythe and Warminster courses, John Oakley and David Thompson joined the Depot at Fenham Barracks before they were due to join the First Battalion in Kenya. Major Alistair Neilson commanded, Colonel Reggie Pratt was Regimental Secretary, Tony Perrins was Adjutant and Dick Blenkinsop commanded the Training Company, with David Welch and Richard Gordon-Steward as training officers. The latter were detailed to look after the new pair and, in particular, guide them through the intricacies of a Regimental Guest Night. The hapless pair were made Mr Vice (John Oakley) and the President (David Thompson) for the event.

The Territorial Band for the evening was placed in the games room, which was at the end of a long corridor some distance from the dining room. An arrangement was made that at the crucial moment the Mess Sergeant would drop his napkin at the dining-room door. On seeing this signal, the band would play the National Anthem. Unfortunately, the Mess Sergeant was taken ill at the last moment and the Mess Lance Corporal, a new lad learning the ropes, was dropped in at the deep end to deputize.

The guests that evening were the Newcastle Assize Judges and Recorders and, therefore, it was to be a fairly formal occasion. The dinner started promptly and all seemed to be going well. Of course, David Welch and Richard Gordon-Steward could not resist the urge to wind up John Oakley and David Thompson as to the extent of their duties. What they had to do and say was built up into a major theatrical performance. David Thompson had been fiddling nervously with the silver bell-push which substituted for a gavel at the Depot.

The first crisis came when the acting Mess Steward placed one of the two decanters of port in front of Major Alistair who immediately filled his glass, thinking that the judge on his right had passed it to him. Luckily this was sorted out and the two decanters had been passed to all before coming to rest in front of the nervous President and Mr Vice. Their great moment had come.

As David Thompson rose to his feet he struck the bell firmly, but no sound came. At the other end of the table John Oakley – and this was before he was made a little deaf from his duties as Mortar Platoon Commander some years later – did not react. He carried on his conversation with David Welch. Meanwhile two of the guest judges, seeing David Thompson rise, rose majestically out of their seats. Alistair Neilson, already fussed by the port incident, thought he should do the proper thing and also rose from his seat. David Thompson sat down to mend the bell and the two judges followed suit. As David Thompson rose again, having sounded the bell with success, the Mess Steward, standing at the doorway, dropped the napkin and the band struck up faintly down the corridor. With everyone bobbing up and down, chaos seemed to reign and still John Oakley had not uttered a word, let alone the answer to, 'Mr Vice, the Queen', before the band played, as if there had been the request in the first place. Nevertheless, he stood up and when the music stopped was able to announce the toast. To this day David Thompson wonders if Richard Gordon-Steward had sabotaged the bell.

Mike Kitching went straight from school to do his National Service with the West Yorkshire Regiment at Imphal Barracks in York. It was a severe shock to the system. Things were not as they should be and the quality of performance was poor, with bullying by NCOs, not getting paid on time and food running out at the cookhouse. Mike Kitching needed to find an alternative to Cambridge because there was a shortage of money despite the offer of a place through competitive examinations. He felt he should explore how to convert from National Service to being a regular and escape to the mystical-sounding Sandhurst. These thoughts were met with disinterest from the training wing officers, except for Lieutenant John Baty who was on a posting from the Fifth Fusiliers to the Yorkshire and Northumberland Brigade Headquarters. He spent time encouraging Mike Kitching to learn more about a regular army career. Eventually he went to Sandhurst and through the offices of Major Robert Ferguson MVO joined the Fifth Fusiliers just a year behind Anthony Parsons and Ian Cummin.

His first proper contact came with the funeral of a young Fifth Fusilier Officer. Mike Kitching was persuaded to go to the funeral from his Young Officers' Course at the School of Infantry which was before he had joined the Battalion. His first meeting with his fellow officers was at a pub nearby. It is perhaps unfortunate that funerals are often occasions where officers meet friends whom they have not seen for some time and a party follows. This was no exception and they all had a very successful lunch. To the horror and consternation of all of them, the funeral organizer asked six of them, who were, like Mike Kitching, in uniform, to be pall bearers. The long, slow march carrying the coffin of their departed brother officer on their shoulders was an affair they would all prefer to forget. The coffin weaved and wobbled a great deal on its last journey, and it was to their immense relief when it was safely laid to rest.

Lindsay Stemp joined the Regiment in January 1960. He had just passed out from Sandhurst, and much to the envy of his brother cadets his first posting was to be Hong Kong. Indeed Lindsay considered that this was one of the attractions that drew him to the Fifth Fusiliers, so thin was his claim. He knew nothing of the Battalion, coming from a completely non-military background. His Company Commander at RMAS had been the very flamboyant Major Robert Ferguson who had 'spotted Stemp' and seen that he was 'unattached', and as the Regiment had at best a rather spasmodic officer recruitment system, he clearly thought that it might be a good idea for Lindsay Stemp to join. Stemp considered that he must have just been given a rocket about not doing enough about getting chaps into the Regiment and spending too much time hunting and going to deb balls in London. Lindsay Stemp has vague memories of being introduced to Field Marshal Festing in Woolworths in Camberley (he was Colonel of the Regiment at the time) but otherwise he has no memory of any regimental interview. Robert Ferguson was the most eccentric character who designed his own uniforms in a sort of cultured Teddy Boy style which was considered to be very 'with-it' at the time. He was certainly the Regiment's greatest asset at Sandhurst through sheer eccentricity, if nothing else. Lindsay Stemp was later to discover that there were to be many eccentrics in the Regiment, some more genuine than others.

The Battalion was billeted at Queenshill, in the New Territories, when he joined it. The camp was a mosquito-infested, hutted affair of the grimmest type. It was in very poor shape and, soon after his arrival, the First Battalion was threatend with an 'unfit for war' tag on the annual test exercise by a Gurkha Brigadier who obviously thought that Geordies should be Gurkhas. Mercifully, after a few months the Battalion was moved to Fort Stanley on the Island, the most beautiful barracks, stunningly set on a promontory looking out over the sea and the wonderful sunsets for which Hong Kong is so famous. A new CO, Robert Leigh-MacGregor did a magnificent job in bringing the battalion together and making it more professional.

Most of the senior officers were unashamedly old-fashioned in their professional outlook. The Staff College seemed to be frowned upon, in fact there was only one officer whom Lindsay Stemp remembers held the magic letters 'psc' after his name and he was considered to be far too keen as a result.

Life was not without its fun though, and Lindsay Stemp looks back upon Hong Kong as the time that he enjoyed most of all in his army career, even though he was the most chaotic officer who was always going from one crisis to another. He was even told that he was the second worst officer ever to be known in the Battalion. He believes that this could have been quite a generous estimate of his ability at the time, for it seemed that he had been taught nothing in his two years at Sandhurst that was in any way relevant to a subaltern's duties. It took him many years to settle down and he is sure that there were many platoon sergeants who tore their hair out in trying to control Second Lieutenant G. L. Stemp. When he left Hong Kong to fly home for his much-needed Infantry courses, the *Hong Kong Standard* included a reference in its gossip column to 'a fun-loving Lindsay Stemp having left the Colony', to which the long-suffering Colonel Robert was quoted as saying, 'Thank God for that!'

Chapter II

From towards the end
of the War to Gibraltar

The end of the war was a confusing time with both battalions on the move. The First Battalion ended up in Tripoli where it was put into suspended animation, with many reservists and long-serving conscripts being released. The Second Battalion, which was part of the Fourth British Division, was moved from Valos to Angelokhi in northern Greece, and then, in August 1946, to Verria, west of Salonika. The Italian campaign was over but the Civil War in Greece continued between the communist guerillas, in central and northern Greece, and the restored royalist government supported by the Allies. The Fourth British Division took over from the Fourth Indian Division.

The Second Battalion took over from the Rajputana Rifles (known by some as the 'Large Banana Trifles'), who offered to sell the officers some stone jars of liqueurs at a knock-down price. They were bought but it was found that the liqueurs had crystallized. There was an exciting mess meeting when they were written off. The country people, and their animals, were close to starvation after the German withdrawal and their 'scorched earth' policy, so much so that Colonel Anthony Sperling was attacked by two very hungry shepherd's dogs and was lucky to escape intact.

In December 1946, the Second Battalion moved to Athens by sea en route to Gibraltar, spending Christmas Day at anchor at Piraeus. Here, a draft from England, including a certain Fusilier Forbes Burn, (later Lieutenant Colonel (QM) Burn), arrived from the Depot.

Earlier, the Battalion had been given orders to close down a brothel in a well-known Mediterranean city. The Adjutant and the Regimental Sergeant Major were chosen for this somewhat unusual task and, dressed in their best uniforms, the pair approached the house of ill-repute where they found a long queue of Italian soldiers patiently waiting for the establishment to open.

The RSM started pushing past the soldiers and was met with some resistance. The general inference was that these two upstarts should take their turn and not try to queue-barge.

'Make way for the Captain,' ordered the RSM desperately.

'Ah! It is a captain. Of course, he must go first.'

Before that, the Regiment had been serving between Egypt and Syria on snow-clad mountains and scorching plains. Now their new division, the Tenth Indian, which was relatively new to those parts, was concentrating in Gaza. The Battalion had worked and fought closely with Indians and were looking forward to integrating their machine-gunners in support. General Headquarters (GHQ) had approved block leave for the Battalion, and the Commanding Officer had kept the divisional staff informed.

Why the Divisional Commander claimed to have known nothing about this block leave has never been understood by the Battalion, nor admitted to by the divisional officers. Colonel Forbes took his jeep with his personal 'Recce' team up to the 'Rose Red City' of Petra, keeping radio contact with Battalion Headquarters. Kingsley Foster, the second in command, held the fort. Most of the Battalion opted for the well-known rest centres in Cairo or Alex. The more adventurous went farther afield, while their Rhodesians and South Africans went the whole hog, arranging air travel. The newly-appointed Adjutant blithely signed the free train passes. Had he read an amendment to an addendum to Middle East Standing Orders, comprising several volumes, he would have thought twice but active service conditions did not give time or space for these burdens. Who was this feckless, callow fellow? The editor requires a 'third person' narrative so he can only be revealed as 'the writer of these notes'.

Lt Davies of the Command Pay Office, Jerusalem took less than a week to get a bill for over a thousand pounds to his victim, the signer of the unauthorized warrants, and was promptly rewarded for his astuteness – the final demand was signed 'Temporary Major'. How long he was to enjoy this will never be known. For the Adjutant, luck, perhaps an unusual or misplaced word in this context, intervened. The King David Hotel was destroyed by a Jewish terrorist bomb the very next week and all records were destroyed. However, this was a mere side issue to the main tale.

Most of the Battalion burst out of camp for the fleshpots in their trucks, ribald, joyful songs echoing throughout the divisional area as they were whisked off to the single-line track. Next morning Kingsley strode into the Mess, suffused with his radiant enthusiasm and affection for whatever company he found himself in, to proclaim that the Divisional Commander had personally phoned to demand an inspection by him of the entire battalion together with vehicles for 2 p.m. that very afternoon. Kingsley went on to detail Captain David Burrow to meet the General at GHQ and lead him to the parade. They would later give him a toast to their future under his leadership. Some of the older hands felt uneasy. The message seemed curt, less than cordial from their new Divisional Commander, and how on earth could they expect to shift 60 mainly tracked vehicles with so few drivers in such a short time?

Hell had erupted, howling engines, jarring, scraping metal, the final moan of batteries, distorted, bellowed orders, dense odious fumes and, overwhelmingly, the deep powdery sand pounded and churned by centuries of invading armies. Dicky Mewburn, Val Jones and Jack Harrison with recovery vehicles and the few drivers still around hauled the trucks and carriers clogged up to their axles. Dead on the hour, in a gap in the swirling ochre cloud, David Burrow's head and shoulders were clearly revealed above the ridge ahead.

He was staring towards the Battalion with a desperate intensity. His image remained for three seconds at most before vanishing in a spiral of dust. David later assured them that at that moment he had been careering through the Sikh cookhouse area with the General rampaging at his tail. People have fantasized about the 'Angels of Mons', Pan the God of Mischief, Will of the Wisp and such visions. The plain fact was that David, who only recently had escaped from capture by a German patrol and found his way back over uncharted desert, had lost his way. They were to be granted 90 minutes' grace, but were finally in order and fairly correct.

Three jeeps, which had cruised with dignity past the Gurkha guard, arrived nearly two hours late, their occupants sand-caked, sweat-stained, bedraggled. The General stiffly lowered himself from the jeep. Kingsley called the band to attention. 'The Battalion is ready for your inspection' was in many ways as corny as an old 'western'; the noble survivors round their wagons accept that the relieving senior officer's face betrayed not one touch of love or admiration.

'You are unfit for battle,' he intoned.

His purple-pantalooned Lieutenant aide-de-camp loyally nodded assent. Kingsley was to assume command, pending GHQ confirmation, and the General requested that he see Colonel Forbes as soon as he returned. Again 'luck' intervened – luck for the Battalion and not the General, who two days later was fatally injured by a passing truck. The 'unfit for battle' tag was forgotten.

John Winn had his own story about luck. He did not consider himself to be lucky at all. Each campaign brought him a new wound and, although he told the story, the wound from the Italian campaign from a phosphorous grenade whilst visiting the thunderbox might have been funny in retrospect but not so funny at the time.

He told the story of how he had had a most serious road accident in Egypt and had had the most horrific litany of injuries. He was eventually evacuated to the King Edward Hospital for Officers in London where he spent a very uncomfortable number of months. The usual answer to this terrible tale was, 'Gosh, John, you were very lucky.'

'Lucky,' he would rail, 'Do you think I was lucky to spend six months in hospital in pain with nearly every bone in my body broken?'

The desert war was deeply engraved on the minds of those who took part in it. One Fifth Fusilier officer, some years after the war, shared a tent with another officer who had been a 'Desert Rat'. Early in the morning a very large mug of sweet milky tea was placed by the other officer's bed which was then half consumed. After this he shaved with the rest of the mug of tea. In the desert, water was scarce. Only tea was brewed and this was used for both shaving and drinking. History does not relate if this habit survived married life or even if that officer ever did get married. He must have been a very sticky person to kiss.

Chapter III

Gibraltar

In Greece, the Second Battalion was still a machine-gun battalion but, on arrival in Gibraltar on New Year's Eve, 1946, reorganized as an infantry battalion. This required a new company, Support Company, which was commanded by Major Paul Ward recently transferred from the East Yorkshire Regiment. Gibraltar, for the fusiliers, was full of guards and piquets. There were, amongst others, the Battalion quarter guard, fire piquet and frequent ceremonial at the Governor's residence at the Convent. Here it was that the Governor's wife, 200 years ago, persuaded her husband to send Phoebe Hessel, the only serving woman Fifth Fusilier, back to her husband in England. There were special guards on a shipload of Jewish immigrants on their way to Israel, or worse, on their way back after interception or rejection. Spanish people were not allowed to live in Gibraltar and would come to work each day and had to return each night, usually loaded with contraband.

Training was difficult, sport restricted and the fusiliers' leisure hours were supervised by no less than six police forces (Gibraltar Constabulary, Security Police, Upper Rock Police, Royal Naval Police, Royal Military Police and the Royal Air Force Police). No wonder that escape for a few hours into Spain was popular, where other perils (and another police force) awaited, not that the formidable Spanish police of the Franco era, in their black patent-leather hats, were unsympathetic. A common cause of friction was a happy band of fusiliers, in the cheap seats at La Linea bullring, fortified by Spanish beer, chanting, 'How-way the bull'. After a night in the cells, the company officer hurrying to the police station usually found the cell doors open. No one ever seemed to be charged, despite the Spanish claim to Gibraltar.

In spite of this, or even perhaps because of it, old soldiers still recall Gibraltar in the 1940s as one of the best stations of all. This may be strange but most soldiers look back on old stations with nostalgia, the present one with disgust and the next one with eager anticipation.

When Gerald Style joined the Second Battalion in Gibraltar, Colonel Anthony Sperling was commanding with Major Tommy Hamilton as his second in command. Norman Rogers was Quartermaster and an ex-Coldstream Drum Major, Mr Johnson, was a smiling and smart Regimental Sergeant Major. There was very little military activity on the Rock. The officers used to play tennis at the Naval Officers' Pavilion, and there was cricket and sailing at the Yacht Club. This was about the only contact they had with the Gibraltarians. Officers would go to La Linea (Bodega Jerezana) or Algeciras (Reina Cristina) for dinner, but there was always the hazard of getting back to the Fortress before the Spanish closed their gates at the frontier. For those without cars, it was a long walk back to British lines and Gerald Style never discovered the truth as to which officer crossed the British end of the frontier on his hands and knees.

The Second Battalion was disbanded on 5 July 1948 and became the First Battalion the same day. Lieutenant Colonel Basil Leech took over from Lieutenant Colonel Anthony Sperling DSO. The remnants of the First Battalion in Tripoli came over soon afterwards. The Second Battalion Colours were sent home to the Depot and the First Battalion colours were brought out by John Green, the Regimental Signals Officer. His plane was diverted due to bad weather to Casablanca and, to avoid losing the colours to thieves in the night, he wrapped himself in them. Anyway, that's what he said.

Colonel Basil Leech, who succeeded Colonel Sperling, was very keen on sailing. Conditions in the harbour and in the bay were ideal. There was a fleet of Sharpies (very basic), and a class of Snipes and Victories which were proper yachts. The Navy lent the Battalion whalers and a large cutter for more robust sailing in the winter. There were encounters with the Algeciras Club which were great fun, and *St George's Gazette* tells tales of being left on the mooring at the 5-minute gun, being becalmed and protests of quite a vicious nature.

Colonel Basil introduced road runs, and this meant starting at Casements, running along the harbour side, followed by a long and steep climb to Moorish Castle. Unfortunately Colonel Basil was a keen beagler and so he had little sympathy for the stragglers. When Gerald Style took over as CO in Lemgo he remembered his loathing for cross-country running, and avoided it himself by ordaining that those over 35 would do 'old man's PT'. Those under 35, with perhaps an equal loathing, were left to groan round the Westphalian countryside.

The Regimental Band was in good form under Bandmaster Evans and Sergeant Tate was Band Sergeant. Regimental bands always lead a special existence, being musicians in uniform. Any good musician worth his salt made a good living moonlighting in local night spots or playing for local dance bands. In times of proper war they became stretcher bearers but in limited warfare, bands were often left at brigade depots and had the onerous task of appearing at military tattoos between their dance engagements.

The Corps of Drums, the drums, bugles and pipes of a full military band, were reincarnated under Drum Major Parfitt. They always stayed with the Battalion and became the headquarters defence platoon under the nominal command of the Adjutant with the Regimental Sergeant Major taking, in the view of the Corps of Drums, all too keen an interest.

Drafts and reinforcements were sent to Gibraltar by sea. On one of these voyages, on his posting to the First Battalion of the Fifth Fusiliers, the Officer joined the passengers on the rail as the troopship moved slowly through the Straits of Gibraltar. They were all eager to catch the first view of the Rock. It was early in the morning and dawn was just breaking with the promise of a grey day. Not many people were about and the group of passengers could not have been more than a dozen. The Officer tried to recall passing this way as a child in 1925, en route to India, but had no memories of it. Nor could he recall the convoy slipping through the Straits in 1942 when he was with the Second Battalion bound for Algiers. The convoy must have passed through during the night to avoid the enemy, for he had no memory of that event either. Absorbed with these thoughts, he was not aware that the boring, silly old buffer, Major Jones, who had seen it all, had moved to the rail beside him. Major Jones was dying for the chance to educate the uninitiated with the sudden, 'There it is. The first thing you see is Europa Point.' This outburst, coupled with a dramatic, outflung arm and a finger pointing to a faint, small smudge on the horizon, brought him back to the present. He was aware of Major Jones's eyes upon him. The Officer's attention, however, was of a short duration as his mind returned to what had been exercising his thoughts much earlier on, causing him to miss any further education. He had become preoccupied with the wisdom of a decision he had made the previous evening.

He had been Duty Officer with a final responsibility for clearing the open decks of all service passengers. There were, to the best of his knowledge, no civilian passengers, only male and female members of the Forces on posting to stations in the Med. It is amazing how intimate some friendships can become in the short space of two days at sea. It was perhaps with this in mind that the OC Troops sent him on this errand on the evening prior to disembarkation. Having cleared the lower decks, he then returned to 'A' deck, making as much noise as seemed decent to the occasion, to ensure that all was as it should be. There, on a deckchair, was a pair of trousers with no owner in sight. He looked around. He called. He went away and returned after a suitable interval of time. The trousers were still there, no owner had come to claim them. There was nothing to suggest who the owner might be and disembarkation in the morning could well present a problem for someone. At the time, it seemed to him that the best solution was to pin the trousers to the noticeboard at the head of the main flight of stairs, opposite the Pursuer's office, with a notice saying, 'Found on "A" Deck. Owner please collect'. The instinct to ask that they 'be removed' was resisted as being superfluous to the occasion. Naturally, on his way to the deck that morning, the Officer looked to see if the owner had been about in the night and retrieved them, but they were still there.

Therefore, standing on the deck coming into Gibraltar, his thoughts were not with Major Jones and, with a muttered excuse, he left the group to go down to the Purser's office to put the trousers in a less conspicuous position before more passengers were on the move. Who was to know that he had pinned the offending article to the board? As soon as he started to remove them, knowing looks were exchanged and, despite protestations, a doubtful reputation was in the making. He cursed the thoughtless lover.

All through the morning, as they steamed towards the harbour, the sky remained full of dark clouds. It was not the sunny reception that he had expected. The trouser business left him feeling ill-tempered even though they had been thrown into a corner of his cabin. Altogether the morning's events had left him in a frame of mind that made Gibraltar seem a less entertaining prospect than he had hoped.

He had discharged his duties and, because he was travelling alone, he was a free agent to move about the ship to await disembarkation, so he joined the throng at the ship's rails to watch the passing show. Then, to his dismay, he found that he was alongside Major Jones who recognized him. He was the sheep that had got away. There was no doubt about it, he was in the firing line. He avoided the Major's eye but knew that it would benefit him little. He looked away and up to the black clouds surrounding the Rock, darkening their approach through Algeciras Bay. Then in a moment of weakness he asked, 'Does it rain much in Gibraltar?'

'Not much', the Major replied, seizing the opportunity to play the Ancient Mariner. 'What they get most is a heavy dew.' It was a signal. The statement was a catalyst. The clouds opened, the rain fell from the sky, tropical in its intensity. They all ran from the open deck to find cover. The Officer was saved.

He saw Major Jones again just before he disembarked, and noticed with pleasure that he was remaining on board. He touched his arm to gain his reluctant attention and remarked with deliberate sourness, 'My God! I do hope it never rains,' and felt all the better for the saying of it. Maybe Gib had more to offer than he had thought.

Returning to his cabin to collect his belongings, he found Major Jones's batman with a large paper bag and a note which read, 'Could you please put my trousers in the bag and give them to my batman.' Perhaps after all Major Jones was not such a bore to everyone, and not such a silly old buffer either.

Fusilier Little arrived at Gibraltar with a draft of recruits and, much to their surprise, they were greeted by a sergeant who took them to a bar near the entrance to Moorish Castle. They were even more astonished, and Fusilier Little, an ex-merchant seaman, was delighted when the sergeant plied them with free booze. Was this the usual hospitality for a draft about to begin foreign service with the Regiment? Would there be lovely señoritas waiting for them behind those previously forbidding gates? A few bottles later, a flushed, totally at ease and boisterously relaxed bunch of raw recruits were cruelly brought back to earth from a lovely dream of Valhalla. Instead, apoplectic officers and the RSM, looking like Beau Gestes from Fort Ville-neuf, appeared to incarcerate them inside the barracks. It transpired that the generous sergeant was trying to appear mentally unstable so as to 'work his ticket back home'. He had ordered the booze and charged it to the Regiment. Still, it made a happy introduction for Fusilier Little to the Regiment he remembers as the finest in the British Army.

There were unlimited quantities of good booze and opportunities to indulge. One subaltern overdid it at a Corrida de Toros in La Linea and was arrested by the fearsome State Police for throwing cushions into the bullring. He spent an uncomfortable night in La Linea jail and required consular support to get him out.

A subaltern in Major Dick Hensman's company, misguidedly and against strict laws because of the prevalence of rabies in Spain, brought back a delightful spaniel puppy. Inevitably, it developed signs of rabies and this was confirmed by the research laboratory in Tangier. A load of vaccine was obtained and this was injected every day, very painfully, into the stomachs of the Company Commander and those who with typical English friendliness to dogs, had allowed themselves to be licked or had touched the rabid spaniel. The subaltern was not very popular and even when he reached field rank, felt he never got the respect he thought was due to him.

Sailors constantly coming and going might have been a provocation, but trouble was rare, often because both sides tried to entertain one another. Three submarines, for example, took parties of one officer and six Fusiliers each on a diving exercise. On one of these a leak was noticed by the Fusiliers as the submarine submerged. Not wishing to be laughed at, the Fusiliers kept quiet, but the excitement when the Captain noticed the leak was considerable. Someone had not closed the hatch properly, but they all lived to tell the tale.

Whilst in Gibraltar, the order came that soldiers should henceforth go to bed between sheets. Thus three centuries of 'blankets next to the skin' came to an end. The problem was how it was to be introduced. A company commanders' conference was called and Reggie Pratt was ordered to conduct a pilot scheme. No better choice could have been made. Platoon commanders and sergeants were briefed, difficult matters of bed-making and kit layouts were solved, and one airing per week was declared. Who but Reggie would have dared to hang 120 sheets from barrack-block verandah railings for one whole morning a week?

Reggie Pratt was his usual Irish self in those days. He had one of the first cars to appear in the Battalion after the war. Water was partly rationed on the Rock and he received a memorandum from the Quartermaster. This stated, 'I notice that you are using part of your barrack building as a garage. Please say if you are using fresh water to wash your car.' The reply was, 'No, whisky. My parents are frightfully wealthy.' Some quartermasters had a self-imposed mission to protect the Queen's purse, often in the face of what others may see as their duty to produce the best for their battalion. The motto of those quartermasters could be, 'Never let efficiency interfere with the system.' One of the authors still resents the fact that he was sent up Mount Kenya for three months with only the very unpopular, and no doubt cheaper, 'Compo' Type 'C' rather than with a mixture of types. It would have meant spending money on petrol for a truck to go to the depot for more types of 'Compo' rather than use up what was left in the store. The sufferer will still not look at tins of meat and veg.

The people of Gibraltar were, on the whole, unfriendly towards their military garrison and, therefore, the officers and the men had to find their pleasure in La Linea. One officer was recommended, by a friend, to a restaurant near the bullring whose speciality had an unpronounceable Spanish name and came in the form of two large chunks of meat done up a special way. It was alleged to do the most marvellous things to one's 'vitality'. On going to the restaurant, the officer found that the size of his portion was much less in size than his friend had described. On his return, he reported this to his friend who could only say, 'Oh dear, I am afraid the bull must have won.'

The National Health Service arrived. Regular officers were obliged to apply to join it, and several refused. This was because of the old unwritten understanding that an officer, being a gentleman of substance, received only nominal pay, but was given free medical attention in peace and in war. No longer, now they had to sign up.

This wealthy officer image had affected the father of one of the authors in the First World War. Pay was five shillings a day and the minimum mess bill, payable by the fictitious 2nd Lt St George, who neither drank nor smoked, was seven shillings and six pence per day. Young war service officers, whose average stay in the trenches was 21 days before they were killed or wounded, went to their deaths worried about debt. The Colonel was astonished to hear that not all his young officers had a private income and the author's father had to take courage to speak to the Colonel on behalf of his brother officers. After this, the rules and the expense of mess life were temporarily changed for the duration. Not that expensive always meant best or even good. The Sergeants' Mess always ate much better for no extra cost at all. The Regimental Sergeant Major would have had the Cook Sergeant's guts for garters if it had been otherwise.

The *Gibraltar Chronicle* described the revival of the St George's Minstrels as a 'Troupe with a 50-year-old history'. The officers invariably provided a sketch and the participants always thought their efforts were hilarious. In any event, the soldiers always clapped politely even though some of the 'jokes' might not have been to their taste. In the concert reported by the *Gibraltar Chronicle*, Sergeant Tate and Lance Corporal Parratt did a memorable Salome sketch, and Captain Bill Little must have been a great success, with non-Geordies, with his Geordie sketches, although his accent was beyond reproach. Officers had to be careful using a Geordie accent. It had to be good, otherwise it was resented because it was patronizing. In another posting one company commander tried to mimic Fusiliers and got the nickname of Joker. It was not complimentary. Regimental Quartermaster Sergeant Hoe left the Battalion shortly afterwards and his tales of 'Sonia Snell to whom an accident befell', and the 'Life of Lance Corporal i/c Sanitary', were subsequently sadly missed. He was succeeded by RQMS Boniface.

In 1948, Major Dick Hensman, as W Company Commander, was in

charge of the Guard of Honour for the C-in-C Home Fleet, Admiral Sir Roderick McGrigor. Things went smoothly enough until the Admiral trod inadvertently on the toe of the very distinguished and senior major. It was reported at the time, in the *St George's Gazette*, that, 'Still, all went well with a stoic amount of forbearance for damage to an otherwise shiny boot.' Not much of a topic to report and it gives a flavour of the times. In Gibraltar, priorities were different in 1948 to those of 20 years later and even more so in today's modern army. It should also be pointed out that officers wore handmade brown boots which they had to buy themselves, without much help from Her Majesty or the myopic parsimony of the Treasury.

The sergeant in charge of the Regimental staff at the Governor's residence was told he should refer to the Governor as 'Your Excellency'. After a while, the Governor thought that the use of 'Your Excellency' every two words was a bit overdone and the sergeant was told to use the good old 'Sir'. Early one morning the sergeant was having a 'puff' in the garden when a voice said, 'Good morning, Sergeant II – .'

Shocked out of his reverie he replied, 'Mornin', Guv'nor.' His Excellency, it was reported, could only beat a hasty retreat in a state of hopeless mirth.

A more hilarious incident took place at the Ceremony of the Keys. This event was watched by many tourists on the balconies surrounding the main square of the Casements. The Governor and other senior officers were inspecting the Fifth Fusilier Guard of Honour which was immaculate as becomes the 'Shiners'. Then out stepped a Fusilier, complete with a large Spanish straw hat and a watering can. To the delight of the onlookers, he began to water the various coloured marker spots which he did with straight-faced dignity behind the Governor's party. The RSM then appeared, trying to unobtrusively shoo off the dedicated and apparently completely oblivious gardener.

The RSM made it in the end, but all decided that the Ceremony of the Keys would never be quite the same again. The Fusilier was trying to 'work his ticket' to an early discharge. It says much for the discipline of the Governor, his entourage and the Guard of Honour that they managed to keep straight faces. However, the audience was doubled up with laughter and it certainly brought some humour to the Fusiliers' lives. History does not relate if the gardening Fusilier got his early discharge. Probably a spell in detention and a casting in the St George's Minstrels was the more likely outcome.

THE CONSCIENTIOUS GARDENER.

24

Chapter IV

Warminster

The Battalion had just returned from Gibraltar to England, and with it had arrived many new cars which were placed in front of the Officers' and Sergeants' Messes. However, those who had served at home had not been able to acquire such tax-free lovelies. Nevertheless the young Baxter felt the need to have transport and therefore took himself off to Bristol. There one afternoon he purchased a neanderthal juggernaut that had been manufactured by Mr Jowett of Bradford in 1929. When the car was ready for receipt he took with him his bride-to-be to enjoy the return journey to Warminster in immaculate and plush upholstery. Unfortunately, as he left Bristol, the gear lever came off in his hand and they spent the rest of the evening at Temple Meads station waiting for a kind aunt to recover them to Warminster.

In due course the vehicle was ready to go to Warminster, and Baxter delivered himself and his wonderful motor car to the Officers' Mess where, because its registration letters were WE, it received some of the ruder names ever applied to such magnificent carriages. It was a machine which required as much mechanical love as it required petrol and the engine spent more time in Baxter's bedroom than actually under the bonnet of the motor car. One afternoon he carried the engine, a 2-cylinder model, down to Messrs Marks's garage in Heytesbury, where the man promised that he would do a top to bottom overhaul for seven pounds! Oh that we had such a vehicle today. It would get to London and back on about a table lighter-full of petrol and still do the journey along the motorway as fast as the likes of BMWs or Mercedes. In fact in the fullness of time the vehicle was sold to a district nurse of Bury St Edmunds.

Opposites in the Army often acquire nicknames, such as the tall being called Shorty, the large and fat called Dynarod. Thus, names of responsibilities such as Intelligence Officer might not necessarily always go to those who were regarded as being possessed of any great intelligence. Certainly a very well-known and distinguished officer, Tony Perrins, who was Battalion Intelligence Officer, fell for the fashion of acquiring a black labrador puppy. However, he named the dog 'Fusilier' and could be seen on most evenings in the week marching around the camp shouting 'Fusilier', to be followed by myriads of soldiers enquiring exactly what he required. The dog in the meantime would be half a mile away chasing rabbits down by the Wylie. There may be some logic in calling a dog Fusilier, but not when surrounded by 720 soldiers of that rank.

During most of its time at Knook Camp, Z Company was the unit for demonstrations to be done for the intakes at the School of Infantry. One such demonstration was being watched by senior officers from NATO and other senior UK staff colleges, showing the battalion in the advance. In those days the infantry were equipped with an instrument for clearing minefields, towed behind a rocket, which exploded along a great length of earth and blew open the minefield. In view of the seniority of the people present, it was not considered safe to fire the rocket so close to the crowd. In consequence, the explosives were laid in the ground to be detonated electrically. The rocket itself was attached to a train of what happened to be much lighter pieces behind it and was in due course fired. Unfortunately, the Battalion had not practised this particular piece of theatre and the rocket with the much lighter load behind it became like a Christmas party balloon and started to zig-zag all over the ranges. It finally veered straight towards the stand of spectators who, viewing this as they would the riders of the Apocalypse, ran in all directions in vain attempts to escape from this horror. Thus they were not ready when the rocket-detonating crew fired the detonators in the ground. The sight of senior officers gazing skywards desperately trying to see what had gone off behind them had to be seen to be believed.

In June 1950, the School of Infantry had its annual summer dance, and one P. Baxter, who was about to marry Anne Reading (now his wife), was shamed by the nature of the conveyance in which he was to carry her off to the ball, this being his 1929 Jowett, which Baxter still considered to be a splendid contraption for most occasions, but not this function. In order to impress his lady-love, the lovelorn officer was persuaded to borrow his Platoon Sergeant's vehicle, the thought being that a sergeant was bound to have a rather more prestigious contraption. Without time for any other change you could imagine his horror when a rusty blanket-covered aberration of an ancient Ford van arrived. To try and cover up the worst of its limitations, Baxter unearthed a splendid quilted eiderdown to cover the front seat. Anne was not too amused at this early stage of their courtship when the eiderdown was revealed, and fellow, less couth officers were heard to remark, 'Is this a means to an end or an end to a means?'

The dance was a great success, particularly for those who helped a certain young lady to unhitch the balloons at the ceiling of the ballroom by lifting her, but more by those who unwittingly had trapped the bottom of her dress to the floor before the great lift.

Chapter V

Bury St Edmunds –
The Way to Korea

In June 1950, North Korea invaded South Korea and the USA, which had military units stationed in South Korea and Japan, requested help from the United Nations to repulse the aggressor. Much international discussion took place, but as far as the Regiment was concerned, very soon it would be on its way to South Korea. Mr Attlee having agreed that Britain would play her role, 29 Brigade, amongst others, was to be sent to Korea. Unfortunately a battalion in 29 Brigade had been found unfit for war, and would take the Fifth Fusiliers' place as demonstration battalion. The First Battalion of the Fifth Fusiliers would take theirs in 29 Brigade. The niceties of finding a battalion unfit for war to be the demonstration battalion at the School of Infantry results purely from the Fifth Fusilier motto '*Quo fata vocant*' (where the fates call). Therefore, in August 1950, the Battalion moved to Bury St Edmunds to start its training for Korea. The First Battalion was not able at the time to take national servicemen under a certain age unless they had volunteered, and this meant that the Battalion lost virtually all its soldiers as a result. The Government therefore called the first-line reserve and the 'K' Volunteers. The latter were men who were prepared to volunteer for Korea and had previous service. The Fifth Fusiliers took on board 1,200 men from these to form the new battalion and its own field reserve.

These were all men who had served in the last conflict, some of whom had even been members of the 9th Battalion of the Fifth Fusiliers who had been taken prisoner of war at Singapore, and some had been looked after by Korean guards. It would bring an interesting dimension to the ex-prisoners of war if they decided to go and seek their previous aggressors and drive their old guards into captivity. Fortunately, British soldiers do not react in this way. The reinforcements had known five years of peace during which time a great number had married, had children and started their own businesses; others patently wished to escape from that environment and were only too pleased to return. The canteen on the first two or three nights was full of men drowning their sorrows because they had had to leave home, and others celebrating the fact that they had had to do so. The problems that had to be dealt with in paying off, or attempting to settle hire purchase debts, or mortgages which the wife couldn't afford to pay, were legion.

Those who were only too pleased to come back used to raid the town like cow-rustling gauchos having fun off the trail, to the point where a local publican complained to the Commanding Officer, and his hostelry was duly placed out of bounds to the gauchos. Inevitably, he made a fortune for about a week whilst all the rest of the Battalion went to see why it had been placed out of bounds. In order to maintain an element of good behaviour in the town on evenings out, a Warrant Officer and 40 men became the town patrol and in fact, on one occasion, saved the local police superintendent from having all his clothes removed by two Fusiliers who stated in their defence later that they only wanted to see what made the policeman tick. An anecdotal extract from CO's orders would make a wonderful TV script for *Soldier Soldier* and many will remember the Fifth Fusiliers' own 'Fusilier Tucker' in real life.

The Fifth Fusiliers' training took place on Stamford Bridge training area around Thetford and in less than two months they had to bring the old hands back up to date for full-time war. They were delighted to see that they had got rid of an anti-tank instrument called the PIAT, and an American Liaison Officer and a Master Sergeant came with a 3.5-inch bazooka anti-tank weapon. The nature of the Master Sergeant's dialect was so strong, and his choice of technical phrase so bizarre in relation to the instrument, that none of them could understand a single word that he said. The Fusiliers sub-sequently discovered, when returning to the Officers' Mess for tea, that the American Liaison Officer coming from New York hadn't understood a word he had said either!

Dialect is a fascinating thing and their own Anti-Tank Platoon Sergeant perpetrated a similar situation when explaining how the American anti-tank mine detector worked. He came from a tiny and obscure village in the Cheviots, and very little of what he said in relation to the instrument registered with the mixed audience, as their reserve soldiers did not only come from Northumberland.

During this time the Fifth Fusiliers also received suitable clothing with which to equip themselves for a winter in Korea, including a heavy wool sweater and a sniper suit, neither of which increased the local temperature by more than about half a degree. In addition, and at great expense, they were also issued with a pair of boots FP. After a great deal of research had gone into exactly what FP meant, they were informed by the Ordnance BOWO with great pride that FP stood for 'Finnish Pattern'. They had been ordered in 1938 in case the Russian-Finnish War came to more than just a joke, and were now issued 12 years later to troops on their way to Korea. The Fifth Fusiliers were lucky to have brand-new boots – ha ha.

Chapter VI

The Experiences of a Draft
Conducting Officer

Having completed his Young Officers' courses at the Small Arms School, Hythe and the School of Infantry, Warminster, Ronnie Cowe duly received orders to report to Strensall Barracks at York in early 1951. Strensall Barracks was the Headquarters of the Yorkshire and Northumbrian Brigade where drafts were formed for the journey to Korea by troopship.

Ben Smith and Ronnie Cowe had joined the Regiment together and were to find themselves in charge of a draft of 80 Reservists and 'K' Volunteers. The Reservists were Second World War veterans recalled to the colours from the reserves, whilst the 'K' (Korea) Volunteers were soldiers of fortune who had signed on for the duration of the Korean War in return for a bonus. Ben Smith and Ronnie Cowe were the youngest in the draft.

The two young officers were comforted to find at Strensall, Major Ralph Mortimer, of the Regiment. He was an impressive character who wore a black eye patch and seemed, to the two young officers, very old and very senior. After a few drinks, he was inclined to tell young officers stories of his service both during and before the war. However, as he often told three stories at one time, many young officers were most confused and, because of this, were judged to be 'young whipper-snappers of little sense'.

Ben Smith and Ronnie Cowe were summoned to Major Mortimer's presence and were told of their impending task. He very generously took them both out to dinner at the Station Hotel at York. After dinner there was a hair-raising drive back to the barracks in Major Mortimer's car and, as he bade them goodnight, he told them to report to his office next morning to be briefed on their draft conducting duties. This pleased them because neither their eighteen months at Sandhurst nor their six months at Hythe and Warminster had enlightened them on their imminent duties.

So far, so good. Everything seemed very much in hand. The young officers had met their draft and they seemed a decent bunch unlikely to eat the young officers en route. As ordered, Ben Smith and Ronnie Cowe turned up at Major Mortimer's office. They had pencils and notepads at the ready and the briefing began.

'Here is a copy of your movement order. You will see that you depart from the barracks at 0800 on Monday morning, arriving at York Station at 0830. Your departure time from York is 0900. Form up your draft on Platform Four and do not allow your Fusiliers to break ranks for any reason whatsoever.'

The two young officers glanced at each other hopefully. Perhaps, with a briefing as detailed as this was so far, they might make it to Korea without any major mishap.

Major Mortimer continued, 'You see, what can happen is that the Fusiliers will ask if they can go to the lavatory, or if they can grab a cup of tea. It is vital that you must not let them do this because what happens is that they take the mugs onto the train. Then when the train leaves they hurl the mugs out onto the platform and we have to pay for them.'

This advice was delivered in a rising crescendo and the young officers made their notes ready and their minds alert for the next phase of the briefing. So far the draft had not left York.

'That's it then,' said Major Mortimer.

'But what happens when we get to London, sir?'

'All in the movement order,' and with that Major Mortimer waved the young officers out.

The young officers returned to their draft. These were to be the first group of Fusiliers they were destined to command. They decided not to impart the advice on cups of tea in case it put ideas into the Fusiliers' heads. The young officers thought they would play it by ear.

The draft was a motley bunch, entirely streetwise. They were from all walks of life with a variety of accents mostly unintelligible to the young officers. There was an exception. This was the soldiers' stand-by expletive which was introduced in every conceivable grammatical construction. Ronnie Cowe remembers asking one of them why he used the word so much and his answer was, 'I'm f——d if A' know.'

However, they were a cheerful lot and surprisingly good natured, despite having left homes, jobs and families to take part in a war on the other side of the world in a country few of them had ever heard of before. Events at York Station went exactly as Major Mortimer had predicted. The young officers' efforts to prevent mugs of tea getting onto the train were not entirely successful. As the train pulled out a hail of crockery sailed onto the platform. Ronnie Cowe's last sight of Major Mortimer for some years was of him waving his fist at the departing carriages.

In the 1950s there existed a Services transit dungeon in the London Underground system known as the Goodge Street Deep Shelter. Very useful in any time of nuclear conflict but although General MacArthur had thoughts of using nuclear weapons on the Chinese in Korea, it was not, as far as it was known, his intention to use them on his allies, however awkward they might get. This was where all drafts passing through London spent the night, both for Korea and Kenya.

It was therefore to this subterranean tomb that the draft's movement order consigned them. To get there, they all had to take to the Underground. There was one change and the young officers were convinced that they would see no more of their draft. To the amazement of the young officers, everybody made it to Goodge Street where a meal was provided. It was not long before more than hints were made that it would be a good idea for everyone 'to see a bit of London'. The two young officers were left with the distinct impression that any confinement to the tomb would lead to a mutiny. Passes were duly approved to 2300 with dire threats of the consequences of being absent at 0700 the next morning, which was when the draft was due to start its journey to Southampton. However, all turned out well and there were no absentees. Within 48 hours they had put to sea in the troopship *Fowey* en route to the Far East and Korea.

The voyage was fairly uneventful except for an incident at Aden where the ship was moored offshore. In the evening a commotion arose on board the ship which involved much shouting and cries of 'man overboard'. All hastened to the rail and they were amazed to see a figure clinging to the anchor chain. Another figure could be seen swimming for an Arab bumboat which was tethered to the anchor chain. Some soldiers trying to jump ship, the two young officers were told. They had, apparently, tried to drop a kitbag into the small boat but this was not successful. Evidently they were the worse for drink because no one in his right mind would try and desert at Aden.

Then there was an announcement over the ship's loudspeaker, 'Would the officer commanding the RNF draft report to the Ship's Adjutant immediately.' The would-be 'deserters' were Fusiliers. The young officers watched the two Fusiliers being picked up by a Royal Military Police launch to be consigned to the ship's 'brig' for seven days by the Officer Commanding Troops on the *Fowey*. The cells were situated on the lowest deck right in the prow of the ship. It was a noisy and uncomfortable place in high seas and they slept in narrow bunks rather than the hammocks used on the troop decks.

Eventually they arrived at Kure. This was the Commonwealth Base Depot and the draft was paraded for disembarkation. A headcount disclosed an extra man – there were 81 Fusiliers instead of 80! After the many opportunities for Fusiliers to abscond, this was hard to believe. Repeated headcounts failed to solve the problem. It was eventually sorted out at the Reinforcement Depot, where it was discovered that the Royal Ulster Rifles draft was one man short. One rifleman had decided to transfer to the Fusilier draft where he had made friends and had acquired a beret and hackle.

Two or three years later, the Lieutenant to Captain promotion examination contained a question on the duties of a draft conducting officer. Ben Smith and Ronnie Cowe passed, although their experience was not exactly as the good book had laid out. However, they had fully briefed themselves.

Chapter VII

From a Hill in Korea

The reversal was sudden, a night attack in great force had overrun some of the Fifth Fusilier forward positions and, although the positions were recaptured during the day, a general withdrawal was forced upon them by the overwhelming weight of numbers along the whole front.

The sharp edge of winter was already upon them but the Fusiliers had not felt the full weight of its lash so they did not realize the consequence of what they were abandoning as they hastily rejected stores as being too heavy, or too bulky, to carry that night, as they withdrew under the cover of darkness. On through the flame-lit night and the iron-grey morning they drove, southwards, clear of the enemy and, as they journeyed through the early dawn, the north winds started to lift the first few flurries of frozen dust from the ice-bound paddy fields, whirling and writhing like brown and white mist-snakes as they accompanied the column in menacing companionship. It was obvious now that everyone was pulling back, far enough to realign or even abandon the war. At long last a halt was called; in a bleak area of deserted, ruined villages, on a line of low hills, they stopped, faced north and prepared for the next assault, accepting their fate with the weary resignation of hard-pressed soldiers.

The temperature dropped, biting hard on tired bodies while the icy wind flicked at worried minds as the winter tightened its grip on the earth. The cold had struck deep, too deep; the soil had become icebound resisting all human efforts to dig trenches, so that nothing but the heaviest equipment would make an impression on the earth, and of that there was none. Boiled water turned into ice before their eyes. Vehicles froze, immobile, to the ground and weapons became useless as metal froze to metal. Sleep was to become the long winter's nightmare as now the full import of their hasty decisions was borne home.

There were few blankets, few sleeping bags and no fuel for fires, except the little gained from the despoiled huts of the population fleeing before the advancing enemy. All the while the wind blew straight as an arrow, straight from the north, into their screwed-up faces; and it blew with a hard ruthlessness agonizing them with fine razor-cuts of exquisite pain. No thoughts existed but escape from the wind's bitter, constant nagging, the Fusiliers had no wish but for still air and warmth.

At the foot of the hill there were the remnants of a small village where, in an animal shed, a low fire was maintained for the morning, to which they staggered like drunkards, craving the meagre warmth and the sleep of which the cold had robbed them. Wrapped in greatcoats, they lay through the night like brute animals, huddled in depressions in the snow. Their bodies were stiff and unresponsive from the crushing force of the freezing wind that whistled in malicious discord about the summit of the hill. Orders were simple and repeated to gain any hold in icebound minds, and they grunted to each other like simpletons, forgetting everything in their hunger for the fire. To the flank, a mile or two above them, and observable from their hill, there moved a long, slow, black thread of refugees, constantly pouring away from the enemy. They moved, some million or more, close packed on their only permitted route, along the now disused railway. They too were harried by the wind's full fury; with no cover, no respite, no warmth except from a few slow-burning fires left to them in pity. Hungry, their thin clothes plucked and fretted by the wind, clutching a few belongings, families trudged south holding on to each other so as not to get lost in the moving mass; trusting in their national hardiness to overcome the winter.

At night they sat and waited as the cold crept deeper into their bones or, with many others, made the desperate search for children separated in the jostling march. Their plaintive cries, tossed and torn by the wind, came in sad whispers across the snowbound night. The mornings, too often, found groups, mostly children, frozen in sleep where they rested. Like nightmare statues of grief they dotted the passage of the slow retreat.

Searching the village for wood, two soldiers unearthed a bundle of rice straw wrapped in a thin, fibre mat. With sticks they teased and pulled it out from under the hut and, finding it held together by a thin layer of ice, broke it open. The sides fell away to reveal a child, a young girl, abandoned, frozen to death in sleep. They stood looking at it.

'Poor bastard,' said one.

'Poor bastards,' echoed the other looking towards the railway line.

Their faces revealed their anguish and their eyes were pierced with an agony of compassion which belied the rigours of their life. Their minds, crucified by the thoughts of their own children and families, made them lift their hands in helpless despair, in pity for themselves and the whole sorry mess. Inarticulate, they looked at each other and swore.

Chapter VIII

Korea

J. J. Thompson writes:

that the late summer of 1950 heralded the invasion of South Korea by the troops of communist North Korea. The North Korean Army had violated the border between the North and the South by crossing the line of the 38th Parallel. This was the agreed line separating the two states who were political enemies.

The United Nations held a hastily convened session which was in the absence of the Soviet Union who had decided to withdraw temporarily from the Security Council after a dispute. It was decided that the attack was against the principle of the Charter of the United Nations and that action was to be taken against the North Koreans by sending an army under the auspices of the UN. It would be under the command of the Army of the United States who already had some troops in Korea from the end of the 1939–1945 war. This presence was with the agreement of the Soviet Union in the treaties following the defeat of Japan.

The British 27th Infantry Brigade was hastily despatched from garrison duties in Hong Kong and was soon engaged in the early fighting. These early battles were fought, with the North Koreans advancing all the way south to a point just north of Pusan, the most southerly port in South Korea. At that time the British Government was asked for further help and it responded by sending another Infantry Brigade and supporting Regiments. Royal Navy units from Far East waters were also sent to support the ground troops.

The 29th Independent Infantry Brigade was despatched from England in November 1950. This Brigade contained the First Battalions of the Royal Northumberland Fusiliers, the Gloucestershire Regiment and the Royal Ulster Rifles with the 8th Hussars deployed as a tank regiment, 45 Field Regiment Royal Artillery and the 5th Squadron of the Royal Engineers. The Brigade was under the command of Brigadier Brodie. All the UN forces in Korea were under the command of General Douglas McArthur, the veteran commander from the war with Japan in the Pacific.

The Battalion was transported to Korea in the *Empire Halladale* in October 1950. The Fifth Fusiliers found themselves on the six-week voyage to Korea, which was a country that most of those who had not served in the Far East had hardly ever heard mentioned. After the ship left Singapore it did not call into Hong Kong. This may have been for security reasons but some thought it might be because too many might take the opportunity to jump ship. After passing Hong Kong the ship ran into a very serious typhoon. It was so shattering that even the infantry officers were pressed into service as lookouts, mainly for mines. The average soldier on the open bridge in the huge seas that were battering the ship was incapable of looking at more than the soles of his boots. Many thought that the exercise had little benefit except keeping officers employed in trying circumstances.

The ship disembarked the Battalion at Pusan and it was sent to Kaesong, a few miles inside the North Korean border. What they found was a great cultural shock. It was like returning to the seventeenth century or even further back. Those Fusiliers who survived the Korean War – and the British cemetery at Pusan shows that many Fifth Fusiliers died for the cause of freedom and the United Nations – returned to Great Britain much more enlightened than when they left. They had suffered many trials and hardships but most were born with stoic humour. Although Korea was, to most Fusiliers, a godforsaken country, they left better and prouder men.

Fusilier Preston Little remembers that on arrival at Pusan, the Fifth Fusiliers were greeted by a large banner archway on the quay which proclaimed, 'Through these portals pass the finest Goddam Fighting men in the World, the US Army'. Not the most tactful greeting to a regiment joining an international and a United Nations approved force. What also annoyed the Fusiliers was the fact that an Australian soldier, who was already ashore, had beaten the Fusiliers to the draw by shinning up the archway to paint 'Bollocks' in large letters on the banner. However, he was there and then made an honorary Fusilier for his efforts.

The Fusiliers finally disembarked and boarded an antiquated train which was drawn up near the quay for them. The train, which was without the benefit of the 'usual facilities', was to take them to Kaesong on the 38th Parallel. On the journey they had to look out for possible guerrilla activity. Therefore, each carriage had to post an alert Fusilier armed with a rifle or semi-automatic Sten gun. The prevailing sanitary conditions, or in reality the lack of them, made it necessary for the train to stop, at intervals, for the Fusiliers to relieve themselves.

At one of these stops, the Regimental Padre, because he thought the dignity of his office required more decorum, had strayed further out than the rest to perform his duties which would enrich the Korean farmland. However, whilst the Padre was concentrating on this task, the train was ordered to move on by the commander who was unaware of the Padre's embarrassing predicament. The Regiment was treated to the rare spectacle of a red-faced churchman frantically trying to catch the train and pull up his trousers at the same time. Eventually the stumbling, tripping and panting Padre was finally hauled aboard by grinning Fusiliers. Somehow the Padre managed to retain his composure although it must have taken quite an effort to do so.

Lieutenant Paddy Baxter and 12 Platoon travelled separately from the rest of the Battalion with its baggage. Getting water for shaving and the odd cup of tea was an operation in itself. This entailed getting the engine driver to fill a steel helmet without its fittings with hot water. However, whilst it was all right to fill one helmet, when the whole of the platoon and its accompanying mortar battery asked for hot water, it took a few hours to get enough steam to get going, so the practice had to stop. The train stopped in Seoul and the platoon felt it most incongruous that Christmas cards were being sold by the traders. Many were the local Koreans' ideas of what a western Christmas should look like and, although many were purchased, few were sent. Most were kept as mementoes.

The Battalion's first action was at Sibyoni and then it withdrew south to reform a defensive line right across the whole of the Korean peninsula. The Chinese had now decided to enter the war and the Chinese Army invaded across the Yalu River. In February 1951 there was a battle to the north of the Han River and the well-reported Battle of the Imjin River on St George's Day 1951.

There was one event that Fusilier Little remembers with a little shame which was, nevertheless, tinged with a little more than satisfaction. This was the removal of some 'spiritual' refreshment from the mobile Officers' Mess on New Year's Eve of 1950–51. The Intelligence Section and the battalion snipers were sharing bivouacs on a night that was bitterly cold with deep snow around. Their meagre ration of bottled Japanese beer had been frozen solid and split cleanly in half making a beer lollipop. However, this now thawed-out version of a poor substitute for Newcastle Brown had been consumed. The Intelligence Section and the snipers listened to the cheerful chatter coming from the direction of the Officers' Mess wagon. One of the Fusiliers, Den Prout, an audacious scouse from the Wirral in Cheshire, began to bemoan his lack of means to toast the New Year. Gradually Prout and Little came to the conclusion that they would do themselves and their comrades a great service if they were to liberate a little of the festive spirit from the officers.

With some trepidation, they used their skill at fieldcraft to ghost their way to the trapdoor at the rear of the wagon. Cool as ice Den Prout silently crawled up the steps to the trap and stole through the hole. They could see the feet of the assembled officers and, joy of joy, an assortment of hooch within easy reach. The intrepid scouse silently and nimbly selected a few bottles and passed them down to Little's eagerly awaiting hands.

They were greeted with great gusto by their comrades on their return and they all enjoyed the illicit booty. Sadly it was to be the last celebration on earth for Sergeant Williamson who was killed in action some days later. Surprisingly, after all these years, Prout and Little still feel guilty about what they did. However, they have convinced themselves that the action was justified if only for the sake of Sergeant Williamson whom they all liked. Little is still in touch with Den Prout who knows that their guilty secret has now been revealed. Although both Prout and Little can understand that there may be some who still feel angry, they offer their much belated

THE BOOZE BANDITS

apologies to those who may have been inconvenienced by the raid and hope they can be forgiven.

Little knows that Tony Perrins, who was Intelligence Officer at that time, suspected Little and Prout. However, Little believes that the officers gained their revenge later when, on a bitterly cold night, they were detailed to help dig in the Officers' Mess truck in frozen ground. He could not help but notice the glee in a certain major's and other officers' faces as, sullenly and muttering to themselves, Little and Prout sweated at their laborious task. Little supposed it was poetic justice.

Little would like to think that he and Prout managed to exonerate themselves at the Battle of the Imjin. The pair, with Corporal Milnes and an 8th Hussars tank, played their part in trying to halt the enemy hordes who swarmed down from the hills around their position. Fusilier Prout displayed the same ice-cool audacity as, covered by Little, he disposed of a leading bunch of Chinese with a grenade. They later spent hours in turn using the tank's Bren gun, hopelessly trying to stem the tide of the enemy, but it was to no avail and they had to endure a nightmare ride on the tank from their position.

They picked up many stragglers from the Brigade and many were killed, or taken prisoner, in this action. During the journey they passed the body of the greatly respected and loved Colonel Kingsley Foster who had been killed in his jeep. They thought he was indestructible. Perhaps their booze raid had been meant as training for this latter action. Or maybe punishment, or both.

A large number of those who served with the Battalion in Korea were Z Reservists, like Corporal Arthur Bland. Many of them were surivors of the Italian winter campaign and others had fought in Burma. This meant there was valuable experience in the Battalion. Fusilier, later Sergeant, McInnes told of how he was firing from a trench at an enemy attack when he noticed that his neighbour, a reservist, had one leg on the rim of the trench. He asked why and was told that once the enemy reached a certain point he would be off. When they reached that point he was off to live to fight another day. In this way he had survived many an action.

Bland had inseparable pals in Fusiliers Wanless and Duggan. On their way out to Korea an inter-company boxing tournament was arranged in the ship. Duggan had volunteered Wanless for the team, which occasioned some ribald comment and mirth. At a meeting where the ABA rules were explained, it was pointed out that the target area was the hairline of the head to the belt line. At this Fusilier Wanless announced his withdrawal. This, he said, was because he was nearly bald and, therefore, suffered a great disadvantage in that he presented a greater target. He got his own back by chasing Duggan round the ship for several days. He even forgot to moan about the fact that the only record on the ship was 'Those far away places'.

Sergeant George Garner was taking a draft to Korea on board HMM *Dunera* and, just prior to the Captain's inspection, the Deck Officer had come round and spotted some socks hanging on the overhead pipes. All he said was, 'Get rid of those bloody socks, Sergeant.' So he threw them all through the porthole. He did not know what to say to the lad when they returned. He was Orderly Sergeant in the ship at one stage, and the sergeant from whom he was taking over said that the record for Reveille for the next morning was set up, so all Sergeant Garner had to do was switch it on. Next morning he was up with the seagulls and put the switch on. He was on the mess decks bellowing his lungs out with, 'Let's have you, Wakey', when he heard on the tannoy, 'Come to the cookhouse door, boys'. He could have passed out. One of the lads said, 'I say, aren't you early, Sarge, for breakfast?'

Everyone had a good laugh at Sergeant Garner's expense, especially the ship's RSM.

They arrived in Japan, at 'Kuri Port', which was very hot, and were put up at Kuri Barracks. Then they were issued with mosquito nets and sorted out their kit. They were also issued with white kitbags which they were to fill with all their unessential kit, not required for combat. Garner moreover had to revert from Sergeant to Fusilier.

In Kuri, on St George's Day, one day before the Battle of the Imjin, the Barracks Commander gave the draft permission for a day out in the town. They all dressed up to explore and found it very interesting. After about six hours, whilst having a drink of Asahi or Tiger beer or saki, pandemonium broke out. The town was flooded with military police with trucks and tannoys blaring out, 'Any soldier from the First Battalion the Royal Northumberland Fusiliers will climb aboard these trucks and return to barracks immediately.'

That ended their brief spell in Kuri. On return to barracks, they were briefed. There had been a big Chinese attack and they were put on Globe-master Air Transports for Korea. Fusilier Garner landed at Kimpo Airport and was sent to what was left of the Battalion. On the way up by train, they were served by the Americans with something which was supposed to be tea. Garner feels that Americans sure can make coffee well, but a knife could stand in their tea and it was as thick as molasses. Needless to say it went straight out of the window. Once there, he was posted to the Medium Machine-Gun platoon, under the command of Captain Charles Chester with Sergeant Clinton as the Platoon Sergeant. The Sergeant told him that the Chinese were only 15 miles away, and off they went up the line after the Chinese recrossed the River Imjin. They dug in on the hills 800 yards from the river, and set up the defence with everything from booby-trapped napalm and 3-inch mortars to minefields. This was expertly done under the super-vision of Charles Chester. Fusilier Garner knew this only too well because he had to reset the fuse on the gate whenever anyone visited the area. He says he got 'the sweat on' a few times doing this.

Sergeant Garner remembers a pal of his, George Barratt from Ashington, who was an avid bible reader. One Sunday morning Captain Chester was doing his round of gun positions when he spotted Barratt reading his bible. 'Having a read, Barratt?' asked Captain Chester.

'Yes, sir. The Good Book says that thou shalt not kill and I cannot do that.'

Captain Chester said, 'Well, Barratt, if they do come and you don't shoot them, the Chinese will bloody well shoot you.' That was the end of that problem.

There was also Corporal Johnson who made friends with a rodent which he named 'Chalky White'. Every second night Chalky White would creep along the sandbags to the gun position and eat the portion of cheese that Johnson left out for him.

One night, Corporal Lowes, Garner's section commander, and Garner decided to spend the night in the command post rather than in the cramped space of the pup tents. So they took their small packs, a blanket and their mosquito nets. They rigged up their nets and got their heads down. After an hour they were awakened by a lot of squeaking. Corporal Lowes shook Garner in some panic saying, 'Garner, grab your kit and we'll get the hell out of here.' The rats were running round their nets like racing cars. They were out in a flash and back to their pup tents.

Patrols from the Kansas Line across the Imjin were called 'Swans'. Humphrey Walker used to complain that those who were good at patrolling, and these were rare birds, did more than their fair share of these very dangerous missions. Fusilier Garner remembers the Machine-Gun Platoon laying down fields of fire to support the 'Swans'.

Another great character was 'Dinger' Bell – a long-time trench mate of Arthur Bland. He was a dour lad from Nottinghamshire, a poacher by trade, whose avid desire was to return to marry his rich little widow. He spent all his time grousing about why they were in Korea, the cold, the Americans and their combat rations, the Koreans and the politicians who put the Battalion in Korea.

In January 1951, there was a rumour that two brigades of Chinese were expected and the Battalion was to dig in to meet them. Dinger Bell said that he wasn't going to fight them since they had done him no harm. However, when the Chinese attacked them early in the morning, he seemed quite unperturbed but went into a grumbling soliloquy about the uncivilized behaviour of a breed of people who drop in on you uninvited without a calling card. When Corporal Bland looked at him, he was carefully checking his ammunition with great relish. However, Z Company was by-passed and when W and Y Companies counter-attacked, the Chinese were chased back about 500 yards to the front of Z Company. Everyone, including Dinger, let fly with everything they had but it was not very effective due to the extreme range. One of the Chinese appeared at a run but then slowed down to a walk. Everyone stopped firing and gave him a cheer. That night Z Company pulled out and learnt that the Battalion had written Z Company off.

This gave rise to another grouse from Dinger. In fact, the only smile Corporal Bland saw on Dinger's face was later in the campaign when he was drawn out of the line to drive the company truck. However, Arthur Bland never tired of Dinger's griping because he got a great deal of amusement from it. He would like to meet Dinger again in order to give him that pint from a frosted glass which he so often yearned for in Korea. Fusilier, later Corporal, Hulme was driving Major John Winn, Z Company Commander, in his jeep from the north of Seoul when it broke down. It could not be fixed because the clutch had gone. Major Winn was not pleased and was having a few choice words to say on the matter when he spotted a large American convoy heading south away from the enemy. Hoping for a tow, Major Winn flagged down the convoy and explained the situation. In the midst of the explanation, an American General, with pennants flying, drew up. The General agreed to a tow, but asked Major Winn to 'saddle up' because he had two 'commie' divisions on his tail and wished 'to get the hell out of here'.

Soon afterwards the company moved up north again and Fusilier Hulme was asked to take Major Winn to the American section on their flank. When they got there, all there was was a pile of empty tins and no Yanks. Major Winn told Hulme to get back as quickly as possible. Later that night, as Fusilier Hulme was about to have forty winks, he noticed some dark figures moving across the front. Thinking they were South Koreans about to relieve them, he shouted at them and was rewarded with a burst from a burp gun. He dived under the jeep as the sky was lit up by tracer bullets. As dawn broke, he spotted two of the culprits and took them prisoner. That night, Major Winn said they had to pull out as they were cut off.

'What about my jeep?' Hulme asked.

'Leave it behind.'

'What about my prisoners?'

'Let them go,' was the reply.

He now knows what Major Winn meant by 'take no prisoners'.

Once the company had got back to the south of Seoul, Fusilier Hulme and two mates decided to drop in at the American artillery battery nearby. On arrival, they were greeted by a large cook sergeant who asked Fusilier Hulme if he would like to trade his Thompson sub-machine-gun. Having been told that they should hand in all weapons confiscated from the enemy, he thought, why not? He asked if the cook had a jeep, but the cook felt that his CO would not stand for that but what about something else? On being told that the company was on hard tack, the Americans generously gave them a good meal and a 3-ton Dodge truck loaded up to the roof with loaves of freshly baked bread. On arrival back at 12 Platoon, his Platoon Commander, Paddy Baxter, nearly had a heart attack. Fusilier Hulme hoped that it made up for the loss of the jeep.

Soon afterwards, Fusilier Hulme was told that he had won the draw to see Newcastle United play in the Cup Final at Wembley. He thought it was all a propaganda stunt and did not believe it until he was on the plane back to England. However, after the two-week visit he was back to Korea and the war again.

One incident certainly did make the national press. A certain company second in command was stunned to see his wife coming to greet him in a lull during the fighting quite near the front line. Was it a dream? It was not. His wife had managed to get herself to Japan and had persuaded an American pilot to take her to Korea. She had then thumbed lifts up to the front line. History does not relate the full details and who got into trouble.

Lieutenant Paddy Baxter missed the action on St George's Day because he had to return to England for his father's funeral. He returned to Korea in Her Majesty's Troopship *Empire Pride*. This was not the largest ship in the world and had no accommodation for women. However, three nurses, named Faith, Hope and Charity by the officers, joined the ship at Singapore to go on to Hong Kong, although the ship was to go to Pusan first and then back to Hong Kong. The officers going to Korea had a far more

"KEEP IT UP CHAPS, JUST A COUPLE MORE HEAVES AND WE'RE CLEAR OF THE MUD." PMGLITTLE.

entertaining voyage after Singapore than the very dull all-male company on the earlier part of the voyage. The nurses admitted that they found the men in Singapore very dull and looked forward to meeting real men who were going farther east. When Lieutenant Paddy Baxter returned to Hong Kong he met Charity again and, later, found that she had married one of the officers. He wonders what happened to Faith and Hope.

When he got back to Korea, he found the Battalion had dug itself in on the Kansas Line. This was like a modern Maginot Line, a bit like the defensive positions of the First World War. He felt the company he joined had been there for some time and, in relative terms, were quite cosy. During the day the company left the hill to live at the bottom. If the enemy had come, they would have raced up the hill to occupy their positions. At night when it rained it was a bit of a haul up the hill and Major John Winn, the Company Commander, led the company up the hill in their birthday suits to keep their clothing and equipment dry.

Fusilier Garner went to Osaka on a course where he met the famous 'Mad Mitch'. He was the only officer Garner had met that gave his dog seven days CB. When he came into the mess hall he would bring his cane down on a table with a crash and plates would jump a couple of inches before he shouted, 'Any complaints?' The soldiers would answer, 'No, sir'. It was not as if any other answer was expected, although the food was good. After the course, they were taken by sea to Pusan where Garner met 2nd Lt Foxton, who was later killed in the last of the Battalion's battles in Korea. Foxton asked what it was like. They replied that it was not that bad and that they took each day one at a time. Foxton told them that the Battalion was going to leave Korea quite soon for Hong Kong, but he was glad to join the Battalion after all the officer training he had gone through. He went to Z Company and was killed trying to take out two machine-gun nests.

In the latter part of their time in Korea, on the afternoon of 5 Ocober 1951, Z Company was ordered to take a hill, code-named 'Newcastle United Football Club', but renamed 'Heartbreak Ridge' by the Fusiliers. Coming up to the hill in the dark, and in the mist, finding the exact place where they were was difficult. When the mist cleared they found themselves on a lower hill with a large hill towering over them. They decided that if the Chinese were on the higher hill they would be sitting ducks, but were still not sure where they were, so they asked the gunners to fire a few rounds at a known point to get their bearings; the guns duly fired. Captain Dick Blenkinsop, who was there to control the Battalion 3-inch mortars, then asked what would happen if Z Company was on the target and the enemy had gone. Lieutenant Baxter had never seen a hill being cleared so fast. Fortunately the shells went far over their heads and it was clear that Z Company was well on the right course.

As they reached the top of the hill, they came under fire and Lieutenant Paddy Baxter told Fusilier Hulme 'to see to it', as he was the nearest to the firing. Whilst under cover behind a rock, he shouted, 'Knock it off, you blokes, we're Z Company.'

The reply came, 'Oops, sorry, we're Y Company.' They then found more Chinese than they expected, one of whom took a shot at Lieutenant Baxter, hitting him in the chest with the bullet coming out of his back. Fusilier Hammil, who was standing next to him, said, 'You've been hit, sir.'

Lieutenant Baxter had noticed this and the shock sent him to the ground. Fusilier Hulme meanwhile saw that Lieutenant Baxter was wounded in the lung and spotted who had fired the shot. He aimed his Sten gun but it jammed and would not unjam, despite carrying out the first IA. In his haste, he dropped his Sten gun and chased after the enemy with nothing in his hand except a smoke grenade. Realizing his error, he threw the grenade and beat a hasty retreat.

He found Lieutenant Baxter with his bad wound and applied the officer's own field dressing to him. After improvising a stretcher for him, he noticed that the bullet had gone straight through him. Rather than use his own field dressing, in case he might need it later for himself, he tucked Baxter's jacket under him and, helpfully, told him not to make any sudden movements – not that he could. He then asked Baxter if he wanted morphine, and received the reply, typically, 'I have got enough f'ing holes in me already.'

In that last action in October 1951, when Lieutenant Paddy Baxter was wounded and Sergeant Smith killed, Corporal Bland found himself in command of what was left of 12 Platoon of Z Company. At that stage, Bland was clearing a machine-gun nest which he had surprised. He took six prisoners and, as each of them came out of the dugout, he passed them to his pal and section 2 i/c, Tommy Thompson who was also the section Bren gunner. Thompson was saying 'Eeny meey miny mo', punctuated by prods from the Bren gun, as each Chinese was passed to him. He looked so comic that Bland started to giggle almost hysterically. Then, as the prisoners were taken away with happy grins on their faces, Corporal Bland collected his 14 men, and was continuing the advance when out of the blue they were overrun by some survivors of 11 Platoon. They had a multitude of Chinese on their heels and several of 11 Platoon were wounded.

Their numbers were not enough to hold the Chinese and, discretion being the better part of valour, Corporal Bland directed his lads, in some undignified haste, down the hill. The 11 Platoon Bren gunner – Bland thinks Leach was his name – covered the withdrawal sufficiently to discourage the Chinese. Shortly after reaching the company area they came under mortar fire when Bland saw his mate, Billie Parks of 10 Platoon, staggering about. He went over to him and found he was partly blinded by blast. Parks later told Bland's wife that Bland had saved his life, but Arthur Bland modestly states that was nonsense. This was the second time Corporal Bland had found himself in command of 12 Platoon and Colonel Baxter is surprised he never got a medal for his efforts, but he feels the great thing is that they both survived and are still alive.

"I'VE GOT TOO MANY HOLES ALREADY TO BE PUNCTURED BY THAT!"

At this last battle, the Machine-Gun Platoon was positioned on the left flank on a small hillock just below some paddy fields. Unfortunately they were spotted by a Chinese observation post, and shells started dropping on their area. They were sweating again. However, Charles Chester just sat calmly on the hill with his binoculars giving the artillery target references so that they could counter-bombard.

Having got over that 'little difficulty', they had to cross the paddy fields to get into position for the attack. Half the platoon had crossed when they were spotted again by someone whom Garner describes as 'that bitch of a Chinese woman soldier'. With his mate Busty Stanley and the Korean porters, Garner hit the deck like a pack of cards and yelled at the porters to get down.

After a lull in the shelling, they joined Charles Chester and the rest of the platoon. They had thought that Garner and Stanley were 'goners'. However, they did lose two Korean porters, who were never seen again, before they got to their position and gave covering fire. The First Battalion of the Fifth Fusiliers took the objective but suffered many casualties.

About this time the Fifth were due to be relieved by the First Battalion of the Royal Leicestershire Regiment. Fusilier Little was detailed to be one of the advance party which was to go to Hong Kong. They were to go by road to Seoul and then, by air, to Kure in Japan. The party was headed by Captain Jumbo Wilson with Corporal Jim Johnson and Fusilier Alfick. Most of the journey was done in the hours of darkness in a jeep driven by Jumbo Wilson. For the sake of security no lights were permitted.

When they were approaching the reasonable safety of Seoul, Jumbo Wilson decided to put on the sidelights only to be confronted by a huge American military policeman waving the jeep down with a torch. The MP poked his angry head into the driver's side of the jeep. He demanded to know if the driver was not godamned aware that he was in an active service area, and did he know that lights were strictly taboo?

Captain Wilson paused and with dignified indignation enquired of this lapsed colonial, 'Are you not aware that you are addressing a captain of the British Army?'

'Sir,' came the reply, 'are you not aware you are talking to a colonel in the Army of the United States of America?'

Game set and match to the military police. After a short lecture on driving behaviour, they were allowed to proceed with a somewhat chastened, silent and chagrined Jumbo Wilson. The three Fusiliers were afraid to catch each others' eyes for fear of exploding. Perhaps, later, Captain Wilson might have seen the humour of the situation.

Korea was no picnic. The Battalion was awarded four Distinguished Service Orders, eight Military Crosses, two Distinguished Service Medals and seven Military Medals. There was also a George Cross awarded for bravery as a prisoner of war. The Battalion lost 67 killed and had 245 wounded.

Chapter IX

In Hospital

In the First World War the life of a subaltern was about 21 days. In the Korean War almost every platoon commander was either killed or wounded and company commanders did not fare much better. The cemeteries in Korea show the number of casualties suffered by all ranks in the Regiment headed by their Colonel. Many of the latter ended up in hospital in Japan.

The Battalion's Medical Officer found himself in an American Military Hospital after being wounded. One morning an American General came round the ward dishing out Purple Hearts, the United States Army medal that shows that you were wounded in action. He reached the MO's bed and the MO was duly dished out a Purple Heart. Unfortunately, being a polite Englishman, he said, 'Thank you, General.'

'That man's a Limey,' said the General. 'Take his medal back!'

When Lieutenant Paddy Baxter was wounded on 5 October 1951, it was a tortuous journey back to hospital which he started on a stretcher where he was met by a bulldozer tank that, because it did not have a turret, was able to have the stretcher fitted across it. Thus Baxter was got back to the Doctor. After initial treatment, he was sent off in an ambulance from the Indian Field Ambulance. This was driven by a Sikh who spoke not a word of English. As Baxter had served in the Indian Army he could speak Hindustani, and he encouraged him to drive faster. He thinks that the driver thought he had a madman as a passenger, and so the driver thought that he would drive like a madman. It was like a crazy taxi journey through a crowded part of Calcutta, and they went like dingbats.

He was then brought in front of the good Indian Doctor whose name sounded like 'cup-of-tea' read fast. The Doctor took Baxter off the stretcher into the surgery and asked what was wrong. Baxter explained that it was this bullet that had gone through him. The Doctor gave him a cup of tea and a cigarette. The tea went down the right way but the cigarette smoke started to come out of his back. This galvanized the Doctor like an electrified squirrel to stop him drinking tea, and he was so horrified that he could not get rid of Baxter quickly enough to the Norwegians.

The Norwegians were to do Baxter's first operation. At this stage he was beginning to lose a certain amount of interest in the proceedings. There he met the great Norwegian surgeon who had, as it happens, visited the Battalion a few days previously. Perhaps he was looking at the cattle before they went to the abattoir. 'Oh yes,' he said, 'I remember you. But I will let you know that I am the best carver in Europe.'

He was sharpening an enormous knife at this stage, but then Baxter lost further interest as someone seemed to have hit him on the head with a sledgehammer. He came to and was then sent on to the American Evacuation Hospital at Seoul.

The helicopter deposited him on the playground at the hospital. Baxter was the last of the four stretcher-cases to be taken in and was left for some time on the playground. He remembers being visited by an army of clergy

48

who asked him if he was Catholic. Was he a Roman Catholic? No. He was obviously then condemned to Hades. Was he a Turk? No, he was not a Turk. Someone came to fetch him, just as more helicopters were heard, and he was raced through the hospital at great speed, hanging on like a wounded Indian tiger until he arrived at the ward. By this stage, his only cover and possessions were his boots. The nurse looked at him somewhat coldly when Baxter asked if he could have some pyjamas. 'Oh, you're British.' She then put him on the bed that Baxter felt was still warm from the person who had just died in it. He was, however, pleased to be in a nice warm hospital being looked after by what he assumed to be properly qualified people.

There was a man on his right on a stretcher. Every four hours in came a gum-chewing orderly who stuffed a great handful of grease up the poor man's fundament. This caused the man to scream like a stuffed pig but after a while he calmed down before the next visit by the orderly, who never uttered a word. After a few days in came the Doctor who prodded the man and said, 'Hey, soldier, it is time to change your treatment.'

The poor man on the stretcher raised himself with great difficulty on one elbow and with a look of hope in his eye, asked, 'Do I get to stick my finger up the orderly's arse?' This made Baxter laugh until he was nearly sick and he must have pulled nearly every stitch in his back.

Lieutenant Baxter was in this hospital for another week, and various people and doctors came to see him. Their main concern seemed to be the fact that the lieutenant's hair was on the long side and he was offered a visit to the hospital barber, which he refused. He felt that he was in hospital to be cured rather than to be smartened up. What were they going to do about his right lung? Nothing, it seemed, because that specialist was not due back from leave for a few days.

He was also concerned that his dressing had not been changed since he had arrived and was beginning to hum a bit. After making a fuss about this the hospital thought the best thing to do was to get rid of the pestilent Baxter. So he was put on an aircraft to Japan.

He was flown to the hospital at Kure, arriving in the middle of the night and was brought into the ward, cursing like a stuffed pig because he was getting somewhat sore from his long sojourn on the stretcher. He was greeted with, 'Don't you come cursing into my ward,' spoken in a beautiful Irish accent from the lovely Sister Flo Hines.

Baxter replied in an Irish accent, 'I will curse as much as I bloody well like.' Needless to say, they both got on like a house on fire. Lieutenant Baxter was in the hospital's excellent hands from then until February 1952.

Second Lieutenant Ronnie Cowe had been wounded earlier and by the time Baxter had arrived had made enough progress so that he could sneeze without causing major problems. One of the nurses said to Baxter, 'Oh, Mr Cowe can now sneeze; is he not a good boy.' Baxter went over to Ronnie Cowe and told him that if he did anything that Baxter could not do it must only be on the pain of death.

The wounded from the battles of November 1951 began to arrive at the British Commonwealth Military Hospital at Kure. They came via the American MASH towards the end of November, and were mainly from the King's Own Scottish Borders, the Royal Leicestershire Regiment and the Third Royal Australian Regiment.

Lieutenant Geoffrey Havilland of the Royal Leicesters was one of the wounded and he recalls there were many interesting characters who were patients. There was a Scottish chaplain who, to the chagrin of many, was the recipient of a bottle of 'medicinal' whisky every day. He disconcertingly made a habit of adding a good measure of it to his breakfast porridge. There was also an engineer officer who was obsessed with mines. He spent his time bribing the ward orderlies to purchase supplies of 'caps'. The Japanese version of the 'caps' used in toy pistols were much larger and more effective than their puny British counterparts. He would spend Wednesday night laying a minefield with his Japanese bangers so that Thursday's Commanding Officer's inspection would be enlivened.

Geoffrey Havilland particularly recalls one Lieutenant Paddy Baxter of the Fifth Fusiliers. He had been severely wounded in October 1951 and had remained in what is now called 'intensive care' well into December. He was in a separate room, with tubes attached to him and there was a constant hum of the pumps working under his bed. Lieutenant Baxter was already bored with his own company and with his incapacity. Even at this early stage, and others cannot remember when he was not, Lieutenant Baxter was a garrulous creature – he needed to talk. The walking wounded were allowed to visit him under the watchful eye of the Ward Sister, Major Jane Carson (who was later to be the Matron of the Cambridge), however he craved the bright lights and the companionship of an Officers' Mess. The nearest one could get to a mess was the Kure Officers' Club.

This club was only available to those who had been discharged to the convalescent depot, which was next to the hospital, but not to the inmates of the hospital. There were many breaches of the rule, and often the more mobile from the hospital and the more inebriated absconders were berated on their return by Jane Carson or one of her over-zealous minions.

Baxter had every intention of visiting the club, and it was inevitable that he disconnected himself from the tubes and pumps to take himself the short distance down the hill to it. This was a social success but a medical disaster. He subsequently received the full force of Major Jane Carson's tongue. She was, of course, more concerned with the good Baxter's well-being than with the disciplinary aspects of the prank.

Eventually, he was released from the isolation of intensive care and, following yet another long operation on a Thursday morning, was reunited with his fellows in the main ward. The engineer's Thursday minefield had by now become even more sophisticated. As usual on this day, the patients were lying at attention in their beds as the inspecting retinue moved through the ward. This consisted of the commanding Medical Officer, his Adjutant, the Surgeon with her Anaesthetist, any specialist consultant, the Regimental Sergeant Major, the Ward Sister and her acolytes, medical orderlies and at the end of the line, a clerk taking notes with great difficulty. At the first explosion everyone jumped. There were more explosions and Major Jane Carson was leaping around like a frantic frog, demanding that the culprit own up. There were more bangs and then a small and sleepy, 'It was me, Sister, I cannot tell a lie,' from a very groggy Baxter, just resurfacing from the anaesthetic.

On one of these inspections, Major John Winn's favourite trick was to fill a hospital bottle brim full and keep it handy until the inspecting team arrived at his bed. He would then produce the steamy and foamy receptacle and demand another immediately as he wished to go again. The orderly, mindful of the formal occasion, would try to persuade John Winn to keep quiet and wait. This was always refused in a loud voice, much to the embarrassment of the orderly and the inspecting team.

On most of these inspections, the Colonel would stop at Baxter's bed and ask him what was wrong with him, despite the fact that all the information was written on a placard at the end of the bed. Baxter got so fed up with this that for each inspection he invented a different wound. The Colonel never seemed to understand that his leg was being pulled.

Lieutenant Colonel Baxter recalls that at night, when all the lights went out at about 9 p.m., all those who could walk would drag those who could not up to the loo. This was because the idea of attending to the needs of nature in the way demanded by hospitals was pretty disgusting. A proper loo was heaven. If the Ward Sister had arrived at the crucial time she would have had a heart attack at seeing what looked like a re-enactment of the painting of the retreat from Moscow.

On one occasion, when Baxter was due to have one of his many operations on his lung, he received the pre-op shot a bit early. By the time he was due to be wheeled from the ward to the operating theatre he was wide awake, although feeling semi-drunk. He was dressed ready for the operation in his rugby socks and the hospital garment that is tied up at the back leaving the usual space down the spine to the anus. He persuaded the young and obedient Japanese orderly to get on the trolley so that the half-naked Baxter could push it. Off they went through the hospital at speed, until they approached the operating theatre. Here, there was a tiny slope and so Baxter thought this was an opportunity to stand on the back of the trolley and freewheel down to the theatre. As he got to the bottom, his speed had increased, and he crashed into the operating theatre where an operation was in full swing.

There was the occasion of the New Year's Eve dance. Only those who could get up were invited. Ronnie Cowe and Paddy Baxter were able to go to the dance and Baxter was very taken with the looks of the Assistant Matron. She had the most superb eyes he had ever seen, and her uniform made her most attractive. The evening wore on and a little alcohol had passed a few lips, so that Baxter was in good form by midnight and he became more determined to dance with this goddess. As the music started he took her by the arm saying, 'Please dance with me.' He then went into a most fantastic jig which happened to be in time with the National Anthem because it was the end of the evening. The Matron's eye as she regarded Baxter and the Assistant Matron would have made him get back into the woodwork if that were possible. The next day he met the Matron on the stairs and she took one look at him, only just surviving from the night before, and said, 'How is my musical friend?' Baxter wished he could have run screaming from her.

When patients left the hospital in Kure they were asked to fill in a sort of visitors' book with kind comments. When John Winn was asked to do this, he thought about it and said he did not feel he should because looking after him was their job and they should not need written plaudits. He was hauled in front of the Colonel who demanded that he should write in the wretched book, despite the fact that he would only be repeating his thoughts on the matter. Eventually, he was ordered to write in the book and he wrote a ten-page essay setting out all he thought was wrong with the hospital. The Hospital Colonel was so incensed with this that he copied John Winn's remarks to the Brigade Commander in Korea. Brigadier Brodie was no fool and no more than a great laugh was heard of the matter.

Whilst Baxter was in hospital in Hong Kong with jaundice, the King died and all the staff wore black armbands. All the nurses wore white uniforms, and so he asked one of them if she agreed that the white uniform was a sign of virginity. She agreed and he asked why she was wearing a black band. She got the message very quickly and Baxter only just escaped with his life.

Chapter X

Hong Kong

F ollowing the tour of duty in Korea the Battalion completed its overseas posting in the New Territories of Hong Kong. They were quartered at the unlikely-named Norwegian Farm Camp near the Chinese border. Hong Kong, at that time, seemed in line for a takeover, by force, by the Chinese Army. The Battalion was there to act as a tripwire to deter any aggression against Hong Kong. In the hills behind the camp were prepared positions which the Battalion would have to defend if Hong Kong were to be attacked.

The Battalion was indignant to find that it was taking over from the King's Regiment (Liverpool), which being the 4th of Foot was one senior to the Fifth Fusiliers. This fact rankled with the Fusiliers as they enjoyed a long-awaited binge in the camp NAAFI and they imbibed many bottles of San Miguel beer that night. The Battalion later received a diploma from the brewery for having broken the record for the number of bottles sold to a regiment, and were almost as proud of that honour as they were to receive the 'Imjin' battle honour which was the last to be placed on the Regimental Colours. When the NAAFI closed, a united mass of Fusiliers, headed by the Corps of Drums doing their drunken best to lead them while playing the Blaydon Races, marched through the camp waking all of the Fourth of Foot.

They were finally halted on a bridge over a stream by the outspread arms of the irate, but nevertheless brave, RSM of the 4th, who with the untouchable confidence of his unique breed, warned them to disperse and make their way peacefully to their beds. Needless to say there were some menacng voices who advised the Fusiliers to chuck the 'b——r over the f——g bridge', but common sense and well-ingrained discipline prevailed.

However, news of the incident had reached the 'Governor's' HQ. They were summoned next day, sheepishly thick-headed, pale and filled with foreboding to present themselves at the NAAFI. There they were confronted by the Commanding Officer of the Fifth standing on the stage trying to look stern and forbidding. He gave them a short reprimand on their disgraceful behaviour, then with a wry grin pointed to the black eye he was sporting. He said, 'Despite what I have said you may note that we had a slight disagreement with the officers of the Fourth ourselves last night.' He would have left to thunderous applause, but his stern look reappeared and he left them with grins of approval on their faces. They loved him; he was a real Fusilier.

During their tour in Hong Kong the 'Glorious Gloucesters' arrived by ship on their way back to England. Not all in the Brigade thought that the

Gloucester's action deserved all the plaudits they received. The Fifth having suffered many casualties, did not allow themselves to be cut off and did not surrender in large numbers. The Gloucesters did not, in the eyes of the Fusiliers, warrant the great US media attention they received. This was combined with the fact they were returning to England before the Fifth and the local Hong Kong press were also talking about them in terms of endearment, when most of those on the ship were new draftees. They made sure that there was a welcoming party waiting for them on the quayside, and that particular bunch of 'Glorious Gloucesters' found it impossible to land to enjoy what Hong Kong had to offer.

There were a number of stand-to practices of the defensive positions. Each company was aided in its task by a troop of tanks, a section of mules and an open-topped vehicle, misnamed a Bren gun carrier. It was the task of the mule section, with its local Chinese handlers, to carry the supplies to areas that could not be reached by wheeled vehicles.

It was the duty of the Company Second in Command to bring up supplies with the mule section. They loaded up with the usual difficulties heightened by language problems and the well-known stubbornness of the mules. One of the Fusiliers looked at the pile of barbed-wire rolls to be taken up the hill. 'Load them on it? Nivah! Not me,' and shuddered at the mere thought.

It was from that moment that the morning began to disintegrate into mule hunting, and one errant animal cut its swerving course away from the loaders with such sure-footed skill that it caused a Fusilier to remark, 'Bi! Ah wish he plaide fur or rugbi teem.'

The loading began to eat away the time and questions about the delay were being passed down from company HQ up on the hill. At last the first two mules set off up the hill with their two handlers and a Fusilier guide. As they neared the top, the path narrowed to the width of a mule. At that moment the Company Sergeant Major came down the hill. It was a case of the unstoppable meeting the immovable, however, one of the mules then decided there were better things in life than delivering rolls of barbed wire to Fusiliers to whom he had not been introduced, and he put his head down in preparation for a different course of action. The CSM, an old soldier and wise in signs of animal behaviour, turned and ran, being joined by the two handlers and the Fusilier. The two mules, not to be outdone, started to jettison their loads and took up the challenge of the race. Later the CSM stated that being chased by mules was not in his list of duties.

This incident curtailed the use of mules and much of the stores had to be manhandled up the hill until a better idea came to the Second in Command – what about the Bren gun carrier? A suitable route was reconnoitred and the loaded vehicle set off up the hill. All went well until the vehicle slid on an outcrop of rock, turned and shed one of its tracks. It was impossible to repair the track in that position and the Second in Command had the inspiration to call up one of the tanks. After many attempts to budge the carrier, the Troop Commander took over and successfully got to the carrier so that it could be moved and repaired. It was then ready to follow the tank downhill. The Troop Commander thought it would be better to back down the hill but halfway down there was a shout of 'FIRE' as billows of smoke came from the rear of the tank. Its camouflage net had caught fire. With prompt resolution it was cut loose and tossed over the side. Alas, this was not the end of this unhappy tale for there had been a long dry spell in the area and a serious hill fire in the young tree plantation followed. By the time the conflagration had been brought under control it was generally agreed that this stand-to exercise had been interestingly different. It was, however, an unhappy Second in Command who took to his bed that night. Some kind person had told him that the Hong Kong Government would charge one pound for each tree that was damaged.

The Battalion returned from Hong Kong on the *Empire Pride*, the same vessel on which Lieutenant Baxter had returned to Korea after his father's death. When they called into Colombo, Andrew Scott found a jeweller selling small silver St George and the Dragons, and told the man how clever he was to have duplicated the centrepiece of the Fifth Fusiliers' cap badge. The man must have been galvanized into activity because he managed to produce another 50 at the drop of a hat.

Baxter was put in charge of the St George's Minstrels concert which was to be performed in the Mediterranean. As it was an all-male ship the womens' parts presented a difficulty, so a Royal Army Service Corps driver was dressed up for the part. The ship managed to produce the make-up, the various goodies bought for wives and girlfriends were lent and a real bra was produced and suitably filled. When fully made-up, he really looked the part, so much so that when he came on the stage, there was a large and very audible intake of breath from the audience, who had been incarcerated without women for some time. The poor man had to be kept under guard for the rest of the voyage from men who were hunting for this woman on board.

The ship arrived in Liverpool on 25 August 1952 and the Battalion was taken by train to Brancepeth, arriving late at night. Many friends, wives, girlfriends and relations had waited for some time to welcome 'their dear boys back from their glory in Korea'. It was a very emotional occasion. The whole scene was lit up by the lights of the buses that had brought the relatives, making quite a sight. Later in the night, it was said that the whole area was heaving with Fusiliers renewing acquaintances with their wives and girlfriends. One of the Fifth's nicknames was 'the Fighting and F——ing Fifth'. They certainly lived up to the last part that night.

Chapter XI

The Homecoming

On 25 July 1952, the First Battalion embarked, for the second time, in HMT *Empire Pride*. The first occasion had been nine months earlier when she brought the Battalion back from Korea as far as Hong Kong, following its year's outstanding service in the Korean War. Now, she was bringing the Battalion home on a voyage to which everyone had been looking forward for a long time. Ahead of the Battalion lay a reception the like of which no battalion of the Regiment had, in all probability, ever experienced before. The City of Newcastle, led by its Lady Mayoress, who towered above the scene of planning and preparation, was going to provide a welcome for its county regiment which would live on in its memory. Alderman Mrs Grantham was that lady and, from the moment she first greeted the Battalion on arrival home, they took her into their hearts.

Painstakingly and generously the Lady Mayoress and the City Council, assisted by the Colonel of the Regiment, Major General H. de Morgan, the Chief Constable and Major Robert Ferguson MVO, Commanding the Regimental Depot, had arranged a programme of considerable proportions over the weekend of the 11th and 12th of October. This included a march through the City of Newcastle, a reception and luncheon for the entire Battalion in the Old Assembly Rooms, followed by speeches, and then attendance at Newcastle United's match at St James's Park as guests of the Chairman and Directors. In the evening, the Sergeants' Mess would hold a 'Welcome Home' Ball at Fenham Barracks to which the Lady Mayoress and other civic dignitaries had been invited. On the Sunday there was to be a Memorial Service in the Cathedral attended by the Duke of Northumberland and an impressive assembly of guests, in addition to a large gathering of Old Comrades. Once again the Battalion would march, with colours flying and led by the Band and Drums, from Fenham Barracks through the City, to and from the Service.

All this lay many weeks ahead as the *Empire Pride* docked in Liverpool on 25 August, while in the meantime the aim was to get everyone on leave as soon as possible. After disembarking and transferring the baggage there followed a slow and tortuous journey by train over the Pennines to the small station of Brancepeth in County Durham, where the Band was waiting. The Battalion had been delayed several hours and what had been arranged to take place in daylight was now to be done in darkness, beginning with the short march of about a mile to Brancepeth Camp where the Battalion would become the guests of the Durham Light Infantry. What was to come is delightfully described in 'The Depot Notes' of *St George's Gazette* for September 1952, written by Major Robert Ferguson.

> A tremendous crowd of friends and relations had been gathering in camp all day, and as darkness fell they were all gathered round the square – some singing and dancing, others sighing anxiously with impatience. The Lord Mayor, moving freely among the crowd, did much to alleviate the tension. Many car head lamps lit up the square, and then, soon after 9.30, the band and drums could be heard from the direction of the station. As the Battalion marched on to the square the crowds surged forward with excitement, nearly swamping the parade, which had the appearance of a searchlight tattoo with the lights on the marching figures and the Colours. The parade faced the Lord Mayor in close column of companies, and she most graciously welcomed them home with a few most charmingly chosen words. The Colours were marched off, followed by the Battalion, who were dismissed, and the remainder of the evening was devoted to re-unions.

It is the reunions on that memorial night which glow in Dare Wilson's memory. Among the large concourse of relatives which had gathered in expectation of the Battalion's earlier arrival were a number of dutiful fathers who were well aware of the deprivation of Newcastle Brown Ale which their sons had undergone during the past two years. Knowing how such a thoughtful gesture would be appreciated they had come liberally supplied with enough of the Geordie nectar to provide for the needs of their thirsty sons following their arrival plus, no doubt, a bottle or two with which to drink to their health and safe return from the war. The occasion called for due salutation.

During the afternoon the waiting became tedious and who could wonder at their decision to enjoy the odd bottle in quiet anticipation of the party which was to come? As time wore on, the temptation became stronger, the odd gap or two in the crate would not be noticed. The evening advanced and the party spirit took over as friends and acquaintances got together, and why not, the lads would be here any moment and they would catch up. The stage was now set for a celebration to fit the occasion. Then the Band was heard approaching and the scene which they had been anticipating for many weeks unfolded before their eyes. Mums and girlfriends shrieked in excitement as they pressed closer to catch their first glimpse of Bill, Harry or Jim. In the meantime Dad had the crate to look after so he would remain where he was, sitting on a rug. 'A'll stay heor, bring the lad ower when yo've foond 'im.'

Major Dare Wilson had further to travel than most and had planned to begin the journey the following day. So, having time to spare, he joined the throng to enjoy the atmosphere, assisted by the darkness, which frequently helps in such situations. The conversations he overheard were fragmentary, but some have lingered with him:

Mother:	'Hey, hinny, can ye tell us wheor to find Fusilier Robi'son? We caal him Billy at yhem, but mevvies the Army caals him William.'
Soldier:	'Which company is he in?'
Mother:	'He was in Y Company, but he had trouble with his corns so he went to HQ as a driver.'
Soldier:	'That sounds like Ginger, he's with the baggage party. Y'ed better ask the Quartermaster, he's ower theor with them three tonners.'
2nd Mother:	'I'm looking for wor Bobby – the name's Torner – he's in X Company. We call him Spelk on account he's taal and thin.'
2nd Soldier:	'Wey, misses, he's still taal but he's ni langer verry thin, he's bin on the San Mig' (Hong Kong Beer) 'and he's picked up a bit of a belly. I think he's back on the Regimental Police. Try the Guardroom in case any of his mates are there.'

While the problems within the dispersal area were being dealt with, those on the periphery were of a different nature.

First Voice:	'Is that ye fether?'
Second Voice:	'Ah divent knaa – whe's caalin?'
First Voice:	'Well, it soonds like ye – cum ower heor wheor I ken see ye.'
Second Voice:	'Ye'd better cum to me, lad, I've got w'ats left o' the beor.'
First Voice:	'I'm cummen.' (Pause) 'Let's hev a leuk at ye.' (Pause) 'Ye bugger, yo're pissed; howay man, si-doon afore ye faal doon! Noo then, wheors the beor.'

At this point Dare Wilson felt that the situation was well in hand, and the time had come for a drink in the Mess before retiring. In the morning, the families had all departed and, as far as he could see, Brancepeth was back to normal with the Durham Light Infantry in control again.

Chapter XII

Barnard Castle

After a short stay at Brancepeth as guests of the Durham Light Infantry, the Battalion marched to Barnard Castle. This was done in due form with the Band and the Corps of Drums. It was a long march and one most decorated Company Commander was said to have had blood coming from his boots for the last part of the march. Capain Baxter was Motor Transport Officer and so managed the journey on his newly acquired folding motorbike.

The time at Barnard Castle was a time when the Battalion breathed a great sigh of relief that it had survived the rigours of Korea. Peacetime soldiering was considered by many to be a bit of a joke and it was a time to relax before the next more serious posting. The Colonel was more interested in his next job with racehorses after retirement, so much so that after a visit by the Chief of the General Staff, Field Marshal Lord Harding, he asked Captain Baxter to look after the Field Marshal so that he could go to the races.

For the officers, St George's Day 1953 was a great event and a great party. The three colours, including the Drum Colour, were duly trooped with honour. That evening the Sergeants' Mess Ball would take place, the downfall of many a junior officer. It was always a grand affair and included old-fashioned programme cards. The officers then retired to their tent for lunch and champagne. The sergeants went to another drinks session in their Mess and the other ranks to Newcastle Brown Ale in the NAAFI.

In the Officers' Mess tent the champagne flowed all too freely and much of the champagne seems to have been passed out of the tent and drunk by the girls from Tilleys and their new-found Fusilier friends. The party was judged to be a great success by one and all – that was until the tent was burnt down and the finances were found to be in chaos. New brooms had to be brought in and many letters sent out to all serving and retired officers pleading for funds to put the Mess accounts back into the black.

Serving with the Battalion was a very perfect, competent and brave officer. When someone was in danger of drowning in the local river, he stripped to his underwear (he also had a perfect figure), executed a perfect dive, swam to the drowning man with an Olympic-style crawl and brought the victim back to the riverbank in the approved Royal Life Saving Society manner. All noted that his underwear was perfectly clean, brilliantly white, ironed and creased in the right places.

This same perfect officer invited a colleague to dinner in his quarters. The dinner was splendid and the Fortnum and Mason wines delicious. Conversation led – could we dare say was steered – towards the Post-Horn

Gallop and the fact that a bandsman at Sandhurst played it with a rifle. Nevertheless, the visitor said that he really liked hearing it played. The perfect officer stretched out a long hand to behind the sofa and drew out a post-horn. He then blew the Post-Horn Gallop, yes, you have guessed it, perfectly.

Captain Baxter went to a local dance on the night of the Coronation. He persuaded the local publican, a lovely lady of mature years with false teeth, to have a dance. The dance band did not face the floor and only the pianist could see the dancers. Baxter and his lady were dancing madly away when her false teeth shot across the deck, snapping gently as they slid over the floor. Only the pianist saw the event and was so doubled up in laughter that he gave up which threw the rest of the band. All the dancers were by this time lying on the floor, also doubled up with laughter. This is really a true story, attested by the said Baxter.

Fifth Fusilier Officers' Mess food was nearly always bad, despite officers paying an extra daily 'Messing Subscription'. At Barnard Castle, the Commanding Officer was alleged to have found an officer cutting grass in front of the Mess with a pair of scissors. The Colonel asked him what he was doing. He said he was having lunch because the food was so bad. 'Go round the back,' he was told by the Colonel, 'the grass is much better there.'

The subject of Mess food became a taboo subject. Anyone who dared criticize it was immediately made Food Member of the Mess Committee. The current holder of the post decided he must do something to get rid of his burden, so he obtained some horse manure, dipped it in batter and had it fried. The first officer the dish reached, smelt it, and declared, 'This is shit!' and then mindful that he could be made Food Member, added, 'But it's perfectly cooked.'

Captain Baxter was with the advance party to Kenya. His one remembrance of the journey was seeing the RQMS stripping off for bed into his long johns in a hanger at Khartoum. He was smoking a cigarette but before going to sleep, took out his false teeth with the cigarette still in them. Next morning the teeth were replaced, the cigarette relit and the RQMS was ready for the journey on to Kenya.

Chapter XIII

Kenya

The Battalion was sent to Kenya in 1953 as part of 39 Brigade. Its task was to combat the Mau Mau in the recently-declared Emergency. Records in the Nairobi library, heavily influenced by the need to write history as the political leaders wanted rather than by the real truth, show that the Battalion suffered severe casualties, returning with only 265 men, having been mauled by the freedom fighters (the Mau Mau). The reality was that of the 45 or so Europeans killed by the Mau Mau in the Emergency, very few were soldiers and the danger from the Mau Mau was more to Africans and to isolated farmhouses, rather than to groups of well-trained and well armed soldiers.

The new Commanding Officer, Lieutenant Colonel R. E. T. St John MC (later Major General St John CB MC), travelled out by RAF aircraft to Nairobi with his Advance Party. On clambering down the gangway onto the tarmac, he was faced by three smartly turned out Indians who saluted politely and handed him a letter of introduction.

They were relatives of a man who had served the 2nd Battalion as canteen manager in India in the late 1920s and were offering their services again to the Regiment. The Battalion had travelled out in some secrecy and so the Colonel marvelled at the efficiency of the bush telegraph. However, they had to be turned away as the NAAFI was already installed in Kenya.

General St John recalls the somewhat supercilious reception the Advance Party received from members of the General Headquarters Staff in Nairobi. They were all immaculately turned out in gabardine while the Fifth Fusiliers were in scruffy jungle green. The Fusiliers were directed by them to set up camp at a six-figure map reference, just south of Thompson's Falls. When they got there, they found it to be in the middle of a swamp, i.e. just picked at random off the map.

This was their opening experience of the poor GHQ staff work that was to follow as they struggled to get themselves straight over the next few weeks or so. At one of the orders groups, the Colonel remarked that someone should put up a notice on the outskirts of Nairobi: 'You are now entering the Gabardine Area', with 'You are now entering the Jungle Green Area' on the other side. A few days later such a notice was erected for all to see and the Colonel discovered that this was the work of that staunch Fifth Fusilier, Major (QM) Phil Bell MBE MM, the excellent Battalion Quartermaster, and he heard later that the notice was taken to heart by GHQ.

During their short stay in the Thompson's Falls area they used to frequent the local hotel-cum-pub which was a replica of a typical country pub in the

UK. There they met the white settlers, at that time an unhappy crowd and not particularly cooperative as regards anti-Mau Mau operations. The better-off employed farm managers who were a very mixed bag and always armed to the teeth. One day, a couple of them had a violent disagreement in the bar and one of them shot the other dead. He was tried later for murder and acquitted, which was the usual form for Kenya in those days.

At Y Company's camp at Happy Valley near Thompson's Falls, company officers were briefed by the officers of the Inniskilling Fusiliers company who they were relieving. The Happy Valley set had a reputation. It was rumoured that at the height of their 'powers' they used to visit each other for weekends. After dinner the ladies would pick a ball of coloured wool from the hostess's knitting basket and tie one end to the bottom of the stairs. They then trailed the wool to their bedroom and later the husbands picked a colour and followed it upstairs. The members of the house party considered it unlucky if it led to one of their own wives. This must have been a variation on the Essex car keys theme.

There was also the renowned hospitality of 'Bubbles' to contend with. On the first visit 'Bubbles' introduced her husband who always carried a large .45 revolver in the style of John Wayne. For this visit he started the evening sitting on the floor, singing Wakamba songs. A subaltern, anxious not to incur the wrath and a bullet from Hubby's .45 fell off the end of the sofa in his efforts to avoid physical contact with the slowly advancing 'Bubbles'. She then decided to enliven the party by dancing naked on the dining-room table, however, this was received in stunned silence by the group. Sensing that things were not going as well as expected, and in order to jolly up the party more, Hubby fired off a couple of shots into the ceiling which killed the dog sleeping on the bed upstairs. The Fifth Fusiliers thought that this was a good time to return to camp.

The Officer Commanding Y Company was sitting on the officers' thunderbox. He thought he would add to his relaxation by having a cigarette with this morning chore. The butt-end ignited the petrol vapour below, but the petrol explosion was little compared to the Company Commander's roar of rage. The Sanitation Orderly responsible also got singed but in a different way.

A similar event took place in the Middle East with the Parachute Regiment where Major Freddie Ward was seconded. The Sanitation Corporal had poured petrol into the pit and had thrown a match to light the petrol, thus killing off harmful bacteria. After this duty, the Sanitation Corporal decided to have a puff whilst answering the call of nature. One of the properties of petrol is that it never completely burns off, thus cruel justice decreed that the cocktail of unburnt petrol and other noxious gases combined to create a vast explosion. Not much of the Sanitation Corporal was found. The Parachute Regiment are a macabre lot and the whole of the Regiment swayed with suppressed laughter as they carried the coffin to its grave. An incidence of friendly fire?

Corporal Mills, at that time a Fusilier, flew into Nairobi with the main party. They were taken to Ol Joro Orok, which was about three miles to the west of Thomson's Falls, where the Battalion had a period of acclimatization in the foothills of the Aberdares. Fusiliers had to get used to the thinner air, the mountain forest and woodland, and the thick bamboo. Mills admits that he was scared at first, but most got used to it. The air was so thin that when the bugler had to play 'The Last Post' on the first night, he completely ran out of blow.

The Battalion was scattered along the mountain and, as part of the training, was marched up the mountain one night. Corporal Mills was number two on the Bren gun and he was glad that his number one was a big strong guy from Cumberland nicknamed 'Yoyo', who used to do a bit of wrestling and was a hard man. Although Corporal Mills was Yoyo's conscience and Yoyo listened to his advice, Corporal Mills knew on which side his bread was buttered.

Shortly afterwards the Battalion was moved to the slopes of Mount Kenya where each company was given an area to patrol. Mills's company, X Company, was based on Minns Farm with the platoons scattered over the wider area. Mills's 5 Platoon was at Littlewoods Farm but came back to Minns Farm at Christmas. He remembers sitting on a crate full of empty beer bottles, no doubt the fag end of the Christmas Eve celebration; it was very hot and it was his first Christmas away from home. Major John Winn, Captain Paddy Baxter, all the platoon commanders, the sergeants and even old CSM Paddy Reynolds did their duty and served Christmas lunch to the company.

Shortly afterwards Mills left the company to train and pass a course as a dog handler. His dog was a beautiful Doberman Pincher. He was promoted to Lance Corporal in the Dog Section and rejoined the Battalion at Mitchell Park, Nairobi. When he was walking the dog outside the camp, a staff car drew up and out stepped the C-in-C, General Sir George Erskine. He looked at the dog and asked Mills what he thought about the situation. Mills complained that he thought that the dogs were not being put to proper use. General Erskine told him not to worry because he had plans for him and then went behind a bush to do, as Mills said, what a man had to do.

About a week later the Dog Section was sent up-country, where they joined up with officers and sergeants of other regiments to do an intensive period of training with white hunters, ex-Commandos, trackers and silent killing experts. This was the start of the Special Combat Group and Corporal Mills was proud to have been in at the start. More people were trained in the same way from the Battalion and detached from their regiments to form teams to combat the Mau Mau deep in the forest. Their mission was to pursue and destroy the Mau Mau at their bases. Mills was with this group for a year before returning to the Battalion.

During their stay in Kenya some parents were concerned not to receive any letters from their sons. One of the authors was very remiss in not writing to his parents and his mother often threatened him with what she did to him when he was at school, which was to send him a postcard for all to see. Written on it was, 'Why no letter. Mummy'. Terribly shaming, not because of the postcard but because of the 'Mummy' bit. On 30 April 1955 *St George's Gazette* gave some advice:

> For a time we have felt that some soldiers have difficulty in finding subject matter for inclusion in their letters home. In order to reassure any parents who read this, we publish without comment a specimen of an 'average' weekly letter:

The Forest,
Mount Kenya (3.00 a.m.)

Dear Mum,

As I write this I can hardly hear myself think for the roaring of the lions and ostriches, who will soon be prowling around this lonely little camp of ours, 14,000 feet up on Mount Kenya.

This is certainly Active Service with a capital 'A', Mum. We just got back from no ordinary flog across the moors and through the forest. Six days it was. Each day we did about 20 miles, mostly on our hands and knees and carrying everything but the kitchen stove on our backs.

You'll be thinking that yours truly probably flaked out every day, but no, Mum, you're wrong! This is actually cushy – it's all in the day's work. Of course, if we were Hillary or John Hunt we'd have oxygen, but the CO won't give it to us because he needs it back at base – I ask you.

Well, you would have laughed the other day – we were plugging along in thick forest when suddenly there was a frightful snort just behind us. Fair made us jump – Bill, my mucker, almost swallowed the mouth organ he was playing, and the Sarge, who was carrying my Bren for me, went and dropped it in the dirt (he would!).

Well, we shipped round, and there, about 100 yards away, was our old friend Rhino – not one, but three of the B——s. 'Bale out' yelled Sarge, and we certainly did, but I suddenly remembered my Bren in the dirt. None of your 28 days in the mush for me, chum, so I dashed back to get it.

Well, I picked it up in time as the three rhinos came at me. There was no time to get away, so I faced up to them and let them have it from the hip. Boy! It was easy money, and reminded me of the time three weeks ago when I gave Dedan Kimathi the works – you remember.

I didn't quite get away with it, Mum, because you see these rhinos were charging at 30 miles per hour, and, as I shot them, their impetigo carried them on, and the leading one got me with his horn and ripped my arm open.

It didn't bleed much, so we strapped it up and I carried on. Now we're back the Doc says I was lucky not to lose my arm from 'ganggreen' (which is a poison you pick up from eating compo). He put fourteen stitches in it. It's a bit jagged, but it won't show much.

There we go again – we've just turned out in a hurry as some elephants have arrived and made a pass at old Charlie, who is doing sentry. He's used to them now, and knows the drill – he chucked a rock at them and fired a Very light at the biggest, and they soon gave up. Unlike another mate in the next Platoon, who last week lost his nerve and ran at them. He hasn't been seen since.

Well, Mum, I must close now and try to get some sleep if I can – it's my turn tonight anyway. Don't worry too much about yours truly – I can look after myself.

Much love from your loving son,
John.

P. S. – If Geordie Black writes that I have got my arm cut with a broken bottle at the Marina Cafe, it's not true.

P. P. S. – Geordie Black is jealous cos I've got my third.

Should anyone find it really difficult to think up news, we try to help him by handing out the following proforma:-

Date _____   Mountain _____

                         Height _____ ft.

                         Temperature _____

Dear _____
   Since my last letter I have been keeping very well/I am now very poorly.
I have just returned from a . . . mile patrol which lasted . . . days/weeks.
During the week we killed . . . Mau Mau, . . . Lions, . . . Tigers, . . . Rhinos, and . . . Buffalo.
The battle with the Mau Mau lasted for . . . minutes/hours. I personally accounted for . . . Mau Mau with my rifle/grenades/hands.
I was wounded in the leg/arm/stomach/head/finger. I am now/am not in hospital. I am fed up/enjoying a good scrounge.
I am enjoying army life/am doing 28 days detention.
I am signing on for 22 years/am going absent very soon/roll on my demob.
My mates in my Platoon are a nice lot/a pretty ropey crowd/a shower. That goes for my officer/sergeant/corporal/the whole outfit.
Since I have been out here I have/not saved . . . pounds/shillings/pence. The other day I obtained/was sold/flogged a gold watch/wireless set/panga.
I spend my spare time reading comics/in the NAAFI/lying in the sun/nattering/scrounging/imitating Frankie Laine/staring at a picture

of Marilyn Monroe/kipping/gambling etc.

It is the dry season now so we only get rained on/soaked through twice a day.

Must close now as I am on guard/going on patrol/about to do a spot of spud peeling/Defaulters has just been blown.

Your loving/disgruntled son,

Corporal Garner's Platoon Commander was Second Lieutenant Althaus and the Platoon Sergeant was Sergeant Revell. The Machine-Gun Platoon, not for the last time, had to put their Vickers machine-guns away and become an ordinary rifle platoon, albeit in Support Company. They were proud of themselves because they had won the Inter-Platoon Football Cup. Corporal Garner had to take out what they thought was going to be a day patrol of nine men plus an Askari (an African soldier or policeman) tracker. All they had with them were sandwiches and no cigarettes. After two hours they found fresh tracks and followed them across a river in which Corporal Garner lost his wallet and all his photographs. A group of baboons watched the fun but, although the patrol did not like them, they had to pass them by. They found signs of a chicken having been plucked but there were no signs of anyone making a meal of it. So they ploughed on and he decided to go to higher ground out of the reach of animals to spend the night. They then had their sandwiches which was the last food they were to have for two days. Next morning, Garner decided to go back to base but they had no idea where they were. He decided that they should stay put for another night at the high point again. Before dark they saw a spotter plane looking for them, but by the time they had lit a fire it had gone. That night they could see flares being fired to the north and so Corporal Garner ordered the Bren gun to fire a magazine of ammunition which contained some tracer. As there was still no response he decided to get moving the next morning.

They would follow the river down until it reached one of the cut-lines (firebreaks) in the forest. After four hours they succeeded, and were met by a Kenya Police patrol. They were very hungry and they welcomed the pot of tea and cake they were given. They were also told that a gang of a hundred Mau Mau was heading in their direction. When they got back to camp they were told that if they had been out for another twenty-four hours, they would have been officially reported missing. His Platoon Sergeant told him that he went nearly white with worry, and his Company Commander, Major Hensman, said he was pleased to see them back. They certainly got well stuck into their parcels from home because it was Christmas Eve. To top it all, Corporal Garner was to be guard commander on New Year's Eve, but at least he had a bottle of Tusker beer to share between himself and the two guards. They got the nickname of 'The Lost Patrol' for their pains.

At Trents Farm, Fusilier Porter of X Company set out in the company three-tonner for his weekly trip to Battalion Headquarters. He was expected back at about 1500. At 1530, the sentry at the barrier to the camp reported that the ration truck was overdue. Although a call to HQ had ascertained that Fusilier Porter had left late, by dusk Captain Paddy Baxter decided that a Landrover should be sent out to see whether Porter had broken down, or worse, been ambushed by the Mau Mau.

However, as it became dark the sentry reported headlights approaching the camp. The barrier was removed and the truck raced into the camp, and slewed to a halt behind the NAAFI. As the sentry tried to close the barrier, he was hurled to one side by a charging rhino which went straight through the camp and out by demolishing the barrier the other side. Fusilier Porter reported that the rhino had ambushed him and his vehicle on the main road, and then followed him at high speed down the track to the camp. He then asked the Sergeant to put the sentry on a charge for failing to arrest the rhino for damaging his vehicle.

The Battalion moved to Nairobi for Operation Anvil and, apart from one company at Langata, the detention camp for Mau Mau suspects, set up camp at the racecourse. After a time social debts had been incurred and it was necessary to have a party for those who had been good to the Battalion and others whom the Battalion felt duty-bound to ask. There is a myth that regiments are given an entertainment allowance by the grateful taxpayer. Whilst the Commanding Officer may have a very small allowance, that is quickly swallowed up and most entertaining is paid for out of officers' salaries.

Nevertheless, a party had to be thrown and, in normal stations, this usually takes place between 6 p.m. and 8.30 p.m. when the bachelors hope to take the spare talent out and the married officers go home. Kenya, in the Emergency, was not usual. The party was still going at 10.30 p.m. and the officers thought that it was time the settlers went home and stopped drinking the officers' salaries away. The Commanding Officer had a word with the Bandmaster who ceased playing his repertoire of medleys for the fourth time and struck up with 'God Save the Queen'. Far from taking a hint, when the anthem had been played for the fourth time, the settlers thought that this was a signal to get down to serious drinking. The time was now close to midnight and the Officers' Mess drink stocks were close to extinction. Firm action was needed. The Regimental Sergeant Major was called and there was a short conference with the Commanding Officer. Within ten minutes, the Officers' Mess tent was cleared and the settlers were driving 'hell for leather' for their homes. The ruse? A Mau Mau 'attack' was staged with generous use of blanks and Very lights – the settlers thought that this was a good time to go home.

2nd Lts Danny Seidl (later Colonel) and John Masters joined the Battalion in Kenya in 1954, having spent two years at Sandhurst, the Small Weapons Course at Hythe and the Platoon Commanders' Course at Warminster. This training made them capable of commanding a Division, whereas National Service officers with their three-month course at Eaton Hall and a year's experience in the Battalion, although technically junior, were much more experienced. Sandhurst officers had some catching up to do. They were met by John Moncur, a veteran of Korea (known as 'Ruggles' to the soldiers), and much older in terms of maturity than the two wet-behind-the-ears Sandhurst officers, which was emphasized by his luxurious moustache.

On arriving at the Racecourse Camp at Nairobi, Danny Seidl was posted to X Company and John Masters had the luck to be posted to Z Company at Langata under the command of Captain Humphrey Walker. With Roger Trewick, it was a delightfully relaxed young company mess well away from Battalion Headquarters.

Danny Seidl was in the main Mess with both Second World War and Korean War veterans such as the Colonel, Major Dick Hensman, Major Paul Ward (both Brigadiers later), Major Philip Bulman, Major Dudley Buckle, Major John Winn, Major Dare Wilson (later Major General) and other much older officers living in the Mess, because it was a posting without families.

Later in his career, John Masters, with a father who had been a Brigadier, had some difficulty deciding who was senior because as a child he had had Majors and Lieutenant Colonels vying with each other to take him to the zoo, in order to curry favour with his father. In Kenya he had no such trouble. He was terrified of most of the senior majors, even when he heard that one of them had his lavatory paper sent out from Fortnum and Mason. Looking back, it was really a matter of respect for the individual. He was in particular awe of John Winn who had been awarded an immediate DSO in Korea, although many said it should have been a VC. He wished that his parents had not told him what happened when they had visited John Winn in hospital in Singapore when he was returning to England from Korea after receiving yet another wound. His father had asked John Winn if he needed anything and John Winn, because he had no civilian clothes with him, had asked for some grey flannel trousers. When his father had got home to his quarter he had asked his servant to look out some trousers which were sent to John Winn. Just before he left John Winn returned the trousers with a note saying they were not much use to him because they had holes in the crutch.

Before the Battalion knew that they were going to Kenya, Majors Hugh Holmes and Derek Lloyd had opted to serve with the King's African Rifles. Imagine their surprise when the Battalion turned up on their doorstep in Nanyuki, their Regimental HQ. They had their families with them whilst the Fifth Fusiliers were on a non-family basis. It was later, whilst all units were deployed on operations, that Hugh's quarter was burnt down at night by the Mau Mau. His family luckily escaped, having been alerted by their black labrador. The story went that Hugh was informed out in the field by telephone and that his first reaction was to enquire whether his Army List had been rescued. In this he evidently marked off with blue chalk all those in the Regiment who he thought likely to obstruct his chances of promotion. It makes a good story and was started lightheartedly by his wife, Marguerite.

Major Hugh Wilkin was also with the King's African Rifles and it was he that chalked up a most miraculous escape when caught by a charging rhinoceros in a game tunnel in the bamboo forest. These narrow passages through thorn, bamboo and other uncomfortable growth provide just enough room for a buffalo or rhino to pass through. Although he was injured when the rhino passed by him, he was lucky that there was not enough room for it to turn round and have another go.

Major Gerald Style (later Colonel) arrived in Kenya in 1955, and was met at Eastleigh Airport by Major Dudley Buckle, who was Battalion Second in Command. They went straight to the New Stanley Hotel, one of the two famous hotels in Nairobi, where Dudley Buckle gave Gerald Style lunch. Gerald Style never forgot it because it was the first time he had ever seen, eaten or heard of a Chateaubriand steak. This gigantic fillet was quite superb and Major Buckle paid the bill without a moment's hesitation. They then went round the Nairobi Game Park, on the edge of the city, and saw Gerald Style's first lions and baboons. After that, straight up the road to Nanyuki, part metalled and mostly red murram. In the dry season the murram dust would cover everything and everyone.

Captain Gerald Style was to be Adjutant, following Major Dare Wilson. He never forgot the painstaking briefing about the colours, what to do with them and what not to do. There was further briefing about the Adjutant's sole command, the Corps of Drums when he was assured that the Corps of Drums were the hottest tactical sub-unit in the Battalion and that the Adjutant should lead them frequently into the jungle on patrol. Gerald Style did this just once and it was a most frightening experience. He had the feeling that there were rhinos and buffaloes round every bush. With Corporal Goodger as Section Commander, he took as an insurance, the Regimental Sergeant Major Frank Bingham and the Medical Officer with him. As it happened, nothing untoward took place as they tramped through the jungle near the Mawingo Hotel. With memories of Major Hugh Wilkin, Gerald Style wondered how he should ever manage to climb the huge trees to avoid a charging animal. However, it was said that a person could climb anything with a rhinoceros or buffalo coming at them at 30 m.p.h.

The Mawingo Hotel was famous for its role in the film, *Mogambo*, starring Clark Gable and Ava Gardner. When the film appeared in Kenya, there was a shout of delight when Clark Gable pointed towards Isiolo saying, quite inaccurately, 'That's gorilla country'. The management of the Mawingo Hotel were very good to the Battalion, giving young officers a free weekend with the luxury of a decent bath and, above all, a break from the rigours of the thunderbox. The hotel was, for a time, an extension to the Officers' Mess at Airfield Camp for those who could afford it.

Corporal Hulme's job was to blow up any bombs that had not exploded and this often led to confrontations with more than irate farmers. Once, with his platoon on patrol in the jungle, Corporal Hulme came upon an angry rhinoceros. The patrol asked him what they should do and he told them to get up the nearest tree until the danger had passed. Once, after building a fence to protect the local headman's building from the Mau Mau, the platoon was just leaving when the local 'pin-up girls' stood outside their huts doing the 'can-can'. The main difference between them and the *Folies Bergères* was that the local girls were showing the lads that all they had to wear were their smiles.

The Corps of Drums provided useful escorts for trout fishers, like Gerald Style, in the streams coming off Mount Kenya. An escort was necessary as the stream beds were always well covered with vegetation and provided regular routes for Mau Mau gangs. The Mau Mau seldom ran into the Battalion patrols, probably because Geordie could not resist a smoke or a talk, however quietly. The Mau Mau senses of sight, sound and smell were legendary. After a few years in the forest, their senses were like the animals and the noses of those whom the Battalion captured moved very like those of tracker dogs.

Lieutenant Colonel Ronnie Cowe cannot recall the occasion for which Captain Humphrey Walker considered it necessary to buy a pig. Humphrey Walker was Second in Command of Z Company whilst Ronnie Cowe held the same job in X Company. The Battalion was scattered some miles apart on the edge of the Aberdare Mountains and Humphrey Walker contacted Ronnie Cowe to suggest that their two companies should share the cost of a pig which he had located. They both thought it would make an excellent feast for their men.

They duly met and made the purchase at a farm near Z Company's base camp. The pig, of course, was alive and certainly kicking. Nevertheless the journey to the camp in the back of a long-wheel-based Landrover passed without any severe injuries. Ronnie Cowe enquired how it was intended to slaughter the animal and Humphrey Walker assured him this presented no problem.

'I have a butcher in my company,' he assured Ronnie Cowe. 'He's slaughtered dozens of pigs.' This placated Ronnie Cowe but not for long.

They arrived at Z Company's tented camp which was on an open plain, with latrines dug on the perimeter. One of these was a fairly substantial hut standing on its own and was for the use of the company officers.

The pig had not been a very cooperative passenger in the back of the Landrover, and everyone was relieved to get it safely into the hands of the butcher. The butcher then proceeded to wrestle the unfortunate animal towards the officers' latrine where, no doubt against all principles of hygiene, he intended to despatch it. With some effort the pair of them were finally enclosed and the bystanders withdrew. It was not long before a great commotion erupted and the walls of the little building started to reverberate with squeals and shouts, eventually collapsing like a pack of cards with the pig at full trot up the plain leaving the 'butcher' flat on his back in the wreckage.

They then ran for the Landrovers, and gave chase, finally using a rifle to bring down the pig before he could reach the forest. The resulting feast was enjoyed by all except for those involved in the acquisition of the main course.

This was Ronnie Cowe's most eventful rations foray as Second in Command of the Company – the other being the purchase of turkeys from the NAAFI at Nairobi the following Christmas. On arrival at the NAAFI, in a 3-tonner, he was amazed to find that the manager had erected a compound at the rear of the building which was full of live turkeys. His consignment was eight of these lively and noisy fowls. In those days the refrigeration facilities at the NAAFI were rudimentary, designed only for essentials such as beer!

The driver of the 3-tonner, Fusilier Pink, was a taciturn and resourceful fellow and between them they managed to tether their feathered cargo in the lorry. The company cooks were a bit nonplussed to hear them arriving. That night they had a line of tethered turkeys around the cookhouse and mayhem reigned well into the night. Ronnie Cowe did not enjoy that feast either. He felt that it was not the same when he had got to know the turkey!

On one Commanding Officer's orders, those attending collapsed with laughter when Fusilier Armstrong responded to the Regimental Sergeant Major's order to 'double up' by literally bending down so as to make his face touch his knee. RSM Frank Bingham nearly exploded.

Fusilier Geordie carried on as best he could whatever the environment and whatever the problems that might beset him. He had impeccable taste in his choice when it came to philandering. When in Nairobi there was a steady build-up of 'angst' in high places concerning social diseases. Captain Gerald Style was detailed to take an 'Adjutant's patrol' around the native quarters in Eastleigh. This area was particularly famous for the glut of tall, thin, beautiful, and elegant Somali ladies of the night. With all this went the usual security risks, and the girls seemed to have an infallible bush telegraph which sent messages round with incredible speed if a police or military police visit was expected. Not surprisingly, his patrol drew a blank, although the patrol did not look under beds or in wardrobes where miscreants were known to hide. It was the gentlemanly approach, where a breach of privacy seemed in itself to be an impropriety.

Z Company was on detachment at Langata Camp which was the main Mau Mau detention centre. Escapes from the camp were rare and the escape alarm that Z Company practised was never used. Mostly Z Company was involved in sweep operations in Nairobi where an area was surrounded, and the male population were paraded in front of hooded Mau Mau prisoners who had been persuaded to identify those who had taken part in the bestial Mau Mau oathing ceremonies. At one of these, Captain Peter Douglas was taken to task by one of the Special Branch officers, who told him that one of his hoods had been 'com-prom-missed'. He went over to his rather humourless Brigade Major, saying, 'This bloke says his hoods have been com-prom-missed.'

The reply was, 'Don't you mean compromised?'

One Fusilier officer was G3 at Brigade Headquarters. At that time this job was as a sort of ADC to the Brigadier. The Brigadier was a very brave man who had a very distinguished war career, but had been removed from his command in Korea for his part in an operation that had resulted in the loss of many Fifth Fusilier lives. He had appealed against his removal from command and the War Office had allowed his appeal. In order to reinstate him, the War Office had to give him a war service brigade, and the only one available was in Kenya with the Fifth Fusiliers. He was alleged to have a liking for women's posteriors, so at any cocktail party the Brigade G3, who was, of course, acting on behalf of his boss, was known to do his share of pinching and then pointing to the Brigadier after the deed.

The Duke of Wellington, in opposing the army reforms that would remove the purchase of commissions, said that it was important that officers should be independent financially because they were then able to tell their superiors the truth, and that an army tied to the establishment would not take part in revolutions. Whilst few would say this view was correct, the former part of his saying was well illustrated in one of the operations.

Y Company had cornered a strong Mau Mau gang of about a hundred in a stream bed and X Company had been called in to strengthen the cordon. Major John Winn, an officer of independent means, was deploying his company when the Brigadier arrived and started moving X Company soldiers about. John Winn called the Brigadier over. 'Brigadier, who is commanding this company?'

'You, of course, John,' the Brigadier replied.

'Then go back to Nairobi and command your Brigade and leave the command of my company to me.'

Would an officer, dependent on his pay and the Brigadier's recommendation for promotion, have the courage to do what John Winn did? The Brigadier, to give him his due, left and nothing more was heard, officially, of the incident.

Second Lieutenant John Masters and 12 Platoon had been sent to set up a base for patrolling and as a secondary task, to guard Embori Farm which was in the foothills of Mount Kenya as the farm manager, Mr Campbell, had been attacked by the Mau Mau a number of times. Mr Campbell was stone deaf and lived in a small rondavel at the farm. When the Mau Mau attacked at night, they fired shots at the rondavel and, like most shots at night, these went high into the ceiling. It was fortunate that Mr Campbell was deaf because if he had come to the door he might have been killed. As it was, each time it happened, he only became aware of it when he woke next morning and looked up at his ceiling.

Mr Campbell seemed to have taken to 12 Platoon, as was evidenced by his generous gifts of fresh milk, discarded by the Fusiliers in favour of tinned milk for tea, and a fresh lamb each day. However, his one aim in life was to get the Platoon Commander to shoot a rhino. The Platoon Commander was not keen, but was prevailed upon to go out on a mini safari to find and shoot a rhino. In a small truck, with Fusilier Hindmarsh as an escort, the intrepid pair set off with Mr Campbell's double-barrelled elephant gun put between them in the cab of the truck. Mr Campbell was not the best driver in the world and, coming to a ford, he stalled the truck. Everything inside slid forward and there was an enormous explosion. 'A Mau Mau attack,' thought the Platoon Commander. No, the elephant gun had gone off, sending both its .500 rounds into the back of the truck. Aghast, the Platoon Commander leapt out, expecting to see a bloody Fusilier Hindmarsh blown into Kingdom Come. It was a near thing. One of the bullets had gone through the cab into the wide blue yonder, however, the second one had passed through the wall of the cab, through a spare tyre, had then skinned the Fusilier's sideburns and had blown a large hole in his jungle hat. The Fusilier was, naturally, very anxious, not because of his near miss, but at the fear of what Company Sergeant Major Forbes Burn would say when he saw the damaged jungle hat.

At an early stage in their time in Kenya, 12 Platoon had been sent on a patrol in the forest. The Platoon Commander and about ten of the patrol had walked past a rhino by only a few feet. It is surprising how well such a large beast blends into the background. The Platoon Commander looked back to see how the rest of the patrol was doing when he suddenly spotted the rhino. A yell of 'Rhino' echoed through the forest and 12 Platoon took to the trees in the approved manner. Corporal Coulson, very speedy on these occasions, and safe in his tree, looked back to see Sergeant McInnes running so fast that he was double marking time on the spot. Eventually the good sergeant made contact and had enough forward momentum to make a tree. However it was a real Tom and Jerry cartoon situation. The rhino rumbled off completely unconcerned at this human comedy.

The platoon were excellent 'OK Corral' makers and they were most put out when Z Company Headquarters took over their encampment before an operation started. They did not object to being put on the centre line so that HQ could take over their construction when they moved on, but not before they had moved out. Once they had built one of their 'homes' and were sharing it with a patrol of the King's African Rifles. The question of night sentries was discussed and a coin was tossed to see who would take from 6 p.m. to midnight and who from midnight to 6 a.m. The KAR lost and took the post-midnight stint. At midnight, 12 Platoon handed over to the KAR. Next morning it became clear that the African sentries had gone to sleep, for right in the middle of the camp were two huge, steaming elephant turds. Elephants are often gentle and silent at night, however, it was probably just as well that the sentries were asleep and the elephants were not alarmed, otherwise the best platoon in the Battalion, that is, in the opinion of all ex-members of 12 Platoon, might have come to serious harm.

Each patrol was equipped with a radio. Training had been given on how to lay out the aerial on a compass bearing in order to pick up the 'Skip-wave' from the 'Heaviside Layer' (Memories of *Cats*) and thereby increase the range of communication. When Lieutenant Colonel Roger St John, the Commanding Officer, flew over the forest in a Kenya Police Tri-pacer, patrols were instructed to call him up. The day came when Second Lieutenant Robin Althaus, deep in the forest, saw the Colonel's plane above him, but he had forgotten the call sign and plaintively called, 'Hello little blue aeroplane'. Not the correct voice procedure.

Sharing the heavier items of equipment on long patrols was good practice, although it did have its disadvantages. Fusilier Potts, who was not very tall, always seemed to have the Bren gun when 12 Platoon was in parts of the forest where the trail was broken up by many fallen trees. This was not unusual. Thus poor Potts would often announce 12 Platoon's arrival to the forest in general and the Mau Mau in particular by falling over every second tree with an unholy clatter and accompanied by equally unholy words. When it was his turn for the wireless set he insisted on operating it. In the forest, reception was not very good, however, sometimes the receiving station could hear the sender whilst the original sender might not hear the original receiver. In order to cover this eventuality the sender would ask the receiver to press his sending button in answer to a series of questions, as often the act of pressing the button could be heard. Fusilier Potts was once heard saying, 'If you can hear me, press your pressel switch once, and if you can't, press it twice.

On one operation, 12 Platoon was the Battalion's longstop on Mount Kenya. This involved a long stay at the end of the plateau in the area above the bamboo line, at about 11,000 feet, and it was hoped that a helicopter height record would be achieved by landing at 12 Platoon's camp. Much work went into preparing the landing strip which, at this height, had to be quite large. It all came to nothing because some rotten so-and-so landed his helicopter on Mont Blanc, in the Alps, at 13,000 feet before the landing on Mount Kenya took place. However, it made a good six-a-side soccer pitch for a competition which Platoon HQ won. The rest of the platoon thought the result very unfair because the Platoon Commander wore chukka boots whilst the rest of the platoon wore gym shoes. At the end of their long stint they returned to Company HQ where Company Sergeant Major Forbes Burn had saved up all the Army Kinema Corporation films the platoon had missed. The Platoon Commander thought it would be a good idea if the viewing was done over a few days, but not the platoon who watched all eight films in the next twenty-four hours. They were not going to be caught out by a sudden stand-to.

Corporal Mills joined one of the Battalion combat teams under the command of Second Lieutenant Yewdell and later Second Lieutenant Danny Seidl. The two teams were put into a newly formed W Company whose other role was the training company. Company Sergeant Major George Connolly was the CSM and took the first opportunity he could to put them through their paces. However, the combat teams were very fit and drilled with zest. Their kit was perfect, mainly because it was seldom used. Mills by this time had been promoted to corporal and had to demonstrate the new Belgian FN self-loading rifle used by the combat teams. This was to replace the old .303 Lee Enfield, but was not issued for a number of years to the rest of the First Battalion due to the usual Treasury parsimony.

At Airfield Camp, Nanyuki a Fusilier could not find his mug when he heard the cookhouse call. Desperate measures were needed as no self-respecting Fusilier goes without his morning cup of tea. He looked around and found an empty Players 50-pack cigarette tin by another Fusilier's bed and decided to borrow it. On his return he heard the Fusilier complaining that one could not even leave an empty cigarette tin around without someone 'nicking' it. The borrower apologized, explaining his urgent need, and was shattered to hear the owner say, 'Well I suppose you won't catch a f——ing disease if you are lucky. I am just getting over f——ing VD and the f——ing treatment heats up a vital part of me. I use the tin to cool it down.'

When the combat teams were disbanded at Airfield Camp, Nanyuki, life for Corporal Mills had gone full circle. The men in the combat teams were no longer green, immature boys, but were now grown men who knew what combat was about. Corporal Mills went back to X Company and took on the duties of permanent Company Orderly Sergeant because he was due for demob on his return to England. In this job, he had to come in contact with the new RSM, Forbes Burn, who had just taken over from RSM Frank Bingham.

Just before the Fifth Fusiliers left Kenya, a young Fusilier had a slight contretemps with a rhinoceros – nothing serious, but hospitalization was needed. When the Colonel went to visit him, he found him very depressed. He reassured him that he would not be left behind in Kenya, but this was not the trouble. It transpired that the Fusilier had been writing home weekly with lurid tales of his adventures in the forest tackling wild game and Mau Mau. This amused his folks at home but they obviously didn't believe him. Now that he'd had a real encounter, he was worried how he was going to convince them it was true. The Colonel told him that he would write to them and confirm his story and the Fusilier quickly cheered up.

At the end of the Fifth Fusiliers' tour, the future granting of independence to Kenya was beginning to take effect. There was a certain British couple employed in the local Civil Service who decided that when Uhuru came it was time for them to return to the UK. When the wife announced this to her office colleagues, who were both African and British, there evidently was some consternation. Eventually an African colleague, with, it was suspected, a sly sense of humour, formed up and announced to her, 'You can't go home. When Uhuru comes, I have won you in a raffle.'

One of the final ceremonies was to honour the Battalion's African trackers. These trackers had been very loyal to the Battalion and often this loyalty embraced blind faith. The number of miracle cures from taking paludrin was legion. To Corporal Mills, the two who served his combat team were special friends and they had often saved his bacon. The Battalion honoured the trackers by mustering a full parade, and each of the trackers was given a medal in honour of their service.

The Battalion went out to Kenya over a thousand strong, largely made up of National Servicemen as junior officers and Fusiliers, which happened to be a very happy mix of Geordie town and country. They made a great name for themselves for their cheerfulness, smartness and performance but, above all, for their consistent good behaviour throughout their time in Kenya.

The Battalion returned home by the troopship, the old *Empire Halladale*, the slowest boat in the trooping fleet. As Gerald Style recalls, the voyage home took three weeks, one of which was spent between Mombassa and the Suez Canal. To survive the ordeal, a strong headwind from the north or north-west was needed. On one hand, this slowed the ship to four knots but, on the other hand, the wind cooled the ship, passengers and crew.

There were many goodbyes, but none was better than when the Fifth's colleagues in Kenya, the Black Watch, left Nairobi station and there was a large farewell gathering on the platform, including the Mayor and the Mayoress. As the train pulled out, clouds of tear gas wafted towards the onlookers who soon had tears streaming from their eyes. 'We knew you would be sorry to see us go,' chanted the Jocks, who had acquired quite a reputation during their tour of duty.

Before Colonel St John left Nanyuki he wrote to, amongst others, the Nanyuki Country Club members to thank them for all the many kindnesses they had bestowed on the Fifth Fusiliers. A few years ago, a god-daughter of his was visiting the club and noticed his thank-you letter framed, and displayed, on the Club's mantelpiece! So the Fifth Fusiliers are still remembered.

Chapter XIV

Northern Ireland

The First Battalion was posted to Hollywood Barracks, Belfast under the command of Lt Col W. A. C. Collingwood (later Brigadier). Its main duties were internal security, aid to the civil power and training. The IRA was not the force it was in later years but, nevertheless, the Battalion was involved in a number of operations, although there was very little danger involved.

At the time, the IRA was only causing minor problems and the Army had not yet been called in at the request of Gerry Fitt and the Nationalists to protect them from the Protestants. However, the Battalion had to guard the Ordnance Depot and the house of the General in command of the army in Northern Ireland. One of the tasks of the Orderly Officer was to visit the guards at these establishments during his tour of duty.

On one occasion, a certain officer had decided that he would not get fully dressed to visit the guards and just put his regimental greatcoat on over his pyjamas. Dressed with his sword in the slit of the greatcoat, he set off. Unfortunately the General was returning from an evening out just as the officer arrived to inspect the guard. The General, being a hospitable man, invited the officer in for a drink, and asked him to remove his greatcoat to be more comfortable. Despite some polite pressure, the officer managed to keep his coat on in front of the blazing fire in the sitting room. Generals are not often fools, having been subalterns themselves, and it was suspected that the kind General knew exactly what was going on.

Lieutenants Alan Hill and Mike Dixon were invited to have dinner with the General one snowy winter's night. They travelled to the engagement, resplendent in evening dress and British warms, on a scooter. Two miles short of their destination, the scooter broke down and they had to run all the way to the General's house. Arriving very dishevelled, out of breath and sweaty, the General was most understanding and even got his ADC to organize the recovery of the scooter.

The Officers' Mess was a place of chaos. Having been overseas for a number of years with just a short break at Barnard Castle, nearly every officer arrived in Northern Ireland with a dog. Unfortunately, most were not house-trained and wellington boots were needed for any nocturnal visits to the 'facilities'. Chewing of essential items of leather was not unknown although, when one officer was accused by the Quartermaster of cutting down a laundry basket for a dog bed, in reality the puppy had reduced a wicker dog basket to a sorry state, it was the last straw and the dog was returned to his parents. Alan Hill's dog, Drummer, dug up the Colonel's garden and ate Second Lieutenant Colin Atkinson's hat. Many dogs returned to 'mother', whilst Alan's went first to the NAAFI manageress and then to Fusilier Blockage's father in Scotland. Eventually the number of dogs was reduced to reasonable proportions.

Mess dogs were not the only problem. W Company Commander, Major John Baume, an England front-row rugby international, had a bull terrier appropriately called 'Butch'. Like his master, Butch was very muscle-bound. His favourite game was to be picked up and thrown against a wall, while his parlour trick was to allow you to push down on his neck and his rear legs would rise, giving a ground clearance of four to six inches. He was devoted to his master to the extent that unless he was tied up during company orders, defaulters often received seven days' CB and a bite from Butch. Butch lived with John Baume in a caravan just outside the barracks and, as a result, he ruled the roost during working hours. He put up with officers' dogs but no cat remained at ground level within the sight and smell of Butch.

There was a small training ground to the rear of the barracks. Although Butch joined in section attacks with enthusiasm he did not quite understand which side to support. Nevertheless, keen to do his best in the final assault, he seemed to sense when he could cause the most chaos without hurting anyone. Many a hidden, heavily camouflaged sniper had his position given away by a visit from Butch.

Second Lieutenant John Nicholson, a National Service officer who now farms near Hexham, was a keen member of the Battalion rugby team which was coached by John Baume. On one occasion the team was playing touch rugby and, as often happens, the game became quite boisterous. Only those outside the scrum saw Butch returning from a rabbiting expedition. Seeing his master being 'assaulted' by other members of the team and being a brave and loyal dog, he did what he thought he was trained to do, launched into the attack and latched on to John Nicholson's thigh. Despite orders from John Baume, it took some time before Butch released his hold.

John Baume left the Battalion shortly afterwards. The rumour that it was related to this incident is not true but although the Battalion was sorry to see John and Butch go, the animals that lived in and near the barracks seemed to visibly relax.

Second Lieutenant Ian Carr joined the Battalion in April 1957. He was a Platoon Commander in X Company and its commander, Major Freddie Ward MC, was the perfect boss. He was intelligent, a devout Roman Catholic, extremely high-principled, and at the same time had a surrealist wit and a sense of humour. A hint of riches to come was given when Ian Carr followed him around as he inspected the company latrines on Ian's first Saturday. After peering studiously down a few lavatory pans, he pulled one of the chains and, as the cistern gurgled and flushed, he turned to Ian with a wry smile and said: *'Après moi, le déluge'*.

However, Freddie Ward's sense of humour did desert him on one occasion. Two National Service officers, Second Lieutenants Mordaunt and Yorke, shared a car whose looks betrayed the fact that it was maintained on their meagre pay. One evening they gave their Company Commander a lift back from a party. Rounding a corner, fortunately at not too high a speed, the door dropped off and out shot Freddie Ward, who was not amused and the two young officers had to pay for a new suit.

Despite the apparent inflexibility of the military code, the rules could occasionally be bent to fit circumstances, as they were in the bizarre saga of one soldier, who shall be referred to henceforth as Fusilier King. He was a very likeable north-countryman in his middle twenties, powerfully built, with a large red face, a square chin, and a stubby nose on which were perched a pair of regulation steel spectacles. He looked like a cross between a German scientist and an all-in wrestler. He was a devout Catholic, a very cheerful soul, and had been allocated the permanent job of keeping X Company latrines in good order.

The snag was that, despite repeated attempts, he had failed to pass the Army third-class certificate of education examination, and so had never received the pay rise to which this would entitle him. He requested an interview, expressed his dissatisfaction with this state of affairs and said, if nothing could be done about it, he wanted to leave the Army when his time was up in a couple of months. There were some fairly high-level consultations about the problem, and it was agreed that Fusilier King was a good soldier, an asset to the Army and that, in fact, given his rather simple view of life, he really needed the kind of protection the Army afforded him. The question was mooted: What would King actually do in the big world outside?

Ian Carr was told to liaise with the Education Officer about the problem. 'Don't worry,' he said breezily, 'he'll get through this time . . . he'll go no further, mind you, but he'll get through this time.'

This sounded promising but, not wanting to leave too much to chance, and as Ian Carr happened to be the invigilator, he told King to arrive half an hour late at the examination room. This enabled Ian Carr to keep King behind alone for 30 minutes after everyone had finished. Then, working at lightning speed, they finished most of the paper together and knocked up an amazing 75%. The Education Officer, who marked the papers himself, collared Ian Carr shortly after the results came out. 'I told you he'd pass,' he said darkly, 'but this is ridiculous!'

So for a while Fusilier King was happy with his pay rise and X Company latrines shone brightly in the firmament. But a few weeks later, he requested another interview. Again he gave his ultimatum: he was fed up with latrines and wanted to take driving lessons in order to become one of the Battalion drivers. Lessons were arranged for him immediately, and soon the day of his test approached. Ian Carr explained to the tester, Sergeant Pringle (later Captain (QM) Bill Pringle MBE), a man with a meticulous sense of duty, that this time he must be generous in his interpretation of the rules because it was imperative that King pass his test. Sergeant Pringle gave Ian Carr a searching look and a wary salute. 'I'll do my best, sir,' he said somewhat grimly.

The morning of the test arrived and the minutes dragged slowly by until just before lunch Sergeant Pringle appeared at Company HQ. Ian Carr could see at once from his distraught face that something was wrong. 'What happened? Didn't you pass him?' Ian blurted out anxiously.

Sergeant Pringle made a weary gesture of resignation. 'Look, sir,' he said bitterly, 'he went through a red light, then he went the wrong way down a one-way street, then he nearly hit a pedestrian, mounted the pavement and hit a lamp-post. I said to him, "OK, King, I'll take over now," and do you know what he said? He said, "Have I passed, Sarge?"'

A few days after failing his driving test, Fusilier King was strolling in uniform on the streets of Belfast when a military policeman told him to take his hands out of his pockets. King refused to do so and told the policeman 'to piss off'. Instead of arresting him on the spot, the policeman followed King into a cafe and took notes while King smashed the place up. Reinforcements arrived and King was taken to the guardroom and put into a cell where he continued giving vent to his rage and frustration by smashing anything he could lay hands on. He was so physically powerful that he even succeeded in loosening the iron bars of the window, while in transit he inflicted injuries on his escorts.

Eventually, he was marched in front of the Commanding Officer, Lieutenant Colonel Collingwood, and a huge list of charges against him was read out. When it was over, the CO said menacingly, 'Have you got anything to say, King?'

King beamed at the CO. 'Yes, sir,' he said, 'How is your little dog, sir?'

There was a tiny, hysterical silence which was broken when the CO managed to splutter in a choking voice, 'March him out!'

King was duly taken outside until all present had time to wipe their eyes and pull themselves together. Then he was sentenced to several days of confinement to barracks with some loss of pay. It might have been a much more severe sentence if he had not asked his guileless question.

Efforts were still made to keep Fusilier King in the Army, but Ian Carr heard that he managed to get his demobilization papers by slipping them into a batch due for signature, and he disappeared without saying goodbye or even letting anyone know he was going.

For the Fusiliers, Northern Ireland was a sexual paradise. Before the main body of the Battalion arrived, the Advance Party Commander had letters either with crosses against pictures of individual Fusiliers from press photographs, or requests for introductions with references from priests and magistrates. Many friendships resulted in marriages, and Northern Ireland girls made excellent army wives.

Not all such relationships ended so conventionally. One Company Commander had the following letter from a mother in Newcastle:

Dear Company Commander,

I am writing to ask you for your help in persuading our young-un to marry Christine here in Newcastle rather than Mary in Belfast because of what you did in solving Jimmy's problem in Kenya. I know that Jimmy has got Mary in the family way and has obligations to her, but we know that Christine would make a better wife as we know her family and her baby is due before Christmas.

I do hope you can help.

Yours sincerely,

xxxxxxxxxxxx

P. S. Please don't tell Jimmy about this, he is so shy.

On arrival in Northern Ireland, a Company Commander had to call in Fusilier Robson (not his real name), to tell him that, despite the fact that he had only been back from Kenya for two months, his wife was six months pregnant. His reaction was somewhat surprising – he did not know why the Company Commander thought it was bad news, because he and his wife had been trying to have a child for a number of years.

'But Robson, you were in Kenya for two years without seeing your wife.'

'That is even more splendid, sir.'

'But Robson, two years.'

'I don't know why you're going on about these two years, there were three years between me and my brother.'

The Army did have some political problems in Belfast. It was in Ireland to maintain internal security, and for that reason, a good relationship with the Royal Ulster Constabulary was essential. The RUC, in turn, offered help in a most delightful and practical manner. The late 1950s was the golden era of visits to the cinema and it was often difficult to get in to see films in Belfast. The RUC said that if the Mess called the station sergeant at the central police station, they could guarantee seats for the Mess if they specified the time and place. This happy arrangement worked well until one night two officers went to see a film by normal means, and were sitting in the fourth row of the circle. At the end of the 'B' film, the lights went up and a platoon of B Specials entered the cinema and cleared the front row of the circle with 'minimum force necessary' and then the lights went down. The two officers were horrified to see the arrival of their fellow officers with a number of low mutters of 'bloody army of occupation' and other appropriate phrases. Needless to say, visits to the cinema, subject to the kind offices of the RUC, ceased.

Captain Peter Douglas had seen the most funny film of his life and persuaded the Mess to see it, omitting to mention that he had seen it after a very successful party. *Viva Zapata* is not the most jolly film, and its humour, without the benefit of generous amounts of gin and whisky, is limited. Peter's judgement was called into question, and some wondered if his decision to retire early was coloured in any way by his perception of his future promotion prospects.

Leg-pulls in the Army tend to be on the cruel side. The Mess in Northern Ireland was no exception. One officer won two shillings and six pence on the pools and decided, with the aid of others in a moment of weakness, to add four thousand pounds to the figure in the Scottish Football Pool's letter of congratulation. He put this letter, with a cheque for four thousand pounds, two shillings and sixpence in amongst a friend's football pool coupons. That lunch, the group waited with keen anticipation for the friend to open his post and join in the good laugh. Unfortunately, the post was not retrieved that day or in the days that followed, and the 'joke' was forgotten, that was until a hysterical figure was seen dancing across the square, waving the cheque in the air, and promising largesse to all his friends. The 'joke' had gone horribly wrong, and it was very difficult to persuade the friend that it was a leg-pull. A dinner in Belfast was not considered by onlookers to be adequate compensation.

Towards the end of the Battalion's time in Northern Ireland, a few medals were awarded for good works. Messes tend to be noisy places, and often incorrect fag ends of conversation are picked up. If you are quick off the mark there may be an opportunity for a leg-pull. One officer fag-ended a conversation and the following exchange took place:

'Medal, did you say?'

'Oh, my god, now he knows.'

'Knows what?'

'About your OBE.'

'An OBE for me? Surely I don't deserve one?'

'Well, you know what it stands for – Other B's Efforts.'

'Never, you must be pulling my leg. What colour is the OBE? It would go well with my Kenya medal.'

Commanding Officer's Saturday morning inspections were a trial. Just before one such a very scruffy Fusilier was found by the Company Sergeant Major wandering round the barrack room. The quick-thinking CSM pushed him into a handy locker and locked the door – and which locker did Lieutenant Colonel Collingwood want to look into . . .? As it was opened, the Fusilier shot out and the CO nearly passed out with fright.

As usual, food in the Officers' Mess was not good. Food Members came and went, all without any perceptible improvement. One Food Member had learnt to produce Devonshire Cream. As he explained to the cook, you stand a quantity of very high cream milk for twenty-four hours, scald it, let it stand for another twenty-four hours, skim it and serve it. The cream was to be served at breakfast and, wisely, the Food Member kept this innovation to himself. Breakfast passed without any noticeable cream.

Furious, the Food Member stormed into the kitchen to demand what had happened to his cream. The cook was quite hurt. He was a bit surprised at the delicacy, but he had personally watched the Food Member eat it with his cereal. A terrible thought passed through the Food Member's mind. He asked the cook to tell him what he did. The cook said he had followed the instructions precisely, he had stood the milk for twenty-four hours, scalded it and stood it for another twenty-four hours.

'What did you do next?' the Food Member demanded.

'Oh, I skimmed off the scum, chucked that away and served the rest.'

Coffee was another problem. The Mess coffee was thin, watery and generally nasty. Despite many valiant efforts, Mess coffee never improved until the Mess heard that there was a very high-ranking cook in Northern Ireland, and an SOS was sent to him. Following his visit, the Fusilier coffee was undoubtedly the best around and the Food Member basked in the reflected glory, that was until the dreaded day came when the old, thin and nasty coffee appeared again. The wretched mess waiter was summoned by the senior officer.

'What is this?' he demanded.

'Oops, sorry sir – left out the gravy browning.'

One of the trials of a battalion is the annual administrative inspection by the General. On one of these, as usual, everything went wrong. Major Matthew Lasseter, one of the Company Commanders, had to accompany the inspecting officer for a barrack room inspection. Just as they were about to start, Fusilier Coultard, very dirty after coal fatigues, tripped past the entourage with a large mug of tea. During the inspection, the General asked to look inside a cupboard on a landing. Matthew Lassiter stood in front of the cupboard with arms outstretched, begging the General not to look inside. Needless to say, the General insisted on looking inside and quantities of very untidy stores and cleaning materials were revealed.

Lunch in the Mess followed, and Lieutenant John Masters, the Food Member, was ordered to produce the best. This was all arranged with the cook and a feast was anticipated. Soup and prawn cocktail passed without incident. The next course was announced with a flourish and the General looked down on a single fried egg winking up at him. The Colonel was aghast, and the General enquired if this was some Northumberland entrée. A strained silence followed until the rest of the mixed grill was served.

Later at the same meal, it was noticed that the celery had been placed on the table in full foliage, stuffed in flower vases. 'Cut the tops off,' hissed the Food Member to the Mess Sergeant. He duly removed the vases and chopped the heads of the celery to the level of the top of the vases, which meant that whenever a stalk was removed the vase was emptied onto the table.

The General was visibly in stitches throughout the meal. 'Best lunch I have ever attended!' he announced as he left, and the Battalion received a very satisfactory report. Generals have been food members themselves in their younger days.

Sergeant Pilcher MM was one of the best active service mortar platoon sergeants in the Army. The official range and limitations of the 3-inch Mortar never impressed him and he could add 500 yards to the maximum range and drop down to 50 yards without trouble. In Northern Ireland,

Sergeant Pilcher had great difficulty with overactive children. One Sunday, one of the children managed to get into the cab of one of the half-tracks whilst it was in a garage. The child started it and managed to demolish the garage wall. It then headed for the corrugated-iron Garrison Church, and the Padre insists that it was his prayers that caused the divine intervention that stalled the vehicle and prevented further mayhem.

Northern Ireland was the first of many stations that the Regiment shared with its friends, the Royal Warwickshire Regiment, whose Colonel at that time was Field Marshal Montgomery. It was always said that his opening remark to an officer that he did not know was 'We have met before.' In most cases it gave him the reputation of knowing everyone, but being the Warwicks' Colonel, he tended to see them quite often and the ruse was not so effective.

One of the Fusilier and Warwick joint ventures involved Alan Hill and Chris Piggings of the Warwicks. They went over on the Strangford Ferry to have a drink in the pub on the other side of the loch. The ferryman always came into the bar before the last ferry went, otherwise it was a 60-mile walk around the lock to get back to one's car and the camp. However, on this occasion, the ferryman forgot to come in and they were faced with the walk. Full of verve and whisky, they decided to row a boat across the loch, little realising that there was a nine-knot current, and they were swept upstream. They finally ended up near a dredger, minus an oar and without a cigarette between them. Luckily a boat came out of the darkness and rescued them, in charge of which was an Irish actor, Joseph Tomelty, with a motley crew and a quantity of poached salmon. They were towed back to their car on condition that they promised not to tell anyone about the salmon and their rescuers' movements.

The following evening the two returned, with a guilty conscience, to see the owner of the boat and pay for the damage. When they alighted from the ferry, an RUC sergeant questioned them about their rescuers, but they managed to conceal the identity of the poachers. Many suspect the police sergeant was not convinced, but poaching was endemic in the area and sensible local police did not get too involved. (This was not the last of the water-borne adventures of the intrepid sea captain, Alan Hill.)

Infantry officers are not known for their brains, and the old army cliché is that an infantry officer was so stupid that other infantry officers thought him stupid. Perhaps this applied to one of the authors who, when he was asked by a pedantic new officer if he was Novocastrian, replied 'No', thinking perhaps that it was an improper suggestion.

The Regiment had at this time two Company Sergeant Majors, the Connolly brothers, George and Tom, who were identical twins. One was CSM of W Company, the training company, whilst the other was CSM at the Regimental Depot at Newcastle-upon-Tyne. For some reason recruits at the Depot did not know this and the Depot CSM would accompany drafts from the depot to the First Battalion. He would take them as far as Liverpool where they would be put on the boat to Belfast, and he always bade them a fond farewell with the following words, 'If you are not properly dressed and smart when you arrive at Belfast there will be a nasty shock waiting for you.'

The Irish Sea is not known for its calm weather and journeys were never of the best. As a result the recruits arrived in a very poor state of attire and not in the best of health. On the quayside waiting for them was W Company CSM saying, 'I warned you, I warned you.'

One of the duties of the Battalion was the task of guarding the Naval Establishment at Londonderry. This was slightly bizarre because stationed at the establishment was a Royal Marine Commando and the thought of these very large and tough men being guarded by the small Geordies was a difficult concept to comprehend. One of the Marines was a National Service officer who was the fly-half of the Scottish international rugby team. His battledress was showing its age and CQMS Gardiner of the guarding company said that he could provide him with a new one. The Marines officer, the Company Commander and the Platoon Commanders went to the stores to supervise the issue where the CQMS handed over the battledress, but suggested that it should be tried on to make sure it fitted. The Marines officer was very reluctant to do this but was eventually prevailed upon to strip down and was found to be wearing women's knickers. Much embarrassment. Apparently what had happened was that he sent his dirty washing back home each week but as his sister had done the same, his mother had got the parcels of clean clothing mixed. Having run out of clean pants he was forced to wear his sister's knickers. Anyway, that was his story.

Chapter XV

Horses and Courses

Major Ben Van de Gucht was reported as saying that the Fifth Fusiliers were uncertain whether they were the 'footiest regiment on horse' or 'the horsiest regiment on foot'. The latter was probably nearest the truth, although it was hoped that this only referred to a certain lack of equestrian ability. Others felt it had a meaning relating to the unhappiness caused by the changes in the social status of the Regiment. Before the war, being a wealthy regiment, most officers owned horses and the Regiment often produced a worthy polo team.

Before the war, one officer, on joining, turned up with the latest brand-new sports car. He was very proud of this possession. His Company Commander, on ascertaining that he did not own any polo ponies, advised him to 'kindly rid himself of THAT THING, and get, as soon as possible, some polo ponies'. He added, with a remark that was to be repeated some years later, 'besides it is a very un-officer-like car'.

On the march, the Adjutant, Majors and the Colonel rode horses and to this day, 'field officers', that is majors and above, wear spurs on their 'Wellingtons' with No. 1 Dress and Mess Kit. After 1945 officers were encouraged to ride and indulge in field sports but over the years, in common with the rest of the upper working classes who earned their living in cities, this tended to die out. After the First Battalion returned from Kenya, officers who rode or shot at anything with a weapon other than a rifle or a sub-machine gun were rare. Very few, and only those who were stupid, ever shot at an enemy with a pistol, because this is the one weapon whose bullet can be guaranteed to injure anyone except the person at which it is aimed.

One officer was a very keen rider as a child, and his loving parents decided to send him for a riding holiday to a stable near Newbury. His riding experience was mainly in what are now called third-world countries, where he would appear at a reasonable hour in the morning to receive his mount beautifully groomed and ready for his lordship. He would then ride over the veldt and return his beloved horse to a team of slaves who would lead it to outhouses out of focus from the house. At the English riding stable, his first view of his beastly animal was in its stable. He then had, not only to brush the brute, but also to 'muck out' the stable. His interest in riding faded with the end of his 'holiday', and he never admitted to any riding ability either at Sandhurst or when he joined the Regiment. He wanted to be a gallant officer who did clean acts of bravery which did not include the companionship of a smelly brute which had to be looked after in a way that involved very hard work.

The Army provides courses on a variety of subjects. The same officer, who it must be said did not have the most beautiful or the most elegant figure, was sent on a Physical Training Course. This was run at Aldershot by a very fit group of gentlemen from the Army Physical Training Corps. He survived the experience – just, and was even graded 'B' for his efforts. Although he is now a qualified boxing referee, a football referee, a diving judge and a qualified volleyball coach, he is pleased to report that these wonderful assets have never proved to be of any use to him.

Whilst he was on an operation in the Aberdare Mountains in Kenya, he and a group of non-commissioned officers were sent on a course on the new self-loading rifle. The intrepid group fought their way down from their mountain lairs to a truck which took them to Nairobi. He reported to the headquarters in Nairobi on arrival on the Sunday night and tried to find more details about the course for the group. After much telephoning, he managed to track down a duty officer who informed him that the course started on Tuesday. This was good news, as a day and a night in the city were just what they all wanted and felt was their due. The young officer dismissed the group, and went to the Muthaiga Club where he was to spend the nights while on the course.

He had a leisurely breakfast next day, did a bit of reading in the library and looked forward to a well-earned lunch. As he approached the dining room his progress was barred by a very GS (General Service – that is very ordinary and without panache) looking officer who angrily asked him why he was not on the course which had started that morning. The Headquarters staff, furiously trying to cover up their inefficiency in not leaving proper instructions, had spent the morning rounding up anyone in a red and white hackle and had only just found him in the club rather than at the uncomfortable transit barracks. He was told that he should never accept the word of a third-rate staff officer – a lesson the future Battalion Signals Officer should have already learnt.

Sandhurst was not a place for enjoyment. The first term involved square bashing until the cadet's brains were turned into porridge, and the delights of the juniors' run with its mud-splash. The second was jockeying for position to become an under-officer. The third was the character grade term, with cadets looking adoringly at the staff who would decide if they got the maximum grade nine or the failure grade one,

Commandants were a mixed bunch. One officer cadet on the first Friday of term spent rather too long out with his girlfriend and had to hitch a lift back. He was picked up by a charming old gentleman to whom he explained his dilemma of getting back into Sandhurst after hours. The old gentleman was quite helpful and added some advice on how to get in, even giving him a leg-up over the wall.

Next morning was a full parade in front of the new Commandant with the cadet being the right marker for his company. When the General came forward to inspect, the cadet suddenly realized that the General was the old gentleman. Somehow the knowledge transferred itself to the rest of the company, there was a ripple in the ranks and a few names were lost for 'bobbing' – that is, your name was put into the sergeant's book to go before the Company Commander or Senior Under Officer for wavering in the ranks. The General was Sir Hugh Stockwell who later commanded the Suez operation.

Intake 12 at Sandhurst were now officers and whilst Sandhurst had trained them to become future commanders of divisions and army corps, they looked forward to their young officer courses. The first was at Hythe where they would learn the practicalities of small arms and the second at Warminster where they would learn the nuts and bolts of being platoon commanders. They also felt they had had it up to their teeth with being handled like teenage prisoners at Borstal, and looked forward to being treated as officers and gentlemen, or, at worst, just as grown-ups.

The first day was a shock. They were 'fell in' and given a little lecture on how to behave. Matters got worse. In the Mess, their fellow officers, their instructors, made it quite clear that they were no more than jumped-up schoolboys who had to be talked down to. The actual small-arms instruction was little better and learning how to run a rifle range seemed to consist of being treated like a recruit on the range for the first time.

At that time, the sergeants and warrant officers of the Small Arms School Corps seemed to lack any sense of humour and presented the .303 rifle as some sort of totem pole to be worshipped, rather than a weapon that was shortly to be superceded by the self-loading rifle. The young officers neither worshipped the .303 nor the Small Arms School Corps, so revered by their officer instructors whose Mecca was the annual Army Rifle Association meeting at Bisley. They were all, in the opinion of most of the young officers, a very 'naff' lot and the senior officer in charge little better.

Second Lieutenants Danny Seidl and John Masters were of the same opinion as their fellow officers on the course on this matter. So was another young officer who was to become, some years later, a very senior officer. It was decided that the senior officers should be taught a lesson on what bad behaviour really was. The Commandant was having a very special dinner party and, after a proper 'O' group, the order was issued that the pigs which were fed on the leftovers from the poor food in the Mess were to be relieved of their piglets, which were to be released at the height of the dinner party in the dining room. It was a very difficult operation because piglets do not take kindly to being handled and a great commotion occurred, however, they were eventually caught and duly released at the most inconvenient time at the dinner party. A better general would have laughed it off and devised a form of punishment that was both humorous and fitted the crime. A more sensitive adjutant might have tried to find out the underlying cause of the problem. Neither of these solutions were even considered and the 'offenders' were brought up on Commandant's Orders and given the equivalent of being confined to barracks.

The situation did not improve and on the last night of the course the young officers had a party outside the Mess in the local pub where large quantities of drink were consumed. At closing time they were delighted to find that the machinery for a local road improvement had been left unattended. All the trucks and steamrollers were started up and a 'wagon train' drove round Hythe making much noise. The police were called and the 'wagon train' fled in various directions. The certain, now very senior, officer lost control of his vehicle, a steamroller, and ended up in the canal outside the Small Arms School. This nameless, now very senior, officer does not like being reminded of this by his so-called friends and colleagues.

A report on the bunch of hooligans was sent by Hythe to the School of Infantry at Warminster. Here the senior officers, who were proper infantry officers, took a different line. They told Intake 12 of the report that had been sent by the Small Arms School but said that as they were now officers they would be treated as gentlemen. Intake 12 behaved impeccably. A few years later Lieutenant Danny Seidl was on a Signals Officers' course at Hythe. On registering, one of the course instructors asked Danny Seidl to which Sandhurst intake did he belong, and visibly paled when told that Danny was from Intake 12.

The only piece of misbehaviour at Warminster was directed at a very pedantic officer. This young man was very keen to tell all those who were close enough to hear of his grand military connections and of his hunting and shooting prowess. Eventually the group decided that this had to be stopped. One of the girlfriends was asked to telephone him to say she was the General's secretary, informed him that the General had noted his military connections and invited the young officer to join his house party prior to going on to a fancy dress ball. Not wishing to let down his parents, the young man hired a very expensive pierrot suit and called on the General at the appointed time. The General himself came to the door – these were before the days of IRA security – immediately saw what had happened and asked the young officer in for a drink to meet the General's family. It was a toss-up to decide which was worse – to appear at the General's door in fancy dress when you had not been invited, or to be invited in, still in a pierrot suit, and have a drink with the General's charming family.

Despite this, the young man still boasted of his hunting and shooting prowess. At last the genuine invitation came and the whole Mess expected to be bored for the rest of the three months with a shot by shot, blow by blow, account of the great day. The young officer returned, but was strangely quiet. After a few days of blessed silence, one officer decided to broach the subject with a little trepidation. Strangely the young officer was not keen to talk about his exploits and admitted that future invitations were highly unlikely. Shooting your host's dog was not an exploit that hosts regard as best behaviour.

A few years later three other Fusilier officers were sent on their Small Arms Course at Hythe. One officer, from another and perhaps more affluent

School of Infantry Instruction to Platoon Commanders' Course: 'Officers are to be encouraged to take their turn when digging in.'

regiment, had a large 1935 Rolls Royce and, one evening, it was decided that a group of them should try a nightclub in Folkestone. On the return journey they played musical chairs whilst the car was travelling at forty miles per hour. This involved the driver getting out from the front seat to the back via the driver's door and the running board to the back door; he was replaced by the person in the front passenger seat; he, in turn, was replaced from the back seat and, thus, everyone moved round one seat – not a practice to be recommended to the young. On arrival at the Mess they found that they had been followed by a police car containing an Inspector. When ten officers got out of the Rolls, the Inspector looked slightly bemused and asked, 'Who was driving that car?' With one voice all the officers answered, 'I was'. He roared with laughter and the Inspector and the officers all went into the Mess for a nightcap.

A Fifth Fusilier officer was sent on a course in London and was put up in the Officers' Mess at the barracks occupied by one of the battalions of the Brigade of Guards. On the first night the officers were dining in and he dressed himself in No. 1 Dress, but was surprised that he was completely ignored by all the other officers. He thought perhaps that this particular battalion had run out of old Etonians, old Wellingtonions and old Haileyburians, and must have been filled with nouveau old Harrovians, so the Fifth Fusilier Officer got on with some reading in a quiet corner of the Mess. On about the fifth night, one of the officers looked at him and then came closer to have a better look.

'Oh, my God,' he said, 'You're not in the Welsh Guards, I am most frightfully sorry. Your No. 1 Dress looks very like the Welsh Guards and we certainly do not talk to them.'

The Fifth Fusilier officer had a most splendid time for the rest of the course.

When in Hong Kong, the Battalion Signals Officer met a beautiful girl and was delighted when she accepted his proposal. She wanted to be married from her home in Dorset and he took his problem to a very understanding Colonel Robert. The solution was the inevitable course, namely a Forward Air Controllers Course on Salisbury Plain, and so Fairyland – Headquarters Hong Kong Land Forces to the uninitiated – provided the orders and arranged for an air passage for the course which was, according to Fairyland, due to start on 17 July.

On 30 June the officer saw his beloved off to England where she was to help her mother with the final preparations for the wedding in August. The invitations were out, the best man selected, the church booked, the choir hired and the cake was made but not yet iced. He returned to the one air-conditioned room at Stanley Fort, the Signals Platoon stores, to be greeted by a phone call from the inevitable third-rate staff officer from Fairyland. He was sorry, not even terribly sorry or devastated, to report that he had got the date wrong and the course started in three days.

'I suppose that means you can't go, old boy,' said the third-rate staff officer.

The Signals Platoon Commander was not too delighted with the 'old boy' bit but was lucky that a godfather had died leaving him £500. Chancing it, he told the staff officer that he would get to the course under his own steam and would argue with him on the matter of the cost of the flight. Luckily Lieutenant Colonel Robert Leith-MacGregor backed him and he went off to British Airways where he bought an economy single to London for that night and took off. The cost to him was £350.

He duly appeared on his course, was sent to Lossiemouth in Scotland to be made airsick by the Fleet Air Arm pilots and was entertained by the Royal Navy ashore. They pretend to be at sea and there were commands like 'Libertymen to the shore boat' meaning 'there is a bus at the camp gate', and 'Duty men to the quarterdeck for cleaning the heads' meaning 'get to the headquarters' hut to clean the WCs'. He always felt that his presence was not entirely expected but things away from the Regiment are never well organized and he never heard what grade he got for the course. He was also used to the rest of the Army treating these peculiarly-dressed officers with a certain amount of circumspection. After all, Humphrey Walker had told him that when he was a liaison officer at NATO he was often greeted with a full guard of honour. Captain Walker RNF was suspected of being some odd form of Naval Captain.

However, he finished the course, got married and went off on his honeymoon which he cut to ten days in anticipation of being called back to Hong Kong. After four more weeks' holiday at his in-laws' house he wondered if the Army had forgotten about him. David Welch had been forgotten after his Regular Commissions Board and John Masters was never the one to voluntarily cut his leave. After some time Captain John Moncur, the Depot Adjutant, telephoned him.

'You may think this is an odd question but where are you?' he said.

Apparently the First Battalion, who knew he was in England, had been telegraphing the War Office demanding that they return him to Hong Kong. The War Office in turn telegraphed back saying that they had no record of him. Eventually a passage was arranged and he returned with one 'W' to Hong Kong. His wife never got over the fact that the only acknowledgement of her existence was an envelope entitled 'W's docs', the Army's 'camp followers' syndrome.

After another month or two he received a cheque for £37, the price the Army paid for a charter flight. He still thought it was worth it despite the large loss. When he returned to Hong Kong some 19 years later he could get a return passage, Hong Kong to London for £99. British Airways was the only airline operating from Hong Kong to London in 1961 but by 1980 competition had set in and there were many other routes and airlines you could use.

Chapter XVI

The Life of the Artist
as a Young Officer

A newly commissioned subaltern can easily develop a crick in the neck from taking too many surreptitious glances at the brand new pips on his shoulders which signify the fact that he has the Queen's Commission. All regiments pride themselves on their differences from the others, and a particular foible of the Fifth Fusiliers was their use of minute versions of these badges of rank – tiny dark objects, which nevertheless seemed to their new wearer to flash and beam like an overworked lighthouse. To have this authority at the age of 19 was a heady pleasure, even though the first engagement for all young officers after Sandhurst was with their peers for yet more training, this time at the various specialist schools appropriate to their future employment – in this case, the School of Infantry at Warminster, with its stark badge of an unsheathed bayonet and its equally uncompromising motto 'Follow Me' – which Gerald Laing later used as the title of a whole series of abstract sculptures made between 1969 and 1973.

The old pre-war attitude to newly commissioned subalterns – that is, that they were beneath contempt and should not be addressed and certainly not conversed with for a year or two – still held sway but was beginning to be eroded by the insouciance of the National Service officers, who had neither the time nor the inclination for such conscientiously crusty behaviour. Nevertheless Gerald Laing's greeting was minimal (if adequate) and he quickly learnt that junior officers should not initiate conversations and that discussion of all but the most innocuous subjects was considered distasteful. The old rule that shop, politics and women were never to be mentioned was also adhered to pretty well, which left young officers precious little to talk about.

These conventions were by that time beginning to fall into disuse; but even so the Army of the 1950s was a very different organisation from that which it is now. Many of the field officers had joined before the Second World War, when officers were expected to attend to their military duties only in the mornings, the afternoons being reserved entirely for recreation. Value, therefore, was placed upon an amateur rather than a professional approach. Keenness or enthusiasm were still frowned upon in certain places, and style often mattered more than substance.

In the view of some more senior officers, there was not only officer-like behaviour, but there were officer-like artifacts as well. For instance, in Northern Ireland the Colonel took a young second lieutenant out onto the steps of the Officers' Mess one day, pointed at his small red Wolsely Hornet sports car, and said, 'That is not an officer-like car.'

He then swivelled his gaze and, pointing to a 3-litre Bentley belonging to one of the captains, he said, 'That is an officer-like car.'

The implication was that the second lieutenant should get rid of his Wolsely as soon as possible, whether or not he could afford a Bentley. The 1950s were a desperately snobbish time. Nancy Mitford's book *U and Non-U*, which dissected and graded nuances of behaviour, was read by thousands with a serious devotion, thus turning her from a satirist into an educator.

The first occasion on which Second Lieutenant Adam Hope, the other newly joined subaltern, and Gerald Laing were taken notice of was after dinner on their first Mess Dinner Night. These dinners were more formal than the usual nightly ones, and were held once a week. Sometimes a couple of guests were invited – colonels from other regiments, or the Brigadier (never any females). Officers wore their Mess Kit, which consisted of short red jackets with facings and waistcoats of gosling green (the regimental colour), stiff shirts and wing collars, black bow ties, and blue No. 1 dress trousers with the broad red stripe of the Infantry. The Field Officers – majors and above – wore tight overall trousers which often displayed their tummies to advantage, and spurs which jangled as they walked. The Regimental Band played during dinner, and after the loyal toast had been drunk, the port passed round, and the Band dismissed, Adam Hope and Gerald Laing were subjected to a violent initiation.

It culminated in each of them being blindfolded and slid fast along the top of the mahogany dining table, to crash off the end upon their noses, and find upon ripping off their bloody blindfolds that they were surrounded by flames, produced by various people holding burning newspapers around their heads. By the end of Gerald Laing's time in the Army such habits had more or less died out; National Servicemen would not put up with them.

Even so, there would often be violent games after dinner, and on one occasion Gerald Laing remembers an unfortunate conjunction between a human flame-thrower who was using brandy as his inflammable liquid, and a horseback fight, which resulted in the shirt of one of the riders being set on fire and its owner being quite badly burnt.

His first duty on joining the Fifth Fusiliers was an unpleasant one. An officer from a Scottish regiment was under arrest awaiting a court martial, and he was housed in a room in the Mess. Because he had attempted to commit suicide his shoelaces had been removed and he was allowed a razor only while actually shaving, during which he was closely watched. His plight was sad and undignified, and rendered more so by the fact that he was in his late forties with the better part of a military career behind him; while those who in turn watched over him were callow youths in their late teens, for no more senior officer wanted to engage in such unwholesome employment and it was therefore shuffled off onto the most junior ranks. The Scottish officer was a Quartermaster Captain – that is to say, he had spent most of his time in the ranks, ascending to the highest non-commissioned rank before being commissioned. Officers promoted in this way were seldom if ever given duties in the front line, but generally had control of supplies and administration. This man had been in command of a transit camp for soldiers' families who were waiting for accommodation to become available so that they might join their husbands. He had had an affair with one of his protégées, the wife of a sergeant. While this was obviously a gross betrayal of his responsibility to both the sergeant in question and of his position, it seemed to Gerald Laing sad that the actual charge which he faced was that of 'conduct unbecoming', for after all he had only been decreed an officer and a gentleman a few years before. Prior to this and for far longer he had been considered the social equal of the sergeant – and as a quartermaster he was even now by no means completely accepted as an equal by the other members of an officers' mess. But the Army sets its rules, and then sticks to them, just as an abstract painter or a conceptual artist must describe the parameters in which he will work, and not transgress from them.

Gerald Laing supposes this first year of commissioned service represented the apogee of his military career. He was still committed to the idea of being a soldier; disenchantment had not begun; and he was not aware of alternatives and the possible richness of life outside the Army. He was at the peak of his training and his Platoon Sergeant, Sergeant Kilkenny, was one of the old type, old enough to be his father and clever enough to run things as he knew they should be run, and at the same time give the impression that it was Gerald Laing who was making all of the judgements and decisions. He willingly co-operated in this illusion since he knew it was the time-honoured method by which young officers learnt the realities of their trade. Thus Sergeant Kilkenny would say to him, 'I expect you want the platoon formed up for inspection at 0800 hours, sir,' or 'Shall I send the men to the cookhouse for their meal now, sir,' and so subtly arrange and implement most of each day's programme according to his experience. Sergeants like this are a thing of the past now; in the modern Army they are often younger than their platoon commanders. These older men made a much more useful contribution however well trained the new sergeant may be, because they were experienced and mature enough to bring to their job a paternal and caring attitude towards the soldiers, with a deeper authority and which, if solidly based, gave out a greater degree of confidence.

In the 1950s, the political situation in Northern Ireland was calm though Gerald Laing is sure that some of the activities in which the authorities were indulging at that time were to some degree responsible for the dreadful events which were to occur later. There were no worries about security; soldiers could move about and join in the social life of the community, in or out of uniform. The IRA limited its occasional acts of violence to inanimate targets, such as remotely sited electricity transformers. No one was killed or wounded on either side during the entire two years which Gerald Laing spent there. However, intelligence reports told the Battalion that the old

IRA leadership, who remembered the Troubles and abhorred extreme violence, were gradually surrendering their authority to a new, more impatient,
violent, ruthless and committed group; and this proved to be the case.

The Battalion operated in support of the civil authorities, particularly as
embodied by the notorious B Specials, auxiliary part-time police who were
invariably Protestant. Even to Gerald Laing's politically naive self it seemed
that many of the Battalion's actions were arbitrary and on the mainland of
the UK would have been impossible – such as, for instance, searching houses
without a warrant simply on the instruction of the B Specials. Though the
Battalion was never oppressive, violent or cruel, these invasions of the privacy
of the people's homes (during which they never found a single weapon)
made an enormous contribution to the feelings of resentment and inequity
among the Catholic population.

Two events in particular stuck in Gerald Laing's mind. One was when
the Battalion searched an abandoned farmhouse which proved to be empty,
except for a cascade of stiff white paper shirt collars of the 1920s style,
mingled with piles of religious tracts, and the mummified corpse of the
family cat lying apparently asleep in front of the empty grate of the sitting-
room fireplace. On another occasion, and again on the instruction of the B
Special the Battalion was escorting, they emptied a remote village hall where
a Republican dance was being held. As the people filed out of the building,
one man was found to have a rude poem about the B Specials sticking out
of his top pocket. The policeman patted him down, and a rattling noise
came from his jacket pocket. Thinking immediately of the favourite weapon
of the Teddy boy, Gerald Laing said, 'It's a bicycle chain. Take it out.'
When the man did so, they saw that it was a rosary.

It would be pleasant to suggest that some sort of moral disgust with these
activities was what prompted his growing disillusion with the Army, but that
is not the case. He was simply bored with the life and the milieu, and at the
same time and with increasing rapidity, even in the limited possibilities of
the Army in Northern Ireland, new horizons were opening up for him.

The Battalion's ineffectual pursuit of the IRA continued. By this time it
had begun to seem more like a myth than a reality; the Orange marches
proceeded unimpeded in their garish and noisy vainglory through the mean
streets of Belfast, and the Catholics were quiet and contained in their
resentment. The patrols went out each night and each night returned empty
handed. Only one note of discord disturbed the somnolent serenity of the
military round, and that was the presence of National Servicemen, unwilling
two-year conscripts, who, like the wandering sea-rat in *The Wind in the
Willows*, seemed to say, 'Take the Adventure! 'Tis but a banging of the door
behind you, a blithesome step forward, and you are out of the old life and
into the new!'

It was difficult for a young man to feel proud of his achievement in having
become a Regular Army officer after two years of arduous training and study,
when he was surrounded by other second lieutenants who had been com-

missioned in a mere six months and who could, if they wished, continue to serve after their obligatory period of conscription was completed. What made it worse was the knowledge that while they carried out their duties with skill and enthusiasm most of them had no intention of staying on and were actively looking forward to a different, more serious and more rewarding career beyond the military. For them the Army was merely an interlude.

Other ranks, too, served unwillingly; most committed themselves to the Army so long as they were in it, and all now seem to look back on it with affection; but some were determined and incorrigible misfits. There were suicides among National Service conscripts, and sometimes eruptions of frustration which culminated in extreme violence and which often achieved the satisfactory end (to both the Army and the individual in question) of a discharge from the service. One such occurred on a night when Gerald Laing was Duty Officer. The Duty Sergeant came to fetch him, saying that there was a disturbance in the NAAFI. When he got there he found it empty except for the defiant and bloodstained, crouching figure of a soldier. He was a gypsy. The discipline of military life had finally become unbearable to him, and he had snapped. He had overturned all of the furniture, smashed the windows, and slashed his wrists with the broken glass. He had then waved his arms about, covering the ceiling, walls and floor with long gouts of blood. By then the other soldiers present had fled. He took one look at Gerald Laing and screamed, 'You're ganner stick me wi' that sword!' Gerald Laing restrained the sergeant and the guard from laying hands on him, and eventually managed to persuade him to walk quietly by himself, with them following at a discreet distance, to the guardroom, where he was put in a cell and, quite soon, discharged from the Army.

Thus the unanimity of purpose and the cohesive commitment of Sandhurst were violated. A sort of Pandora's box had been opened, and who knew what might fly out of it?

In October 1957, the Battalion's tour of duty in Northern Ireland came to an end, and its morose, damp landscape was exchanged for the flat plains and dun colours of Westphalia. Here the Battalion faced the Russian Army. This was the time of M. A. D. or Mutually Assured Destruction. Hundreds of intercontinental missiles with multiple nuclear warheads sat in their silos at opposite sides of the world, awaiting the signal for Armageddon. People felt that a general conflagration was likely, if not inevitable. The thought of it was so appalling that it was, most of the time, ignored.

The British Army of the Rhine, which was derived from the original occupying forces of 1945, together with the American and French armies in their sectors, was intended as the first sacrifical obstacle with which the Russian hordes would be confronted, given that they (and the Allies) were spared in sufficient numbers to fight a conventional war. Sealed contingency plans for all the possible permutations of this prospect were held locked in the safes of the headquarters of every unit.

Nevertheless, life in the Army continued on its even keel. The Battalion no longer had to mount nightly security patrols and so time was devoted to training. This follows an annual rhythm, beginning anew each autumn with small arms training and the exercise of the smallest units, which, as the year progresses and the seasons change, by combining with others, become larger until they participate in the great Brigade and Divisional manoeuvres of the late summer, with their extraordinary confusion and contretemps, and their massive delays and vast deserts of boredom. Then, in autumn, it starts all over again.

In Germany Gerald Laing again found himself involved in the unpleasant business of a court martial, and had to act as the escort to a fellow subaltern who was facing a serious charge. This young man was in a cavalry regiment stationed nearby. He had been captain of the Eton cricket team (this fact was cited as a part of his defence) and had an exemplary background and career thus far, until a 15-year-old German girl accused him of exposing himself to her in the street. She had never met him or spoken to him before; but she said that it had happened and it was simply a matter of her word against his. Gerald Laing remembers being quite surprised that the word she employed to describe his penis was *schwantz* which in fact means 'tail' but is a slang word in German for the male organ. Gerald Laing feels it strange that he cannot remember what verdict was reached in this case. He found it very painful to listen to and was at the same time aware that the Army's desire not to appear to show favouritism militated against the young man in the dock. His life hung in the balance; it was as though the life of convention had been lifted and the thin membrane of daily behaviour rent, so that the grotesque anarchy of the soul was displayed, and all for a simple act, obscene if it had occurred as the girl described and equally obscene if it had not.

Gerald Laing kept a boat at Munster and used it at weekends for outings on the canal. He was at the time conducting a liaison with the Brigadier's daughter and she would occasionally accompany him, but needless to say she behaved with perfect decorum. He had a habit then of exchanging one old car for another in the hope that change would show some improvement; her mother, one evening, with some perspicacity he now thinks, said to him, 'Gerald, will you change your wives as often as you change your cars?'

After a time at Munster, Gerald Laing was posted to the Regimental Depot at Newcastle-upon-Tyne. This was a large and grim late Victorian castellated compound, inside of which were two parade grounds, an armoury, the headquarters offices, some slum-like married quarters for other ranks, the cookhouse, and the Officers' Mess. At the entrance to the camp was the guardroom, at which sentries were posted at all times.

The Depot's task was to take in recruits, and then to keep them amused until there were sufficient assembled to form a platoon of about 30 men. Basic training then began, and when each group had successfully completed the ten-week course it was transferred to the First Battalion, wherever it might be at the time. New soldiers were given literacy tests, which they approached with some enthusiasm, as well as apprehension, because their degree of literacy affected to some extent their rate of pay. Though of course standards varied enormously, some efforts at essays were quite startling and one in particular delighted Gerald Laing. It was written in completely phonetic Geordie and has an almost Chaucerian rhythm, rich and dignified, particularly in the last paragraph, which follows. At the same time it gives a muddled view of the Army from the point of view of the soldier in the ranks.

> We training at the Depot, at last for tin week and, I like the tin week. We get peat tea alose feetball and basketball and HOKIE. We get up in the morning at 5.30 a.m. and get your breakf at heafpastit seven we go for your riefels. Then we go on muster pread and we get sheked for been dute and we go in front of you OC, for the Punehmet and we get a cupel of deg guker or a warinin and wen we come out of the OC the CSM will tork to you for a will and tells you not to get in trudul, or I will stop you go out for a weekend then you, goto the sagent mess and clen the mess the polp hav made, there, your kit has to be bad for muster prad in the monen and it strouts orlover a gen and that wotse go on for a day. We go on the ringens for firen the wene your skoren bad and ther no yore a good shot you go in front of the CO for wasten the army muney with be in the army you canoot to be fune to the offuser.

Gerald Laing's new Platoon Sergeant was a younger man, a stocky Yorshireman from Ripon called Sergeant Goodger. He maintained an almost constant monologue on the subject of women, and Gerald Laing was never able to decide whether he was debating the mystery with himself and then presenting him with his conclusions in order to instruct him, or whether he was simply seeing how far he could go before he shocked him sufficiently for him to protest. Some of his advice seems to Gerald Laing quite sound, such as, 'If you want to keep a wife, sir, keep her well fooked and badly shod,' or, more graphically, 'There's nowt like a drink from the 'airy coop, sir.'

But he was an efficient and robust colleague, with a particularly imaginative repertoire of parade ground threats and insults – a genre for which the British Army is justly famous – such as, for instance, 'Beresford, if you don't get a grip of yourself I'm going to stick my pace-stick up your arse and tickle your cap badge!'

The pace-stick, normally reserved for sergeant majors but employed at the Depot by Sergeant Goodger for basic training, is an interesting if archaic military tool. It is essentially a yard-long pair of wooden dividers, beautifully made and polished, and mounted with gleaming brass. These dividers can be set open at the length of pace at which the Regiment intends to march – say, 30", or more typically, 28". The Sergeant Major places one point of the open dividers beside his right boot, holding the top of the stick in his right hand. Then with great dexterity, he marches forward, turning the stick on its point outwards in a semicircle with each step, and transferring its weight from point to point. Thus his paces are measured exactly as he marches, and a standard for the Regiment is set. It is an intriguing and graceful spectacle, and with it the complex manoeuvres of the parade are measured and drawn out.

At the beginning of 1959, Gerald Laing enrolled for four night classes per week in life drawing at King's College. At that time Laurence Gowing was the Principal, and both Victor Passmore and Richard Hamilton were teaching there. Although he regularly attended his life drawing classes, and reaped some benefit from this instruction, he was disappointed in the art school. Used as he was to a more total commitment to the work in hand, such as was obligatory at Sandhurst, he found the uncertainty and pessimism of art school disconcerting.

At about this time Gerald Laing had a quite serious car accident. He was driving through the city in one of the innumerable Austin Sevens which he seemed always to be buying and discarding, they being the only type of car which he could afford, when he was hit, head on, by a much larger car driven by two members of an habitually criminal local family called Shotton. One of them had just got out of jail and they had been celebrating. Gerald Laing's car spun round and was totally demolished, and he was left holding the rim of the steering wheel, which had broken off completely, which gave the event a bizarre and comic tone. He suffered cuts and bruises and some damage to the vertebrae in the area of his neck; his luckless dachshund got a dislocated spine which gave him a sort of small hump halfway down his back. (This was later cured by a physiotherapist.) Enraged, Gerald leapt bleeding from the wreckage and shouted for witnesses; several came forward and he took their addresses; none of them later appeared in court – it was understood that they had been 'got at'. A policeman appeared, notebook at the ready.

'What's your name, lad?' he asked of the driver who had run into Gerald Laing.

'Feind oot, ya booger, it's yore job!'

'What's your name?' repeated the policeman, more firmly.

'Corly-baalls o'Swalwell,' came the reply, and even in the chaos and pain it struck Gerald Laing as a pretty good response, reminding him of the Border outlaws from whom these Shottons were no doubt descended.

The sick leave he was given after this debacle gave him a little more time to himself, and he rented an attic which became his studio – '. . . quite large, and contains a few assorted items of furniture, such as a delightful basketwork chaise-longue. There is a jutting-out window and a bed, gas ring and gas fire. All for 10/- a week! It promises to be a haven where I can really try and sort things out.'

He took his paintings to show them to Professor Laurence Gowing, who was head of the Art School, and told him of his intention to resign from the Army in order to become an artist. The professor looked quickly at his still lifes of bottles and jars, his figures and landscapes. One of the great gobs of spittle for which he was famous slid on a long salivary string from his lips, and was as quickly sucked back up. He leant forward in that ungainly way common to many who have found refuge in intellectual pursuits and stammered, 'Stay in the Army'.

Fortunately Gerald Laing had just read Somerset Maugham's short story in which the ambition of the young son of a successful Jewish industrialist to become a pianist is thwarted by the opinion and advice of a musical expert, resulting in the young man's suicide. He therefore was to some extent forewarned on the subject of advice which is crushing and frustrating; and ever since he has believed that it is the height of arrogance to discount a person's ambition. It is true that he went to Gowing to seek his advice; but what he gave him was a stone wall.

In spite of this setback Gerald Laing submitted his resignation in September. Within a few weeks notification came that it had been rejected, whereupon he submitted it once more. Naturally his superiors were alarmed by his plans, and he believes that their subsequent actions were inspired by a genuine concern for his well-being. Almost everyone without exception attempted in different ways to dissuade him from leaving the Army and going to art school. The only exceptions to this were Unitt, his batman, and one major's wife, who said, 'For God's sake get out if you can, and don't leave it till it's too late.'

His Commanding Officer, a man whom he liked and admired especially for his brilliant war record, took him to sit in his car in the neutral ground of the Officers' Mess car park. This clumsy but well-intentioned manoeuvre affected him sufficiently to disarm his anger when, havng failed to frighten him with warnings of destitution and the inadvisability of rejecting a well-founded career, the CO then said that if Gerald Laing persisted in his attempts to resign he would put in an adverse report on him, so that he would be obliged to appear before the General Officer Commanding Northern Command. This was a severe and unusual threat, and one which was duly carried out.

His appointment with the General eventually took place; he had decided to be contrite but firm in his wish to resign his commission. The General refused to accept his resignation, and told him that his behaviour was unsatisfactory, and that he would instead be posted to the Lancashire Fusiliers for a six-month probationary period, at the end of which if his attitude had not improved, he would be cashiered. In other words, he threatened that if Gerald persisted in attempting to leave the Army, he would be thrown out in disgrace.

This was extremely depressing, but served only to confirm him in his wish to change his life; and even in the midst of the unfairness and growing cruelty of the treatment he was receiving he could see that, at the back of it all, there were good intentions. Eventually, and after an unpleasant and uncertain period of waiting, the Army also appeared to realize this, and finally his resignation was grudgingly accepted. (Extracted from Gerald Laing's autobiography which is to be published soon.)

Ian Carr, in an anthology on the National Serviceman, *All Bull*, wrote:

My friendship with Gerald Laing began in Northern Ireland, ripened in Germany and has continued ever since. My first impression of him was not favourable: he looked like a typcal regular officer with his stiff upper lip, his supercilious expression, and his dachshund called Andrew. But on my first regimental dinner night (St George's Day, 1957) I found myself sitting next to him and soon realized he was a kindred spirit. At regimental dinners it is forbidden to talk about religion, politics or sex until the Queen's health has been drunk, which happens, of course, only when everyone has finished eating. Talking shop is frowned upon. This leaves precous little to talk about, but on this occasion Gerald spent the whole meal reciting *Winnie the Pooh* in a rather declamatory fashion. There was a great deal of laughter at our end of the table, and it duly attracted the attention of the Colonel who barked, 'What the devil is Laing talking about?'

A captain in the centre of the table dutifully reported: 'He is saying,

> And nobody
> KNOWS-tiddely-pom
> How cold my
> TOES-tiddely-pom
> Are growing.

Or words to that effect, Colonel.'

I soon learned that Gerald Laing was a man who pursued his dreams with demonic fervour. At one time the all-consuming passion had been ballet and he'd taken ballet lessons. He still kept locked away with his prize possessions a pair of old ballet shoes given him by the ballerina Belinda Wright, and I believe they gave him great comfort in moments of stress. Then he had become obsessed with the romantic idea of soldiering, so he went to Sandhurst and got his commission. But the reality of army life was tearing the dream to shreds and, when I joined the Battalion, Gerald was already falling out of love with his career. To add to his general frustration, he was temperamentally even less suited than I to the celibate, all-male existence.

In Germany the intellectual and imaginative poverty of life and the lack of freedom resulted in some very idiosyncratic behaviour. I have three vivid mental pictures of Gerald at this time:

First, striding along the path outside my window and shouting in anguished tones: 'Masturbation is the only answer!' And as he disappeared round a corner, groaning once again, 'Yes, the only answer!'

Then during a cocktail party, when a pair of Royal Army Service

Corps officers were guests in our Mess, Gerald suddenly dropped down on his hands and knees and scurried up and down the ante-room barking like a dog. The Adjutant, his face purple with anger, hissed at him: 'For Christ's sake, Gerald! Not in front of these RASC blokes, please!' And Gerald, who was too far gone to be moved by thoughts of social propriety, bared his teeth and with a snarl tried to sink them into the Adjutant's calf. With amazing agility for such a bulky man, the Adjutant skipped to one side.

The final incident occurred when I was sitting quietly in my room writing some notes. I heard the roar of an approaching motorbike. Suddenly the door burst open and Gerald roared in on his bike, screeched to a halt in the middle of the room, and revved the engine until the place was full of blue smoke. I tried to shout something to him, but there was so much noise my voice was inaudible, and I could see from the fury in his eyes that the words were redundant anyway. As suddenly as he appeared, he swung the handlebars round and roared out again. I got to my door just in time to see him smash like a bullet through the swing doors at the end of the corridor.

In Northern Ireland Gerald Laing had returned to his early love of painting and in Germany he began taking lessons again. He left the Army in 1960 to study at St Martin's School of Art in London. As a painter he had considerable success in America in the 1960s, and is currently a leading sculptor working mostly in bronze.

Chapter XVII

Munster

The First Battalion was commanded by Lieutenant Colonel (Later Brigadier) Dick Hensman OBE. It was an unhappy time for the Battalion. The need to recruit to avoid amalgamation meant there was little selection and it was rumoured that offenders appearing in front of magistrates were offered service with the Fifth Fusiliers as an alternative to prison. Some of the time in Munster was spent in sorting and removing some of the worst.

Thus, in September 1957, Second Lieutenant David Thompson, due to a flu epidemic that laid Lieutenant Derek Buckingham low, found himself as Baggage Officer for the move from Belfast to Munster. Initially, as Assistant Baggage Officer, before flu struck, David Thompson spent several weeks prior to the move making a detailed inventory of all types and sizes of boxes and crates. Those without metal banding had to be protected by wooden crates almost as heavy as the box they enclosed.

The baggage party of about 20 poor souls had been detailed and it was fortunate that, amongst their number, was a splendid sergeant who proved his worth time after time. Sergeant Major George Connolly also accompanied the party but seemed to have other much more important things on his mind.

An early reconnaissance of the docks in Belfast was reassuring, the proviso being that the baggage was not to arrive before 5 p.m. as before then the stevedores would be loading the ferry with its normal cargo.

The great day arrived with David Thompson now in charge. The baggage arrived at the docks just after 5 p.m. leaving two hours before the ferry sailed at 7 p.m. The baggage party got on with its work of unloading the ten tons of assorted baggage but was not helped by the rain and the wind. Everybody else at the dock seemed to have vanished excluding the crane driver who harangued David Thompson for being late. Each word he uttered was accompanied by another beginning with 'F' and with two-fingered gestures. There were further expletives aimed at the British Army in general and the Royal Northumberland Fusiliers in particular. He then disappeared after the stevedores. To compound David Thompson's predicament, he found that the tide was out. This meant that the ship's deck was six feet below the level of the dock with the hold even lower.

Fortunately a seaman came to his rescue and, somehow, a contraption was rigged which was not unlike a children's slide and the baggage party slid each load down into the ship, although it was a slow and precarious business. They had to use a rope to ease the baggage down a 45-degree slope and some of the heavier boxes broke loose. This made life at the bottom of the hold very lively, to say the least.

As the time for sailing drew nigh, David Thompson felt helpless and was unable to accelerate the process. George Connolly wisely kept clear saying goodbye to Maureen, his wife to be, whilst David Thompson fixed cabins for everyone with the Purser. The job was only finished a few minutes before sailing and the party was fortunate to have a calm and peaceful crossing to Liverpool.

David Thompson was summoned at dawn to the Purser's office, to be confronted by a short, very aggressive, bandy-legged Liverpudlian. David Thompson did not get a chance to introduce himself before the Liverpudlian launched out with, 'If your lot touch as much as a box of your cargo we shall have a strike on our hands and it will be your fault. Do you understand?' David Thompson assured him of their absolute cooperation. He was, at that moment, totally in favour of this illustration of union demarkation because he was only too pleased that he did not have the problem of unloading the hold. Within an hour the boxes were on luggage trollies ready to be loaded into transport which had arrived at the dock gates.

The baggage party moved across Liverpool to the railway station and their next hurdle. Whenever you need a trolley you can never find one, and they needed an army of trollies. Eventually they unearthed a large trolley that must have been used by Noah when he loaded the ark, and they began the transfer from the trucks to the van at the front of the train. It would, of course, have been easier if it had been at the back. After an hour of very hard labour the van was loaded to the roof and the baggage party could relax in their reserved compartments with their haversack rations.

All the Liverpudlians with any vestige of authority seemed to be small, aggressive individuals. The guard insisted that the van be reloaded so that there would be a passage through the baggage van to a restaurant car that was about to be attached to the train. By now the baggage party had had enough of being ordered around by tinpot civilians. They gently told him to put his whistle in a place where he might be able to blow it but only with difficulty. They also suggested that it might not be too impossible to put the restaurant car at the rear of the train. The Fusiliers were quite amused to see the guard throw a tantrum of operatic proportion, threatening all sorts of dire consequences. However, on this occasion, the Fusiliers had the whip hand and the train had to leave on time either with the guard or without him. He boarded the train spluttering.

After a slow cross-country journey the train arrived at Parkstone Quay, Harwich and the luggage van was conveniently shunted next to the crane beside the ferry to the Hook of Holland. Unloading the contents of the van to ground level was not easy. The really awkward business was carrying the heavy boxes to the luggage room in the ferry. The door to this room was only five feet high and was only just wide enough for the boxes. The major difficulty was the fact that the baggage party had to duck their heads and step over a foot sill while still carrying their load. There were a few sore heads and this was not due to the duty free.

In contrast to the Irish Sea crossing, the North Sea was rough and so the Fusiliers were not in the best condition to cope with the loading onto the quay at the Hook of Holland. This time there were two smaller wagons which were then attached to the rear of the train.

David Thompson was a complete stranger to train travel on the Continent. However, he was very conscious of the fact that, on arrival at Munster station, they would have to unload the two vans very quickly if the train was not to be delayed. They 'stood to' several times unnecessarily as they approached a number of stations. A railway plan would have been a useful tool but the Army Movements Authority did not seem to be that perspicacious. Eventually the right station hove into sight and David Thompson was first to leap to the rear of the train. Alarm and despondence – no luggage vans! Various thoughts rushed through his mind and it took some time for the NCOs to calm him down.

In their Teutonic and efficient way the Germans had 'slipped' the two vans as they passed the goods depot. The better news was that a coach was waiting to take them to Buller Barracks and they did not need to unload the vans until the next day. Perhaps, after all, the Army Movements Authority did know what they were doing although they could have briefed him better.

They had loaded and unloaded, by hand, ten tons of assorted crates and boxes twelve times in forty-eight hours, with no one coming to blows in the process. David Thompson does not regret that for a modern battalion move, baggage is looked after by a professional contractor using roll-on and roll-off ferries, containers and proper lifting equipment, so that moves are now made with the minimum of fuss. No doubt the extra cost is justified by the savings made in the lack of damage to the baggage.

Amongst a number of minor dramas was the purchase of a motor mower by the Officers' Mess which was required because officers living in the Mess were often disturbed by the sheep whose task it was to keep the grass down. There was, however, a minor row because the mower was lent out to families and it was said that only the most senior of officers ever got on the lending list.

There was in the barracks a Royal Army Service Corps Transport Company and the Battalion was amazed to find that the company had managed to spawn a section of the Ancient Order of Buffaloes. This is some sort of a secret society, not unlike the Masons, and its presence in the barracks caused some excitement among the senior non-commissioned ranks. The trouble was that according to positions held in the Order, it was possible to find a warrant officer having to touch his hat and kowtow to a lowly lance corporal. The RSM and other warrant officers in the Battalion were not impressed with all the obvious implications to 'good order and military conduct' and Fusiliers were not encouraged to join.

One of the pubs frequented in Munster was called Pinkus Muller. German words often took Fusiliers by surprise. '*Frei Fahrt, Einfahrt* and *Gute Fahrt*' caused a certain amount of mirth even when it was explained they meant

'Freeway, one way and have a good journey'. Gerald Style tried many times to explain the significance of this to a Bavarian friend, Lieutenant Colonel Heine Frey, particularly as Bavarians are notorious for their very positive sense of humour. After a number of attempts the penny seemed to have dropped. '*Ach so!*' Frey said, 'it is wind from behind.'

Sex (the absence of) and boredom soon began to preoccupy the minds of all ranks, and the Battalion's alcohol consumption rose enormously. Given that most of the 940 men in a battalion are heterosexual, that they are herded together in barbaric conditions, surrounded by wire fences and guards, in a foreign country whose language they know nothing of, and with the bromide of fear removed, then the only reasonable thing to expect is drunkenness, inefficiency and absence without leave. Humphrey Walker felt that the answer was to employ a large Womens Royal Army Corps band, who could not play music, to visit battalions for a week at a time every three months.

A few shows were put on in the gymnasium to entertain the troops. It seemed a humane thing to do, and it kept men off the beer for a couple of hours. But the moment of truth came for Ian Carr when the Battalion was entertained by one of the popular singers of the day, a tall, well-built girl. As usual, the first two rows of seats were occupied by the officers wearing dress uniform and their ladies in evening dress. The rest of the gym was filled with other ranks in denims. All went as planned until the singer delivered a particularly lively song during which she jigged around and wiggled her bottom a bit. Suddenly, in the middle of it, a diminutive soldier in shapeless denims rose to his feet and yelled triumphantly: 'I've come!' A ripple of unease agitated the sartorial splendour of the first two rows and a few startled faces glanced back. A couple of military policemen bore down on the hapless testifier and removed him bodily from the hall. However, it was difficult to forget the sheer delight of that man's proclamation. It was as if he'd found an oasis in the desert.

On one occasion the Brigade Cavalry put on a display of polo in an area half the size of a football pitch for the benefit of the local population. The hearty and horsey whoops, swearing and other pieces of polo 'fun' left the large German audience at a complete loss as to what on earth the mad English were up to, however, with their usual regulation courtesy they applauded bravely (not unlike the audience at the end of the officer's sketch in St George's Minstrels). In return the British were treated to a fine display of martial music by a German military band. It is remarkable how the sound of a German band differs from an English band. This is partly due to the use of many instruments not heard in Britain and partly due to the charac-teristic oompah, heavy drumming, glockenspiels, flugelhorns and other in-struments. One is reminded of the noticeable difference between a Royal Marines band, a Guards band, Cavalry and Infantry bands and the happy sound of the Household Cavalry bands playing at the trot. In Hong Kong it was possible to buy pirate cassette tapes very cheaply. The editor's wife being of partial Scottish descent, was keen on pipe bands. On playing the tape back at home she found that there was only one minute of pipes. The piratical Chinese obviously did not believe that what he was hearing was music and she was treated to Andy Stewart dance music instead.

The Brigade telephone system was a bit quaint and there were some crossed lines. One notable one was:

Major Amos: 'Who is that, get off the f——ing line.'

Voice: 'Get off the line yourself.'

Major Amos: 'Who the hell are you to say that?'

Voice: 'Brigadier——.'

Major Amos: 'Do you realize who I am?'

Brigadier: 'No.'

Major Amos: 'Thank God.' (Puts phone down hastily.)

Another conversation went:

Voice: 'Sir, we are testing your phone.'

Senior Officer: 'Thank you. What should I do?'

Voice: 'Repeat after me – I cannot eat a currant bun.'

Senior Officer: 'I cannot eat a currant bun.'

Voice: 'Again.'

Senior Officer: 'I cannot eat a currant bun.' (Said with a little exasperation.)

Voice: 'You had better stuff it up your bum, then.'

Ian Carr had been playing the trumpet intermittently as an amateur since he was at school, and in Germany the only emotional release he could get was in playing jazz. The Bandmaster loaned Ian a cornet and when life became unbearable he would slip down to the band room and have a blow with the musicians from the Regimental Band. There were also a couple of officers, Lieutenant Derek Buckingham and Captain Peter Adams, who played guitars and so they occasionally had jam sessions in the Mess. The Colonel and other senior officers lived in married quarters and so knew nothing of these activities.

One night the Brigadier was a guest at a regimental dinner and, during the meal, as was customary, the Regimental Band, discreetly hidden from view behind a screen, played their usual selection from popular musical shows. After the meal the custom was to walk round to the door at the other end of the room and watch and listen to the band before going into the ante-room to indulge in the usual boisterous parlour games. On this occasion, Ian Carr arrived at the door to find the Brigadier leaning languidly against the doorpost and the Colonel standing beside him. The Band came to the end of a piece, and instead of striking up again immediately, there was a pause and the Bandmaster, offering Ian Carr a cornet, said: 'Do you fancy a blow, sir?' Avoiding the Colonel's gaze, Ian went into the room and played 'St Louis Blues' with the rhythm section. The Brigadier was delighted and the Colonel, faced with the obvious pleasure of his superior, shouted with forced joviality, 'How about Tiger Rag?' However, Ian Carr could detect a glint in his eye.

Some days later Ian Carr was invited to dinner at the Colonel's house and, after wining and dining him generously, he shot a question at Ian. 'Don't you think we should bring back flogging?' The resulting argument was intense and, after they had arrived at an impasse, the Colonel suddenly said, 'An officer and a gentleman doesn't play the trumpet!'

HRH Princess Margaret, as Colonel of the 3rd Hussars, visited that Regiment and all the arrangements and parades were immaculate. HRH stayed with the Commanding Officer of the Hussars, for which certain internal arrangements to the furniture were made and certain officers wondered, in passing, whether the special loo seat was left *in situ* at the end of the visit. No such luck, there are no loo seats in ordinary homes sat upon by HRH in the same way as beds slept in by Queen Elizabeth I. It was felt, nevertheless, without poking fun at such attention to detail, that it was eminently sensible that the royal personage should be able to succumb to the joy of returning to the familiar at the end of her daily duties however far away she was from home.

Second Lieutenants Mike Kitching and Bill Welton and their platoons were pitted against each other in an exercise set by Major Gerald Style, Y Company Commander. The platoons had to give the grid reference of their own HQ to each other, defend their own HQ and, at the same time attack their opponent's HQ. Kitching's night patrol was brilliant. They found the opposing Platoon HQ spot on without being observed, attacked with much noise using thunderflashes and returned triumphant to their own base. Early next morning the Company Commander sent for the smug Platoon Commander who was ushered straight in to Lieutenant Colonel Hensman's tent. In an icy, furious voice the Colonel told the Platoon Commander that his platoon had attacked, and burnt to the ground, the private tent of the Commanding Officer of the neighbouring Cavalry Regiment. Second Lieutenant Kitching had to don his service dress and Sam Browne and drive to the site of the ashes to apologize. To this day Bill Welton swears that he did not give Mike Kitching the grid reference of the cavalry CO's tent, but equally, to this day, Mike Kitching does not believe him.

At the end of Bill Welton's National Service he left Mike Kitching a large metal ammunition box saying that it contained a few things that he had borrowed from Mike Kitching. After seeing him off at the station, the latter opened the box in his room and found, to his horror, that it contained an arsenal of weapons and ammunition. Mike Kitching was so terrified of being found with this loot that, in the dead of night, he dumped the lot into the Dortmund-Ems Canal.

John Masters was Machine-Gun Platoon Commander and it was at a time that the Vickers Machine-Gun Platoons were being phased out. So some of the time in Munster he had a platoon, until it was disbanded, only to be reformed for Hong Kong and then disbanded again. He remembers seeing *The Bridge over the River Kwai* with his Support Company Commander, Major John Webb. John Webb had served with the Ninth Battalion in Singapore where it had been a machine-gun battalion. As an ex-prisoner John Webb was interested in the film and it was also rumoured that the main character played by Alec Guinness was based on his battalion commander. In a moment of high tension in the film the Japanese back up a truck and reveal a Vickers machine-gun ready to mow the prisoners down. The only problem which spoiled the tension for the two machine-gunners was that the Japanese half cocked the gun so that it would not fire. This was announced to the whole audience.

John Webb also told the story of how, when he was a prisoner, he wanted to have a quiet read in the jungle. On returning to his work party he was spotted by a guard who enquired what he had been doing. He gave the obvious excuse and the guard demanded to see the evidence, so John took him into the jungle and showed him a fresh elephant turd. The guard looked at John and then the elephant turd, and promptly cut John's rations because if he could produce so much he must be overfed.

Y Company, under the command of Major Gerald Style, was sent on detachment to Winterberg to do the hard work of pitching a camp for a winter warfare school. When in Winterberg a most unexpected offer of entertainment came from a merchant trading in blue films. Because of the first disbandment of the Machine-Gun Platoon, Lieutenant John Masters had been sent to Winterberg to be the 'Administrative Commandant' of the camp where he resided in the luxury of Gerald Style's excellent caravan. He was quite keen to run a blue film centre as he saw much profit in it for regimental funds. However, Gerald Style was not so keen. At the time he stated that he was concerned with the effect on the morals of Geordie (a likely tale), but perhaps, as some unkind officers said, more on his promotion prospects (he was in the zone for consideration for promotion), and (this was probably the main reason) the effect on the Regiment if the news got around, with an excess of histrionic and hypocritical horror and the unwanted intrusion to the quiet life of the camp.

Before the winter warfare instructors arrived, the snow came and covered the whole camp. Two days later the Battalion was given orders to be posted to Hong Kong and the camp had to be handed over to the Warwicks. The problem was that not all of the equipment could be seen and, quite reasonably, the Quartermaster of the Warwicks would not take over what he could not see. The solution was a Board to write off equipment. A drunken officer in the RASC was selected for the job and the price for the write-off was a bottle of duty-free brandy from John Masters. This was fed to the RASC officer after lunch and he then signed off the documents produced by the Warwick's Quartermaster. All were satisfied; nothing for the Fusiliers to pay and no problem for the Warwicks. John Masters's price was two spare machine-gun locks (cost over a hundred pounds) from the Warwicks who had found themselves guarding the Vickers supply reserve in the Middle East and had, quite rightly, helped themselves to more than a few spares.

For some reason or other, the Brigade staff and Battalion Headquarters were never on the best of terms. The fact that the Colonel of the Regiment was also Chief of the Imperial General Staff did not improve the Fifth's perception of its superiority, and the Brigade Commander did not think it should make any difference. Poor Major David Brook, the Second in Command, was almost always selected to pass on any disagreements with any Brigade order. This did no good to his promotion prospects and a very able officer was passed over for promotion as a result. One of the contretemps was caused at the end of a long brigade exercise. The Battalion radio rear link received a message which was understood to mean 'Exercise ends'. The extent of the misunderstanding or its cause has never been revealed, but the result was a disaster. The Commanding Officer, Dick Hensman, missed the final orders group which involved the Battalion in some sort of attack. Unfortunately the wireless message was believed and the Battalion packed up in quick time as they were all keen to go after the boredom of the exercise, and headed home to barracks before the Brigade staff were aware of the situation.

Posterity does not reveal the conversation the next day at Brigade Headquarters between the CO and the Brigade staff. Relations did not improve and the orders to go to Hong Kong were received with great relief by both sides.

Captain Paddy Baxter was made Adjutant, but due to some muddle at Battalion Headquarters there was no quarter for him. He was not delighted, as a newly married officer, to be told that, 'Adjutants should be too busy to have their wives with them.' Eventually he was able to get accommodaton and was able, at his own expense, to bring her to Munster. When Captain and Mrs Baxter arrived at Harwich they were told that there was no room for Mrs Baxter on the ship and Baxter had to pay for a trip for his wife on a Dutch ship that was arriving at the Hook of Holland at the same time. He was not amused to be told by 'some over-promoted nurd' from Movements that Mrs Baxter could not go on the train because a place had not been booked for her. This was despite the fact that the train had dozens of empty seats. Captain Paddy Baxter replied characteristically, 'Look, friend, if you want to be dropped in the bloody water, I'll drop you in the flaming water, otherwise my wife is bloody well coming with me on the train.' By the time he got back to Munster there was an infuriated complaint to Lieutenant David Welch, the Assistant Adjutant, about the behaviour of a certain Captain Baxter and did he know Captain Baxter? David Welch admitted that he knew him very well and was asked to report him for this most dreadful behaviour. Needless to say he did not find it necessary to do so.

The Battalion wives were asked to help the many Eastern European refugees in Munster. One of the wives saw the Brigadier's wife come out of the NAAFI with a very spotty child. She greeted Mrs Worsley with, 'How good of you to take a refugee child into your home.'

'Pat, this is my daughter,' was the reply.

Major John Deighton was one of the company commanders at Munster and had a well-deserved reputation as a county and army cricketer. Gerald Style, who was the Officer Commanding Y Company, was frequently mistaken for John Deighton, both being of ruddy complexion and each having fair hair. Gerald Style says that he was very miffed by this simply because nobody ever mistook John Deighton for Gerald Style. Such is fame in the sporting world. John Deighton led the Battalion team that won the British Army of the Rhine Cricket Cup. Having bowled out the Second Royal Tank Regiment for 5 in a earlier round, they went on to win the final thanks to an astonishing and gloriously unorthodox batting rescue by Sergeant (later Lieutenant Colonel (QM)) Ken Dalby.

An annual event was the cricket match between the Officers' Mess and the Sergeants' Mess. This was a close-fought event and, over the years, honours were generally even. However, an onlooker might be forgiven for mistaking the well-turned out and immaculate team in white shirts, white flannel trousers and white cricket boots as being the officers' team. The poorly dressed team in any old trousers, scruffy shirts and gym shoes would be identified as the sergeants' team. The onlooker would be quite wrong. The scruffs were always the officers.

The Battalion did not have the greatest hockey team and 2RTR avenged their cricket defeat by beating the Battalion soundly in a friendly. The Battalion then drew 2RTR in the first round of the BAOR Hockey Cup. Firm measures and a certain amount of diversionary tactics had to be taken. The defence, Deighton, Buckingham and Kitching, were put into the forward line and the team played out a pre-match charade of laid-backness. Could the RTR lend the Battalion a couple of balls for practice? Could the Battalion wear white shirts because there were not enough regimental shirts to go round? Could they borrow this and that? Could the date be changed so that the Battalion had eleven men who could play hockey. Behind this smoke-screen the Battalion team practised furiously and on the day the whole Battalion turned out to cheer them on. These ploys managed to dent their opponents' morale and the Battalion beat a technically superior team in a tight game, although in the end this was to no avail because the Battalion was posted to Hong Kong before the next round and 2RTR went through.

Towards the end of the Battalion's tour in Munster, after some protracted disagreements with the Commanding Officer, Captain Baxter found himself as second in command of Z Company. On one exercise, Major John Deighton was on leave so Captain Baxter was commanding the company. There was an enormous muddle between Z Company and another Company Commander, a Major. Captain Paddy Baxter, never the one to overlook the truth, told the Major his fortune. He was placed under arrest for his attitude towards this 'Major'. Baxter decided to become very pompous saying that only the Brigadier could release him and asked to see the Brigadier. At this stage he was told not to be childish and get on with commanding his company which Captain Baxter found to be most diverting.

Before the days of bank accounts and cheque books for Fusiliers, soldiers were paid weekly in cash over the pay table, by companies. What a chore it was for everybody! It was a terrible time-wasting routine. There was the ritual of names being called out, soldiers marching up to the table and halting (if the floor was slippery this could mean a crash into the table with terrible chaos resulting). A salute followed, the right hand was extended to receive money, another salute, about turn and back into the ranks to count the 'gift'. They were then sent to the stoppages table, for, no sooner had a soldier been given money than it was taken away from him. There were stoppages for barrack damages (one Christmas one of the jail escapees had spent the evening butting his head through the glass doors that linked the barrack blocks), TV hire, canteen debts, laundry, the company sports fund and losses of kit. What a headache for the Company Second in Command who had to account for it all!

Collecting the bag containing the pay in the first place was bad enough. David Thompson remembers taking an armed escort to a branch of a bank in Newcastle to collect the pay for the Depot. Having identified himself to the cashier, he had to weigh up whether to count the money or trust the bank. As it was always recounted at the Pay Office he tended to trust the bank and not waste time.

At Munster with the Battalion, Headquarters Company was the worst. Paying them out took all day as soldiers were released from their departments in dribs and drabs so that vital work, like the cookhouse, was not interrupted.

An officer who had honed his signatures over the years to one of style and distinction soon found that it was ruined by signing countless pay books and the pay sheets each time money was handed over. There was little temptation to acquire the odd pound or two because the paying-out officer's every move was watched by two witnesses and the company pay clerk.

However, money did go astray sometimes, not only when the notes were new and stuck together. If the count revealed a deficit, unless it was of enormous proportions, the paying-out officer had to pay the difference. Once in Munster a whole company pay bag did disappear and to this day the culprit has never been discovered despite a very serious and unpleasant Special Investigation Branch investigation.

David Thompson recalls another occasion when the whole of a company's pay went missing. The Battalion had assembled in Barnard Castle for a few months just prior to the move to Hong Kong, and most soldiers were due for two weeks' embarkation leave pay. Officers had to collect the company pay bags just before lunch with pay parades due after lunch. These bulging pay bags were a nuisance during lunch in the Mess, and the Mess Secretary was never there at the vital time to put them in his safe or simply did not want the responsibility of having the whole of the Battalion's pay in his safe.

In these circumstances, wise officers clung on to their pay bags, like leeches, during lunch. One officer, however, placed his pay bag under his hat on the Mess hall table.

After lunch, David Thompson had just finished paying out his company when he was asked if he had any spare money left over.

'Why, what has happened?' he enquired.

'Adam has lost his pay bag somewhere and he needs the money to pay out his company'.

Under these circumstances, officers help their chums. Without giving too much away, they hunted high and low, questioned the Mess Staff and asked, as surreptitiously as possible, if anything had been handed in to the guard-room or elsewhere. No trace could be found of the pay bag.

Meanwhile Adam's company was getting a little restive, to say the least. The Paymaster was beginning to ask questions because he was anxious to close his books so that surplus cash could be handed into the bank before it closed.

What had happened was that some dear senior officer had spotted the bag and, bearing in mind what had happened in Munster, had taken it to the Adjutant. It would seem that whilst Adam spent a penny, he had made off with the pounds. The Adjutant, the very dear fellow that he was, decided to let Adam stew to teach him a lesson – not a nice thing to do to a fellow officer.

The sequel was that Adam became the subalterns' friend for a number of weeks. In the end, his first day off duty was when the *Empire Fowey* berthed in Aden.

Chapter XVIII

Two Battalion Paymasters

I t is surprising that, whilst Battalion Padres came and went quite frequently, the Battalion was lucky to have had two loyal and popular Paymasters who stayed with it for long tours of duty.

In Lemgo the Battalion had four Padres but was lucky that the Paymaster, Major Griffiths, remained for the whole of its time there. 'Griff', as he was affectionately called, had come to the Battalion some years earlier when it had sailed for Hong Kong. He left nine years later and his replacement, Major Angus Elliot, stayed longer. Such was the service these two provided that they were both aware of every nuance that made for the smooth running of the finances of the Battalion.

It is certain that they knew more about individuals than many Padres. One Padre left after a year without having achieved any rapport with the Fusiliers, NCOs, officers or the Commanding Officer. He had suggested to the latter, after an exercise at Soltau, that he should stop swearing so much and set an example to his officers and, in particular, the Fusiliers. His successor arrived shortly afterwards and certainly preached a sermon with Welsh fervour but never really settled in or understood the Geordie. He left prematurely which was a pity because he had a most attractive wife who had, it was thought, been a British Caledonian air hostess. Earlier Padres had refused to bury the dead on the field of battle because it was too dangerous and one had been unfrocked for financial impropriety. One was greeted in a pub by a person wishing to be saved. 'Don't bother me out of office hours,' was the reply. However, these were exceptions and many Battalion Padres, such as Pat Scott and Jack Stacey, became great favourites.

Griff and his wife, Hilda, left just before the Battalion was sent to Aden. They had both become so much part of Battalion life that they were sorely missed. Griff enjoyed guest nights. He avoided the rough and tumble of mess games by pleading old age and long service as a gunner. It is said that at one guest night when charades were being played, Griff's team had to enact 'Pee Wee Brown'. The team decided to act 'Pee' and 'Wee' by standing round the Christmas tree pretending to 'decorate' it. Whilst everyone else pretended, Griff, full no doubt of the Christmas spirit, added a sense of reality to the proceedings. He could often be found in the kitchen entertaining the complete Band – all on the Mess Guests account.

Hilda used to get a little fed up on these occasions because she was often woken up in the early hours by an all too well refreshed Griff, and so she resorted to locking up the front and cellar doors but leaving the downstairs lavatory window open. However, she also locked the door to the lavatory from the outside. Griff would arrive at his married quarter mellow and in the happy state when the mind is still capable of working things out but lacks risk judgement. Feeling that he could and determined that he would get inside, Griff would find the window, but would have to climb in head first and spend the rest of the night in the loo. Hilda and Griff seemed quite used to not speaking to each other or through a third party for weeks on end.

Both Hilda and Griff were always willing to help anyone in need. Griff would spend hours sorting out Mess Accounts with Mess Secretaries. This was an unpopular appointment as most officers were often not competent accountants for whom therefore unfathoming the intricacies of mess bills and preparing the Mess Accounts for audit was a nightmare. However, so long as the Mess Secretary made an honest attempt, Griff would burn the midnight oil, delving into the records to set matters straight.

Angus Elliot served the Battalion equally well. He relied on his vast experience, having served in the Black Watch from an under-age junior drummer to Regimental Sergeant Major, before joining the Royal Army Pay Corps, rising to the rank of Major. He served during the time when soldiers' pay started being paid direct into bank accounts. The problem was that some soldiers and their wives thought that a cheque book was an automatic pass into the bank's vaults and that pay day was every other day and not just once a month. Thus by the time overdrafts had been cleared, stoppages deducted, and hire purchase debts settled, there was not much left to last the rest of the month. Angus had served long enough to be able to advise bank managers whom he could or could not trust.

The Regiment owes a great deal over the years to Griff, Angus and their wives, and was also well served by its other attached soldiers from the Royal Electrical and Mechanical Engineers, the Army Catering Corps and the Royal Signals.

1. Gibraltar, 1949. 'Early Days'.
Sgts Goodfellow, Deans, Donald, Beattie, Heweson, Walker.
Sgts Hutchinson (RAEC), Haigh (APTC), McAnulty, Clark, Aspinall, Dunn, Bates, Whittle, WO II
Pittcairn, Jones (RAEC), Hayler (RAEC),
S/Sgt Tate, Sgts Weatherdon, Jordan, Jackson, C/Sgts Burn, Henderson, Williamson, Connolly, Sgts
Bailey, Connolly, Smith, D/Major Rackley.
CSMs Radcliffe, Blanchard, Richardson, RQMS Boniface, RSM J.J.H.Westwood, Lt Col B.J. Leech,
DSO, ORQMS Brown, CSMs Ambury, Tong, Pratt.
Courtesy of Fusiliers Museum of Northumberland

2. Korea, 1950–51. 'Orff Taet Warr', H. T. M. Halladale.
Fus. F. Geard, Fus. F. Dutton, Cpl J. Thompson, Fus. W. Wyner, Fus. J. Rooke, CSM A. Tong.
Courtesy of Fusiliers Museum of Northumberland

3. Korea, 1950–51. Patrol for Korea with 8th Kings Royal Irish Hussars.
Returning from searching patrols in North Korea, British Centurion tanks of the 8th Kings Royal Irish Hussars laden with men of the Royal Northumberland Fusiliers approach the ford on the north bank of the Imjin River. Daily patrols by men of the 29th British Brigade had been taking place since the recent Allied advance but only light contact has been made with the Chinese.
Courtesy of Fusiliers Museum of Northumberland

4. Kenya, 1953–55
Lt Colonel Roger St John MC, CO 1RNF with Regimental Samburu trackers.
Courtesy of Major A. K. C. Hill

5. Kenya, 1953–55.
2Pl, Support Coy, Longowot, Kenya, 1955.
Fusilier Parrott, Fusilier Christie, Fusilier Shields {???}, Fusilier Marshall, Fusilier Donaldson.
Courtesy of Major A. K. C. Hill

6. Kenya, 1955–55.
'Aphrodisiac!'. The RMO, Captain Roy Fleury with friend.
Courtesy of Major A. K. C. Hill

7. Belfast, 1957.
Lord Mayor's Parade, Belfast.
Drum Major Lambert, Cpl T. Hoos, Cpl W. O'Brien, Drummer T. McDonald.
Courtesy of Fusiliers Museum of Northumberland

8. Depot, Farnham Barracks, 1957.
Recruit Coy Comd, Captain Alan Hill and Recruit Coy CSM 'Tom or George' Connelly
(identical twins), can you remember?
Courtesy of Major A. K. C. Hill

9. TA Battalion. 7th Bn (TA) RNF at camp

Sgts G.J.Powell, C.Giles, J.Reid, T.Milburn, N.Middleton, E.Mackie, P.Lunn, B.Scott, G.Cone.
H.Birch, G.R.Henderson, R.Middleton, H.Ratcliffe (MM), B.Steer, J.Fife, C.Dodsworth, J.McGee, W.Robinson.
Dixon, G.Jackson, W.Arnold, T.Gibson, F.Laidlaw, Hunter, W.Sword, Palmer, Newby.
W.Brown, Hedley, Sgt Ollerenshaw, C/Sgt E.Tully, C/Sgt Parker, D/M F.Tuck, C/Sgt R.Jackson,
C/Sgt N. Cosgrove, C/Sgt P.Bailey, Sgts A.E.Wilson, T.Ormsby, E.Bailey, A.Meekins.
CSMs J.Adamson, H.Lamb, H.Naylor, F.Bingham, Lt Col J.L.Sanderson TD (Commanding
Officer), RSM H.Westwood, CSMs J.Jones, J.Donald, W.Henderson, P.Woodcock, Heweson.
Courtesy of Fusiliers Museum of Northumberland

10. Hong Kong, 1961.
Paddy and the Princess.
Major Paddy Baxter and HRH Princess
Alexandra. CSM Les Lamb is left guide.
Courtesy of Fusiliers Museum of
Northumberland

11. Hong Kong, 1960. Mortar Pl, Support Coy, 1RNF.
Fusiliers McAlister, Maddison, Clasper, Gibson, Faley. Sgt Stainforth, Fusilier Thackray,
Sgt Diplexito, Fusilier Culyer, Howard, Welts, Williamson.
Courtesy of Major J. B. Oakley

12. BAOR 1966. 1RNF Boxing Team.
Top (left to right): Fus. Moore, McIntyre, Gordon, L/Cpl Fryer (REME), Fus. Jacques, Tyler.
Middle: Fus. Willis, Cpl Ganning, Fus. Masterton, O'Toole, Bell, Hindhaugh, Sample.
Front: Fus. Masterton, McBurnie, Capt. Hope, Lt Col Blenkinsop, CSMI Kenny (APTC),
Sgt O'Toole, Fus. Holian.
Trophies: 4th Div. Winners, BAOR Runners-up Shield, 20 Armd Bde Gp Winners.
Away: S/Sgt Charlton, Fus. Minto, Fus. Lashley.
Courtesy of Fusiliers Museum of Northumberland

13. Newcastle upon Tyne, 1966.
1RNF exercising their Freedom of the City.
CSM Peter Hoare, Sgt John Hayman, Lt David Cruikshank, Cpl Colin Pick, C/Sgt Norman Ward,
Lt Simon Thompson.
Courtesy of Fusiliers Museum of Northumberland

14. Aden, 1966–67.
1RNF in Crater, Aden. 'Armed Robbery'.
Sgt J. Hall, Cpl T. Johnson, Major Angus Elliott, Bn Paymaster.
Courtesy of Fusiliers Museum of Northumberland

15. Aden, 1966–67.
OP duty, Overlooking Crater, with Main Pass in centre background.
Courtesy of Fusiliers Museum of Northumberland

16. Kirton-in-Lindsey, 1968.
'The last March Off The Colours, St George's Day, 1968'.
Captain Peter Marr, CSM Mick Goodger.
Courtesy of Captain P. H. D. Marr

Chapter XIX

Gypsy Smith

The late Gypsy Smith was one of the best-known regimental characters. He was a great active service soldier who could live off the land without any problems. One of his better tricks, learnt no doubt from his early days as a poacher, was to rock a chicken to sleep which enabled him to conceal the bird about his person whilst it slept soundly – a form of poacher's hypnosis.

He was probably at his best out in the forest on patrol, providing valuable old-soldier advice to the young national serviceman. Back at base, he tended to taunt those in authority and occasionally to get very drunk and have a punch-up. He always stood up for the underdog, and for all his occasional lapses he was respected by all ranks as an experienced, streetwise soldier who knew how to use barrack room law not just to save himself. He was more likely to help a fellow inebriate back to his bunk before staggering home himself. He had very intelligent children, of whom he was justly proud, and a very tolerant wife. She had to be so because Gypsy Smith could be difficult at times.

General St John recalls a number of dealings during his time as CO with Gypsy Smith. There had been many times that he had been up in front of the Colonel, and came the moment when he beat up two members of the Corporals' Club for bullying a youngster, with which misdemeanour the Colonel had some sympathy. Without warning the Colonel shook those present at his orders by promoting him to Provost Corporal and challenged him to prove the Colonel right. For quite some time it worked very well, then news from his family, who travelled the road, deteriorated and he sadly got screaming drunk again and had to revert to Fusilier.

When he was Provost Corporal he decided that the Colonel's son should be put in the guardroom. This did not please Colonel Collingwood and after a reprimand, Gypsy Smith decided that he should leave his post for a good drink and night out. The Lance Corporal left in charge allowed a prisoner to escape, so Gypsy Smith thought the best way to escape his responsibilities was to go absent without leave.

There are many stories about Gypsy Smith, most of them true. One night he was in the cells after a drunken orgy, but was unfortunately very wide awake and very belligerent. He demanded to see the Orderly Officer and, very unwisely, an inexperienced Guard Commander, instead of leaving Gypsy Smith to his own devices in the cell, called in the Orderly Officer. The Orderly Officer, a newly commissioned National Service officer, equally unwisely, went down to see the problem. The cell door was opened and the Orderly Officer was greeted by a swaying Gypsy Smith.

117

'Are you the Orderly Officer?' asked Gypsy Smith.

'Yes,' came the reply from the Orderly Officer who received a hefty blow between the eyes for his trouble, thereby learning a valuable lesson – never get personally involved with other rank drunks; if they hit you they can go to prison.

At Christmas Day lunch, 1954, at Nanyuki Airfield Camp, Phil Bell handed the Colonel a large neat whisky preparatory to his wishing everyone a happy Christmas. The Colonel called for silence and was about to begin when Gypsy Smith came staggering towards him with a large whisky in his shaky hand. 'Colonel,' he shouted hoarsely, 'I challenge you to Bottoms Up!'

'OK,' the Colonel replied, 'but I plead superior rank and you drink up first.' Everyone agreed amidst cheers and Gypsy Smith started to drink, but it proved too much for him and he toppled over backwards and passed out.

In Northern Ireland he was Major John Baume's batman. After cleaning up John Baume's mess kit after a strenuous guest night he told John, 'Next time you have a guest night, I will put out denims for you.'

In spite of this he was employed for most of the latter part of his service with the Regimental Police where he rose and fell through the ranks, rising at one time to Sergeant. This was on the premise that in a peacetime station he was better employed keeping others out of trouble rather than getting into trouble himself.

One evening, as Field Officer of the Week, Major David Thompson was called out to the other ranks' quarters to find that Gypsy Smith had been locked out of his quarter. Mrs Smith had decided that she had had enough. Gypsy Smith was not pleased and had found a pile of bricks which he had lobbed against the upper floors. A large audience had gathered, having been brought out of their homes by the noise of Mrs Smith berating her husband and dodging the missiles as yet another brick sailed through their bedroom window. No one was prepared to stop him and, in any event, it was a show worth watching. Having exhausted his pile of bricks, Gypsy Smith went quietly and spent the night in his own cells.

As usual he was very contrite the next morning, swearing undying loyalty to his wife, Quartermaster, the Officer Commanding Headquarters Company and the Regiment. It was very difficult to punish him and he was resigned to having to pay for the damage.

Some weeks later Gypsy Smith was put under more pressure. He was very respectful to all officers, but if he did not know them by sight he worked on the theory that proper officers wore hats and drove expensive cars. The rest were very suspect. One evening he was manning the barrier to the camp but was about to go off duty. A large, smart car swept up and without more ado the barrier went up and Gypsy Smith gave his usual very smart salute. The car swept in and drove off to Battalion Headquarters.

Early next morning Major David Thompson was none too pleased to receive a rocket from the Brigade Major. He was told that the gate guard had failed to recognize the Brigadier, failed to stop and search the car or ask for passes. Although security was not as tight as it is now, David Thompson was, nevertheless, a little put out because Brigadier Ward was well known to the guardroom even if he was driving his own car and not in uniform.

However, the Regimental Sergeant Major was put to work. New photographs of the Brigadier, his staff car and his private car were posted up in the guardroom. The provost staff were briefed and instructions brought up to date for the guard.

As luck would have it, Gypsy Smith was on duty the next evening whilst the guard was being briefed. The barrier had been raised to let a car out when a little red mini swept in and drove up to Battalion Headquarters. Gypsy Smith had time to see there was one occupant with a cloth cap. Instinct told him it must be an officer going to Battalion Headquarters for there had been much activity that day.

For weeks after that it was almost impossible to get in or out of barracks, particularly if Gypsy Smith was on duty. The Brigadier had complained again and earned his nickname of 'Tricky Dicky' Ward. That evening a new photograph was posted on the guardroom wall – the red mini belonging to the Brigadier's wife.

Chapter XX

Hong Kong Again

The Battalion was commanded at Fanling by Lieutenant Colonel Dick Hensman who handed over to Lieutenant Colonel Robert Leith-Macgregor after a few months; its role was internal security and the defence of Hong Kong. Richard Hughes, the author of *A Borrowed Time a Borrowed Place*, said that if the Chinese wanted Hong Kong, all that was needed was a telephone call from Chairman Mao to the Governor of Hong Kong. It was not a bad station for most in the Battalion, and an excellent station for the social life of young officers. However, from the strictly soldiering point of view it had many disadvantages. There were limited training areas which were very hilly, with movement across them restricted to the logistics of mule loads and jeeps with trailers.

Major Gerald Style, as Second in Command, had the task of taking the Advance Party to Hong Kong. He was welcomed by at least three different potential contractors, however, within a few days of the orders for the posting to Hong Kong, Jalal Din had arrived in Munster. All the officers were measured for tropical kit which awaited their arrival in Hong Kong. As a result of Jalal Din's visit to Munster he was appointed, notwithstanding the determined efforts of the other contractors to outbid him. Jalal Din would deal with tailoring, laundry, charwallahs, haircutting, Officers' Mess catering and many other matters now beneath the consideration of British officers. He even made one of the authors' morning dress for his wedding which lasted until he 'outgrew it' just prior to his last daughter's wedding. Jalal Din appointed an excellent No. 1 for the Mess, although it was suspected that the good food in the Mess was subsidized by the soldiers' char and wads. The contracts for the char and wads was sub-contracted to charwallahs.

Each company had its own charwallah and the contract was sold, by Jalal Din, on a company to company basis, dependent on the size of the company. The best contract was for Headquarters Company. The problem was that the Signals Platoon had been made part of Support Company, unlike any known order of battle for other English battalions, and so there was a battle between the Support Company charwallah and the Headquarters Company charwallah for the right to sell tea and buns to the Signals Platoon. How it was resolved never really came to light although there were rumours of duels at dawn with knives. Some of these charwallahs were well educated even though their qualification might be BA (Eng) Failed. A group of three BA failures used to meet once in a while and at one meeting the conversation turned to a girl they had all been pursuing. One of them had married her, and when the others asked after her, they were told that she was well but had failed to produce any children because she was 'unbearable'. The second of the group said, 'No wonder you failed in English, you mean she is "inconceivable".'

The third then said, 'You both have it wrong, she is clearly "impregnable".'

The sudden news of the move to Hong Kong took many by surprise, except for Jalal Din. The train journey from Munster to the Hook of Holland, from Harwich to Barnard Castle and from Barnard Castle to Southampton was not one to be remembered, particularly when some pig-headed authority forbade officers and men to travel with their wives.

The main body of the Battalion travelled to Hong Kong in the *Empire Fowey*. She was built in 1937 in Bremen for Hitler's proposed world cruise and her steering was the same as the *Bismarck*. This meant it had press-button steering with a number of seconds overlap before any command to turn was translated into action by the rudder. When the *Empire Fowey* first went through the Suez Canal, she took her place in the usual convoys, but she always ended up side on to the canal and, in the end, she was either placed first in a convoy or had a clear way through.

The *Empire Fowey* had on board, in addition to the Battalion with its families, about 150 other personnel, mainly RAF reinforcements for Cyprus and Aden. Dick Hensman, the Battalion's Commanding Officer, travelled in the ship but authority was vested in the Captain who, in turn, delegated authority to the Ship's Commandant.

Accommodation on board was very tight. There were on board a few younger married officers living in offical sin. (The Army did not think that officers should marry before they reached their twenty-fifth birthday and those who did marry early did not get married quarters and received a lesser marriage allowance. However, single officers of the same age felt that married officers got out of some duties because they were not at the right spot at the wrong time.) Officers had to share four-berth cabins, but when a single cabin became free all junior Fusilier officers implored the Ship's Adjutant to allocate the cabin to one particular officer – the unfortunate possessor of feet that had a particularly lethal odour. Some officers felt that the misfortune was less to the possessor than to those who had to share the cabin. On the return voyage, at the end of the tour, the single cabin was allocated immediately, notwithstanding the fact that two regiments were on the ship.

The soldiers were particularly cramped in tier bunks and, at the start of the voyage, had a very unpleasant time. Lt David Thompson was a troop deck officer with his charges on the lower forward part of the ship, just above the cells which were below the waterline. Everything was very cramped and locker space was very scarce. The cells below were overflowing with the absentees captured just prior to departure. David Thompson can still smell the stench from the soldiers caught in a Bay of Biscay gale and remembers their moans and groans, and the pitching, twisting, incessant thumps and vibrations. The metal deck was slippery and there was damp everywhere.

Adam Hope, due to his misdemeanour concerning his company's pay at Barnard Castle, was almost always Duty Officer which included visiting the prisoners in the cells. It was due to his efforts that the Ship's Commandant was persuaded to move the prisoners to another part of the ship. However, Adam Hope's efforts did not endear himself to the Ship's Commandant, a singularly sour and humourless personage who was more concerned with the dignity of his office than his task of making the ship a better place in which to live. As a result, Adam Hope became the Ship's Commandant's whipping boy and hence had the almost permanent job of Duty Officer. The other lieutenants and captains helped as much as they could but it was not easy. At least Adam Hope had friends in the Ship's Engineers' Department and he found a suitable bolt-hole for some respite.

Perhaps it was these new-found friends who induced him to carry out an audacious plan. Officers dined in style in the ship and evenings were mellowed by a few pre-dinner drinks, however they were surprised to find Adam standing near a rope which led round the door into the dining room. Those inquisitive or able enough to investigate might have traced the rope to the Ship's Commandant's chair. He usually made a grand entrance after everyone else had come in and, unfortunately, saw the rope in time. Should the plan have worked and the offending gent been dumped on the carpet on the seat of his pants, it would have been to a standing ovation from all Fusilier officers. Everyone was distressed that Adam, once again, found his tour of tenure as Duty Officer extended.

The final approach to Hong Kong was breathtaking. Coming through the Lamma Channel to Green Island, the greasy sea was littered with fishing sampans. The green and fertile islands of Cheung Chau, Peng Chau, Lantau and the other smaller islands seemed to float out of the early morning mist, and it took some time to dock at the old Ocean Terminal but once tied alongside unloading had to begin apace. David Thompson had one final memory of the voyage. It was of a net of boxes being lifted out of the hold, perched on top of which was a black, shining officer's tin trunk. As the crane boom swung towards the quayside, the net seemed to hesitate and then to catch up the movement, but being a free agent, instead of stopping, the net continued its momentum. The tin trunk however was launched in the air in a beautiful curve to disappear with hardly a splash into the sea. He says that John Masters was not amused to learn that it was his trunk (John Masters has no recollection of this, but memory does funny things. However, the shining box part of the story makes him think it was not his. He never did have anything very shiny and his father's black tin trunk from 1918 was not a thing of beauty).

The Battalion's sea trip back from Hong Kong was the last sea trooping it had the misfortune, in the eyes of some, pleasure in the eyes of others, to undertake. Charter air flights have now taken over.

For the first part of their Hong Kong tour the Battalion was stationed at Fanling, near the farthest outpost of the Empire on the Hong Kong-Chinese border at Lowu. The hills surrounding the barracks were covered with Chinese graves which were earthenware pots surrounding a central construction built into the hillside, set in the best *fung-shui* position. Bodies were buried in the ground and after a few years the bones were polished and placed in the earthenware pots. These were worshipped as many Chinese worship their ancestors, the pots of bones were of great importance to the families whose ancestors were interned in them and totally sacrosanct.

One morning when the duty cooks came to prepare breakfast in the dining hall, they found several sets of bones laid out in proper skeletal shapes on the tables. Great panic at Battalion Headquarters. An excuse for a riot? Would the Peoples Republic of China make a major incident of the matter, using it as an excuse to invade Hong Kong all because of the Royal Northumberland Fusiliers? Because of this incident the SIB were called in to investigate 'who done it'. The finger pointed towards 'W' Company. As a result the Company had to pay for a Buddist Monk to re-install the bones and they also had to purchase a new pot! In great secrecy, the bones were returned to their pots without being discovered by the local Chinese and the invasion of Hong Kong was averted. The relator of this story thought that the incident should not be told, in case now, after nearly 40 years, it could still cause an incident.

However one of the authors, who has worked for the Hong Kong Government, would like to assure readers that this is highly unlikely. The Government has to arrange for the removal of graves for many public work schemes and it is very likely that these graves have been removed. The families often find the cash payments made by the Government to compensate them for their loss of *Fung Shui* has been very acceptable. Very few riots occur and it has been known for graves to suddenly appear in the path of public work schemes. *Fung Shui* literally means 'wind and water'. It is part of the Chinese lifestyle and associated with their religious belief. In our terms, for our home to have good *Fung Shui* it would face south in order to get the best sunshine. For graves, the best position must have a good outlook and in its turn it should not be overlooked.

Many years afterwards Major A. K. C. Hill was catching a train from Ashford to Charing Cross when by chance he happened to bump into 'W' Company's Clerk.

'Oh by the way did you happen to know who was responsible for laying the skeleton out in the cookhouse?'

'Yes Sir, I did it!'

Just opposite Aberdeen, then a small fishing village, now a large town, on an adjacent island, the Government was to allow a big power station to be built. Unfortunately the new power station was overlooked by a large cemetery and the Government surveyors braced themselves for countless claims of loss of *Fung shui* from the families of those buried in the cemetery. Not a single claim. Then when the summary of land sales was published each month it was noted that the prices of plots in the Aberdeen cemetery had risen threefold. Far from ruining the *Fung Shui*, the power station had improved it. The reason – the three tall chimneys of the power station were considered to be like three permanent joss sticks looking after the dead.

On one live-firing exercise with the 3-inch Mortar Platoon, an interesting distraction occurred. The mortars were being fired by a distinguished and highly decorated veteran of Korea, nicknamed Yo-yo because he frequently migrated from Fusilier to Colour Sergeant and back again. At the time of this exercise he was a Corporal. On the day in question he was suffering from an acute hangover and, as a result, the mortars were fired with a 90-degree error. This meant that instead of the bombs landing in the range target area, they exploded in a Chinese cemetery blowing up a number of pots with their ancestral contents. The outcome of the exercise was that the Corporal was reduced to the rank of Fusilier and the Platoon Commander was sent to Netheravon to study how 3-inch mortars should be controlled.

The New Territories in the 1950s and early 1960s were mainly paddy fields and small villages, the fields being fertilized by what is euphemistically called night soil, that is human manure, which gave the New Territories its all-pervasive smell. The approaches to the camps were along a bund and just off these bunds were bamboo and straw huts which housed ladies of a certain profession who entertained lonely Fusiliers. These places were, of course, strictly out of bounds and were often visited by patrols of the Royal Military Police (MPs or red hats). Fusiliers caught in these places were charged with being out of bounds and being improperly dressed 'in that the accused was not wearing a tie after 1800'. It was pointed out to the MPs who framed the charges that those who had been wearing a tie would have to be charged with being improperly dressed for the activity in which they were engaged. This did not go down well with the hated red hats but better worded charges were submitted after that.

The Battalion was a British one in a Gurkha Brigade and this had its problems in that Gurkhas operate with different habits, and customs. The Gurkha and the Fusilier are different breeds with different deficiencies and fields of excellence. British Gurkha officers tend to view efficiency in terms of how Gurkhas operate. Thus in khud racing, a sport that involves racing to the top of a hill and then hurling oneself down again, the Gurkhas being a mountain people invariably won. It was amazing to see them flying down the khud-side in great leaps. They ascended just as well, being fit as fiddles and with an inborn understanding of hills. Geordie, on the other hand, found it hard going. If the Battalion had stayed in the New Territories longer, before moving to Stanley Fort, the Battalion would, no doubt, have done well against the First Royal Tank Regiment who were permanently stationed in Hong Kong.

It was felt by Battalion Headquarters that the Brigade Commander, himself a British Gurkha officer, had it in for any new British regiment coming under his command. This was even to the extent that he made the Battalion do a complete test exercise for a second time. The Battalion hierarchy were not a little miffed by this unsympathetic act and it sadly left a bit of a bad taste, even if the first attempt was not carried out as well as it might have been.

Just before the first disastrous exercise, the Battalion came under the command of Lieutenant Colonel Robert Leith-Macgregor MC DFC. He was one of the Battalion's most successful commanders and, had the Battalion had the misfortune to go to war at that time, he would have moulded it into an excellent fighting unit. He was unusual to have been both a brave soldier and a decorated fighter pilot. In the Second World War, not only did the Army provide pilots for the RAF but there were also a number from the Allies. One of these, from the Netherlands, had a command of English which was quite eccentric having been picked up in his RAF service. On one of the commemorations of the Battle of Britain he was interviewed by the BBC, and part of the interview went:

Pilot: 'I was just returning from a mission when out of the sun I was jumped by a Fokker.'

Interviewer: 'I should add, at this stage, that Fokker is a well-known aeroplane manufacturer.'

Pilot: 'Oh no, this Fokker was a Messerschmit.'

Colonel Robert felt that the first terrible test exercise had been such a distressing shambles because the Battalion was very unfit, one of the reasons for this being that it had had to concentrate on ceremonial duties, such as the St George's Day parade and the Queen's Birthday parade. After the exercise, the Battalion was warned that unless matters improved it would be reported as 'unfit for war' to the War Office, and so would be tested again some three weeks later as enemy to the Royal Marines who were arriving in Hong Kong in HMS *Bulwark*. The remedy was simple, the Battalion had to get physically fit.

For the next three weeks there was battle physical training every morning and Queen's Hill camp was turned into the Royal Naval College at Dartmouth, which meant that any movement in the camp had to be at a run, or in army terms 'at the double'. There were some grotesque sights and none more so than the Commanding Officer's barrack inspection with his entourage doubling around barracks. After some initial problems everyone entered into the spirit of the training and the results of the fitness regime were felt throughout the last few weeks at Fanling and the two years at Stanley Fort on Hong Kong Island.

Then came the second test exercise, against the Royal Marines. The Battalion was first told to occupy a certain defensive position and to await further orders. The Directing Staff (DS) then gave further orders for the Battalion to march into another more forward position some miles ahead, across the hilly New Territories terrain. The DS had worked out that the cross-country march would take three hours and had timed their orders for the Royal Marines to arrive at the same time with some chaos resulting. Content with their scheme, the DS went off for a leisurely lunch and aimed to arrive at the new position fifteen minutes before the three hours, to see the fun. However, once the DS had departed, Colonel Robert ordered the Battalion to double to the new positions and the companies arrived well ahead of the DS schedule and had time to dig in. Once the DS and the Royal Marines arrived, they found the Battalion in an impregnable position and the Battalion could only be declared clear winners of the exercise. No more was heard of any 'unfit for war' tag.

The good report was not achieved without some heart-stopping moments. At the first Orders Group ('O' Group), Lieutenant Mike Kitching, as Intelligence Officer, had to make sure that the whole procedure was seen (by the HQLF Staff and the Commander-in-Chief) to be professionally slick and efficient, having previously marked up all the Company Commanders' maps. Came the time for the 'O' Group, all were seated in a ditch, but where was the Officer Commanding X Company? Lieutenant Adam Hope was acting as Company Commander. After some minutes sounds of crashing in the undergrowth were heard and Adam Hope arrived. 'Sit down, Hope, and get your map out.' After much fumbling in pockets, backpack and pouches there was a triumphant, 'Ah – got it,' as Adam pulled out his crumpled map. Gingerly he unfolded it to reveal it contained badly squashed tomato sandwiches. The IO hastily prepared another map.

At another 'O' Group, much later, on a high mountain top that could only be reached by a narrow metalled path, another Company Commander was late. This time it was Major Paddy Baxter, the Officer Commanding Z Company. Mercifully there were no observers but the CO was getting furious. Lieutenant Mike Kitching raised Baxter on the radio to hear that he was at the bottom of the hill, at least half an hour's walk away. The CO was told . . . more fury. 'Kitching – get on that motorbike and fetch him – NOW.' Mike Kitching was far too frightened to own up that he had never been on a motorbike, however, he hastily asked the dispatch rider to start it, hoping to coast down the hill for Paddy Baxter to drive him up. He set off, but went straight over the edge. Another explosion from the CO. The Adjutant, Captain David Welch, was called over and instructed that all Captains and below must learn to ride motorbikes within 30 days.

So there was motorbike training in the New Territories. About six officers were being trained by Fusilier King, a cockney DR, when there was a pause on a flat road winding between hillocks and paddy fields. Where was Adam Hope? After a long wait, in the distance could be heard the sound of a screaming motorbike engine and he could be seen going quite fast with the gears stuck and the engine racing. In front of him, round a small hill, there was a Hakka woman in her traditional garb of black 'pyjamas' and a large straw hat, carrying a long pole across her shoulders with a bucket at each end, and moving at a trot in rhythm with the bouncing buckets. She heard Adam and moved to the side of the road to avoid him. However, it was too late and he caught the left bucket sending it flying into the paddy field. The pole started to spin round her shoulders like a helicopter blade propelling her fast down the road before she spun off and joined the bucket in the field. If only they had had a cine-camera. Fortunately no one was hurt.

After a year in the New Territories, everyone was pleased that the Battalion was moved to Stanley Fort which is at the extreme end of Hong Kong Island and is a barracks that contains just one battalion, although its pre-war quarters were so palatial that major's quarters were purloined by the staff for senior officers. One of these quarters overlooked the Officers' Mess and the wife of the senior officer in it telephoned Colonel Robert to complain that officers often used the verandah between their bedrooms and the bathroom in a state of undress. Colonel Robert was reported to have said, 'Madam, if you are a lady you do not look and if you are not a lady, does it matter?'

Whilst at Stanley there were two large typhoons which caused much havoc. Ships were sunk in the harbour and blown ashore, one of the Macau ferries sunk, small boats disappeared from their moorings and windows at the rear of quarters were sucked out. Remarkably no one was hurt but it was sad that at the Botanical Gardens the birds in one of the aviaries were blown against the wire of their cages and flattened to death.

On arrival at Stanley Fort it was suggsted that a boat for recreation would be a good idea. The Nuffield Fund was approached and a grant was made. After much deliberation, it was decided that an old lifeboat powered by a Bren gun carrier engine should be purchased, and a deal was struck with the owner of the craft which was moored at Kai Tak. This meant that the boat had to be sailed from Kai Tak to Stanley Bay, so three intrepid sailors, Captains Eric Brighton, John Baty and Alan Hill were chosen to bring the boat round and they duly set off, with a batman to serve drinks, to Kai Tak.

Unfortunately they chose the day for the undertaking that a typhoon was about to strike Hong Kong. They made good progress up to Green Island, in the shelter of Hong Kong harbour, but the seas got very heavy between Telegraph Bay and Lamma Island, they started taking in water and then the engine failed. Luckily for them there was a Chinese fishing boat at hand, a very brave Chinese sailor swam across in the gale force winds and high seas with a line, and the boat was towed into the typhoon shelter of Aberdeen harbour. With great relief the intrepid captains tied the boat very securely to the quayside, and left the batman on board to guard the new acquisition.

The typhoon then struck Hong Kong with full force and did considerable damage to the area. Once the winds had dropped, the captains went to see the craft, to find no boat and no batman. There were just a few spars at the end of the lines and some floating wreckage, but a search of the local bars revealed the batman safe and sound. When the wind direction changed, he had decided that discretion was the better part of valour and abandoned ship to the nearest bar, where he spent the night. The Battalion had failed to insure the boat so had to replace it from their own funds and a small water-ski boat was duly purchased. However, this time the Commanding Officer and the Second in Command sailed the boat to Stanley in fine weather.

The Officers Mess at Stanley Fort was a great bachelor home, but was ruined on one odd occasion by a married officer who had just arrived in Hong Kong and was waiting for his family to join him. He felt that the Mess should have dining-in nights three times a week. There was a revolt and a number of young captains got ticked off by Colonel Robert. What did the Colonel say to the Major? Colonel Robert was far too canny not to see the real situation but had to support the new self-important 'Field Officer'. Nevertheless dining-in nights at such frequent intervals ceased, the wife of the Major in question arrived in Hong Kong and life in the Mess returned to normal so that Hong Kong nightlife could be enjoyed each night again.

There were some memorable guest nights at Stanley Fort. There was the cringing embarrassment of singing Geordie songs from the specially printed songbook, which were conducted by Bandmaster Allen with Major Paddy Baxter on the trombone. There was racing in orange boxes down the four and a half flights of stairs. A visiting Admiral, who was forewarned, summoned his 'Flags' when challenged to enter the race and demanded a swop of trousers so that his would not be damaged. Later that evening the young officers called his and the Colonel's attention to the fact that the ante-room carpet was about to be relaid later that week and was, therefore, neatly rolled up. Then, when the Colonel ordered that the carpet be unfurled, the last roll revealed a giggly, well-oiled Lieutenant Anthony Parsons.

The newly appointed Wines Member decided to organize a blind wine tasting in the Mess before lunch one Saturday. A wine merchant was organized and the thirsty officers duly arrived. Officers of the Fifth Fusiliers do not spit out wine after tasting, they drink it and drink it very quickly. Within a short period the wine tasting was turned into a very jolly party and no judgements were made, or could be made, on the quality of what was on offer. Luncheon was announced and a certain field officer, who sported a large, dark moustache, decided that he had to ease springs which he did into the nearest wine glass and replaced it on the table leading to the dining room. A thirsty captain, who was following, picked up the glass and swallowed the contents in one gulp. 'Christ,' he said, 'that's horse piss.' This was the only classification made during the tasting that was nearly correct.

After many years in the Regiment, Colonel Robert considered that he knew that the order of priority for the Geordie Fusilier was beer, fighting, football and the 'F' word. In Hong Kong drugs were readily available but these did not enter the order of priority. Therefore, it was right out of context when it was reported that a junior NCO had bought HK$5 worth of heroin and had used it, making him very sick and very ill. Battalion Headquarters heard of the incident through an excellent Women's Voluntary Service lady who also said that the NCO was regarded as a figure of fun and an idiot. It was felt that it would be better to ignore the incident and no other cases were ever reported whilst the Battalion was in Hong Kong.

However, a new young police inspector was posted to Stanley and he came to hear of the case. Despite promising not to report it, the case came to the attention of Fairyland and Colonel Robert was asked to report to the Brigadier and explain why the NCO had not been charged and sent to prison. Colonel Robert said that to have done this would have drawn too much attention to the case, and if this had been done some might have thought that they might try drugs to see what the fuss was about. The Brigadier said that the CO should have reported the matter to HQ and the man should be charged. Colonel Robert told the Brigadier that the case had already been dealt with because the NCO had been brought in front of him and he had reprimanded him – and to set the matter straight the CO rushed to a payphone, got the NCO on the other end and quickly reprimanded him. His relationship with Police HQ was so good that the offending inspector was moved to the farthest-flung police post in the New Territories the next day.

Some hundred years earlier another senior military officer had had a confrontation with his superiors in Hong Kong. He was not happy with the outcome and this part of his letter can be found in the Hong Kong Government archives.

Your decision is like the left buttock of a blackamoor. It is neither right, nor fair.

Off-duty entertainment, apart from sport, was confined to the bars and dance establishments of Wanchai, the home of Suzie Wong on the Island and Tsim Sha Tsui in Kowloon, that was except for the excellent China Fleet Club, the home of the Navy ashore in Hong Kong. It also was, and still is, an excellent bargain, hassle-free shopping centre for those who could get passes. The China Fleet Club was the saviour of the Fusilier and his drinking problems. Whilst the Battalion was very grateful for its hospitality, it is not certain whether the China Fleet Club would have been financially viable without the mass cash injection put into the bars by the Fusiliers. However, the Commanding Officer was often threatened with its closure to the Fusiliers by the senior naval officer, Commodore Butler, because of over-indulgence in the bars. Nevertheless, on the Battalion's departure, Commodore Butler was most liberal with his praise and thanks for the Battalion's support of the club.

For the officers, there was Albert's which never closed, and the Paramount which always had a most excellent floor show and Larry Allen at the piano bar. Lindsay Stemp seemed to enjoy life outside 'Army hours' to the full, and certainly his parking methods, in his splendid old Citroen, left something to be desired – forward until you bend the bumper of the car to your front, reverse until you hit the car behind and you are in.

There was one much-publicized and exaggerated incident for which, if nothing else, Lindsay Stemp may be remembered in the Regiment, indeed Anne Baxter has told him that she cannot think of Lindsay Stemp without remembering the Larry Allen Incident. Lindsay himself supposes it is better to be remembered in the context of lavatories than not to be remembered at all.

Larry Allen was, and still is, a pianist of ability on the Far East circuit, where he plays light music in a piano bar setting. In the early 1960s his bar was firmly established as one of the most popular haunts on the Island of Hong Kong. It was a regular place for 'the military' to foregather because the songs were topical, amusing and usually 'risqué'. On the night in question, Lindsay Stemp, having been to one party too many as usual, was in Larry's bar when, in a more puritanical mode, he clearly decided that Larry Allen's songs were becoming too much for sensitive and well brought-up young officers like himself. A visit to the loo and the sight of a proliferation of loo paper through Lindsay Stemp's befuddled gaze had clearly put ideas into his mind because, taking a fullsome roll of paper, he burst into the bar and threw it with a long trail which wrapped itself lovingly round the offending Larry. At the same time Lindsay Stemp was heard to yell at the top of his voice: 'A lavatory roll for Lavatory Allen!'

The incident did not end there because it was repeated on several occasions, each time producing a thunderous response from poor Larry. Anyway, on the night in question, in the presence of half of the Regiment, he slammed shut the piano lid and with a murmur of, 'I'll get that bum,' shot off in the direction of the lift in which the intrepid Lindsay Stemp was in full retreat. Mercifully the lift doors shut just in time to prevent a size fourteen fist connecting directly with the delicate physiognomy of the offending officer.

According to Lindsay Stemp, Larry Allen has been looking for him ever since. In 1982 whilst on a cruise between Hong Kong and the Philippines, John Masters met Larry Allen who was playing at the piano bar in the ship. Larry Allen said he remembers the Regiment with affection, however, Lindsay Stemp was not mentioned. If Lindsay Stemp ever disappears in unknown circumstances please refer initially to Larry Allen and his Piano Bar. But, do not worry, the Far East is not on Lindsay Stemp's agenda.

Although people thought the incident was funny, unfortunately his Company Commander lacked a sense of humour and he can remember being sent off to Stonecutters Island where he was given a very hard time.

One Saturday night four subalterns were dining at the Hong Kong Club at a table next to two senior majors and their wives. Well into the evening, when wine had been consumed in large quantities, the band suddenly played the Charleston, and without any prompting, the four subalterns got onto the table and danced a very creditable form of the dance. Unfortunately the table was not built for dancing, it collapsed under their weight and some china went flying. The staff were totally unconcerned and simply demanded payment for the damage, however, the two majors, who had a reputation as players and not gentlemen, took a totally different view. As a result the four subalterns were ordered to appear before the Governor, Sir Robert Black, in their No. 1 Dress with orders to apologize. The Governor thought the whole thing was all rather fun and entertained them to several glasses of champagne.

At Maxims, which was a nightclub and not a restaurant chain as it is now, there was also a floor show. One night the floor show was Lord Moynihan playing the bongo drums for his wife, Princess Ameen, to belly dance to. It was not the best act in the world and a party next to the Signals Officer and his fiancée let all and sundry know what they thought of it. To the delight of all those present, Lord Moynihan came over to the table and invited the main dissident to come outside for a bout of 'fisty-cuffs'. When the request was refused Lord Moynihan left but a very irate Princess Ameen arrived and turned the table over, providing extra entertainment that everyone enjoyed. Some 30 years later, in Manila, Lord Moynihan died in somewhat shady circumstances.

Once a rather over-zealous Chinese promoter devised a show which went the rounds of naval and military senior NCOs' messes. Highly recommended on a very unofficial net, the show was hired for a one-night stand in Stanley Fort and was to be supplemented by the Regimental Band.

On the night in question a great commotion alerted the Duty Officer to pay a call. Reinforced by the Field Officer of the Week and the Regimental Sergeant Major, they set about trying to get in, which was difficult because all the doors were barred, but eventually they got in to find unbelievable turmoil. The troupe of semi-naked Chinese girls was in action, mostly of an insalubrious nature and one of the Band's clarinets was being used in a quite unmusical fashion. One has to leave the reader to imagine the scene because a detailed description would cause offence to the Lord Chamberlain's Office.

Needless to say the repercussions were quite serious because it came to the attention of the same wife who had had the conversation with Colonel Robert about naked officers. It was her moment of revenge. Colonel Robert had a very tiresome time beating off the usual gang of inquisitors who can appear out of the woodwork on such occasions. True to his colours he beat them off satisfactorily, not being one to be bested by such a trivial affair.

Captains Alan Hill, David Welch and John Masters got married whilst the Battalion was in Hong Kong. These occasions can get out of hand and when Danny Seidl got to his honeymoon hotel his wife was leapt upon by the hotel staff and was whisked off to bed. Danny had unwisely divulged his address and a telegram was sent to the hotel saying that Mrs Seidl needed to be put straight to bed on arrival. Alan Hill decided he would not divulge his honeymoon address and go somewhere out of reach. He wrote to a hotel in the Philippines asking for rates and was delighted to receive a reply addressed to the North Winterland Fuskies, a much better name than the dull Royal Northumberland Fusiliers.

Whilst in Hong Kong, and pressurized by the new Band President, one Gerald Style, the Bandmaster, Mr Allen, arranged '76 Trombones' from *The Music Man*, then being performed on the London stage, into a very good

131

march. To some people's outrage the Band did a special arrangement of 'Hernando's Hideaway' to which they marched in slow and quick time. The idea came from seeing American and New Zealand bands doing, in our staid view, incredible things on parade, but it started something with British bands. Well done the Fifth, another case of doing things differently, ahead of the field.

Throughout the time the Battalion was in Hong Kong all sports were played with varying success. Boxing was one sport in which it eventually excelled. At Fanling the Battalion lost by ten bouts to one against the Lancashire Regiment. Captain Richard Gordon-Steward and Lieutenant Adam Hope were summoned to the Commanding Officer after this disastrous result and were given a clear brief to win the Army Far Eastern Command Boxing Trophy. Together they worked hard on this and produced a good team helped by the brothers Sergeant and Lance Corporal O'Toole. They were runners-up at the end of the first year losing by only one bout and won it easily the next year, now with Adam Hope in sole charge, on the night before the Battalion left Hong Kong. Needless to say, the strict training regime was broken that night, and one of the successful contestants missed the ship and had to be flown to join it in Singapore. His time in detention before the ship arrived at Singapore was considered sufficient punishment.

This was the start of a boxing revival. In the years that followed the Battalion Boxing Team had the following record:

1962–1963 Germany – 1st Division Champions.
            Semi-finalists – British Army on the Rhine.
1964–1965 Germany – 4th Division Champions.
            Runners-up – BAOR.
1967–1968 Runners-up – Middle East Command.

The following, amongst others, boxed for the Battalion: Major Gordon-Steward, Captain Hope, S/Sgt O'Toole, Cpl O'Toole, Cpl Ganning, L/Cpl Holland, L/Cpl Holian, Fusiliers Anderson, Bell, Chapman, Featherstone, Hindhaugh, Gordon, Jacques, McBain, McBurnie, McIntyre, Masterton F., Masterton J., Minto, Moore, Powell, Ramsey, Sample, Tullin, Tyler and Willis.

Whilst the First Battalion was in Hong Kong, National Service ended. Colonel Robert felt that for the Battalion, the end of National Service was a boost to morale, discipline and efficiency. The National Servicemen had been first class and had contributed to all aspects of regimental life, however, they could not prevent causing discontent amongst the regulars with their very natural excitement as their discharge date neared, with the prospect of their early return home. When the last of the National Servicemen departed, the Battalion was able to settle down to being a well coordinated unit with proper career and training planning. The last year in Hong Kong saw the beginnings of a well-disciplined, well-coordinated and well-trained unit.

Just before the Battalion left Hong Kong, Jalal Din, the contractor, heard that the East Surreys were to be the Battalion's successors. Remembering his success in gaining the Battalion's contract by a visit to Germany, he decided to call on the East Surrey's in Aden. He had a good trip and gained the contract but news of the visit got out and this did not find favour with General Headquarters Far East Land Forces (HQ FARELF known as Fairy Land). He was summoned to Fairy Land where he was told that this was unfair practice and he would be banned from being a contractor to British Forces in Hong Kong. However, as usual, Fairy Land's right hand did not know what its left hand was doing which was evident when he got back to his office and he found a letter inviting him to tender for the War Department (WD) contract for boot repairs and laundry for Stanley Fort, which he duly won. He was then summoned once again to Fairy Land where he was told that all contracts for tea (char), buns (wads) and other contractor services such as shop and tailoring would be done by the NAAFI. Naturally he was upset by this and asked Colonel Robert for his advice. Colonel Robert told him to go to the NAAFI and offer his services as their sub-contractor, having first worked out his prices and profit margin. This worked out very well for Jalal Din and nothing really changed except that NAAFI got a cut and the soldiers paid a little more, but not as much as they might have as NAAFI, with their overheads and inefficiencies, would have charged.

When the sailing date for departure became known there was an end-of-term feeling across the Battalion. Jalal Din was not the only person to gain from the information and many Chinese traders thought they would use the knowledge to their advantage. Despite notices both in English and Chinese characters posted in strategic positions saying that traders should not enter into delayed payment contracts, many such contracts with soldiers were entered into. Most families returned home with restocked linen cupboards and artistic table cloths. As the date of sailing drew nearer, the activities of the traders to sell more and to guarantee payment became more frantic. The crunch came when Fusilier 'B', with a wife and a number of children on station, was committed to prison for debt. There was great interest as to how long he would remain incarcerated. As Fusilier 'B's pay book showed no credits and the PRI had strict instructions not to help, it was thought he would never emerge, however he soon appeared with a grin from ear to ear because the trader had discovered that in Hong Kong the creditor had to fund the cost of the debtor's sojourn in prison. The final result would have made the debt insignificant, when set against the cost of prison.

Just before leaving Hong Kong, Captain John Oakley decided to buy a new set of golf clubs from Aluwhalia, the sports outfitter in Kowloon. He had bargained with Mr Aluwhalia junior, and had started to settle his bill when Mr Aluwhalia, senior, came into the shop. He asked John Oakley what price he had agreed. On being told he turned on his son and said, 'My son, my son, you will bankrupt me, but a price has been agreed and I will stand by it.' A good public relations exercise. Some 17 years later, John Masters went into the shop and was greeted with, 'Good morning, Colonel Masters.

How is the Regiment doing?' Despite the gross over-promotion, not bad public relations either.

It was a very excited Battalion that set sail from Hong Kong on Saturday, 17 February 1962. Before disembarking at Southampton, every man had been issued with a rail warrant to his home, his pay, and instructions to report to Lemgo in Germany. It was a very proud Commanding Officer who was able to report to the new Brigade Commander that the Battalion was present on the day and time stated with only one absentee. This man had taken extra leave following a misdemeanour on the ship which had reduced his leave because of time spent in detention.

Postscript

In the New Territories many married officers and NCOs lived some distance from the camp. This meant that only young NCOs had the task of keeping discipline in the camp after normal working hours. One particular Fusilier, who was very big and very strong, made things very difficult in the camp. It was a pity that there was not enough time to take this Fusilier in hand, and so it was with regret that after a number of last chances Colonel Robert had to take steps to get him discharged. Some two years later, shortly after returning to England and leaving the Army, Colonel Robert bought a house in Hertfordshire. Whilst awaiting the arrival of his furniture and belongings in a Holts' van from Newcastle his wife called out to say that it had arrived. At that moment a voice said, 'Hullo, sor, how are ye?'

It was, of course, the discharged Fusilier. He admitted that too much San Mig had been his downfall and he had heard from his mates that they had had a great time in Hong Kong. He was sorry that he had not remained with the Battalion. Colonel Robert felt the same because underneath he was a 'good chap'.

Chapter XXI

Lemgo

The Battalion was quartered in a splendid barracks and was the only unit in Lemgo. Still under the command of Lieutenant Colonel Robert Leith-Macgregor MC DFC, they found that they had to change from being an infantry unit with a considerable internal security role to that of a mechanized infantry battalion in an armoured brigade. The Battalion's four-year tour in Lemgo was probably one of those turning points in the history of the Regiment. After centuries of marching or being carted about in lorries, rifle companies became mechanized. This meant companies and now sections had vehicles and a need for many drivers. Many officers and NCOs had to be sent to Bordon to learn to become driving instructors and also get to know the complications of the Saracen personnel carriers. Companies, particularly on exercise, were attached to armoured regiments as their infantry back-up, and a new platoon appeared on the order of battle in the rifle companies: Support Platoon.

Having been removed to Hong Kong prematurely the last time it was in Germany, the Battalion now had the chance to prove that it could adapt to something completely new. Fortunately for the Battalion, Major George Forte and his 'A' Squadron of the Fourth Royal Tank Regiment eased the Battalion through this transformation.

The Battalion, in the first year, had to be introduced to working with armoured regiments and to a new and complex communications system. There was also the mystery of the Saracen CES (the Complete Equipment Schedule).

The Battalion took over 53 Saracens from the Argyll and Sutherland Highlanders and was soon to learn that there was a wide variety of equipment missing from the vehicles. By the time the Fusiliers took over full responsibility many of the missing items had been replaced from a large Aladdin's cave of spare parts accumulated, over the years, by A Squadron. Some parts even found their way into new 'private' stores in the barracks.

The Army is a very unforgiving master and any missing part has to be paid for by the unfortunate who lost the item or who had signed for the Saracen, which could be very expensive. The result of this was that a bartering system developed behind closed doors and in the corridors of real power, the Sergeants' Mess. In other areas of the camp, and in the field, certain Fusiliers reverted to character and became magpies, some being more skilled at this than others.

It did not take long for impoverished subalterns to learn the tricks of this underground trade if their platoons were not to be billed for deficient kit.

All this was a particular headache for Company seconds-in-command who had to keep control of the Saracens and their equipment. It was no use inspecting Saracen CESs platoon by platoon as bits and pieces would float, as if by magic, between vehicles to hide deficiencies. On one occasion, when all the kit was laid out in front of the vehicle for inspection, a driver was caught passing a spanner to a chum down his trouser leg and through a hole in his pocket.

Captain Frank Burrows was Technical Quartermaster and, as much as he tried, he failed to coordinate an inspection of all the Battalion Saracens on the same occasion. It would have needed more time than could be spared and an army of conscientious and honest checkers with their wits about them to carry out this impossible task.

Equipment did go missing for quite legitimate reasons, but the Treasury does not like lashing out taxpayers' money and the rigmarole of proving a loss was like passing a camel through the eye of a needle. It was not unknown for locals in exercise areas to acquire equipment when Saracens were parked in their farmyards and fuel jerrycans were often left behind when refuelling took place at night, becoming useful containers for tractors.

Drivers were trained to remove the armour-plate in the front of their vehicles to help the Royal Electrical and Mechanical Engineer fitters when fanbelts had to be changed. The Saracen was so complicated that 30 bolts had to be removed before that operation was completed. As a result, if the repair had to be done in the dark, it was not surprising if the odd spanner went missing. Everyone learnt from their mistakes and the Lemgo tour played a vital part in educating the Battalion and taught Fusiliers not to leave their expensive equipment lying about.

The Battalion did not have a large number of its families for several months after its arrival in Lemgo. When the families eventually arrived, the younger husbands, who had found the going pretty rough without their wives, changed overnight into very solid citizens. Up until then, the local Germans were getting a little impatient over repairing plate glass. The Band, also, was most unhappy because its attractive band room had lots of plate glass which became a magnet to anyone trying to 'buy their ticket' out of the Army. The Battalion won in the end with the Quartermaster attending Commanding Officer's Orders, when required, and with a prepared form ready for the guilty party to sign to pay for the damage.

Lieutenant Colonel Gerald Style took over command in late 1962 from Robert Leith-Macgregor and his Second in Command was Major Freddie Ward MC. In a few months Freddie Ward went to Walker, in Newcastle, to command the 4th/5th Territorial Battalion of the Fifth Fusiliers. In his place came Major Dick Blenkinsop, forming an old liaison which started in Gibraltar in 1948. A similar relationship was renewed with the Quartermaster, Captain (QM) Forbes Burn. He was Colour Sergeant of Headquarter Company in Gibraltar whilst Gerald Style was Second in Command to Major Robert Ferguson MVO. Forbes Burn must have been one of the youngest

Company Quartermaster Sergeants in the Army at that time. Later he was Company Sergeant Major of Z Company when Gerald Style commanded it in Kenya. He did what all good Quartermasters should do and acquired in due time the final accolade of Lieutenant Colonel (QM). In the Fifth Fusiliers, like the other infantry regiments with only one battalion, the old and the bold came together again and again. However, for the junior officers and junior ranks, the first eleven years of their service was confined, for the most part, to service in the Battalion. Senior subalterns and junior captains could afford a wry smile when pear-shaped majors reappeared from staff jobs and talked about the necessity of 'getting to know your men'.

For reasons best known to higher command, the Band and Drums were invited to lead the Munich Festival and remain on in the American Sector for a month. A young officer, one Wysock Wright, was selected to be the officer in charge of this jolly. The first event was the opening ceremony and a march through Munich with the Fifth Fusiliers' Band and Drums in the lead. The following evening they had to Beat Retreat outside the American General's residence. That morning, at the rehearsal, it was discovered that everyone had sold their tunics, hackles and sealskin caps and so replacements had to be flown in from Lemgo and Newcastle. From then on they were stripped after every parade and sent back to barracks in denims so that the best dress could be locked away with the Quartermaster.

Robert Parsons has written to John Masters with an account of his experiences in Lemgo in September 1962 and it is reproduced with his permission:

When the Nazis built a camp between the ancient town and the hill, they can hardly have imagined the influence their work would have upon the town. No doubt there was going to be money spent by the soldiery in the town, but at what cost?

In September 1962, the elderly bus that the army ran to fetch and carry travellers through RAF Gutersloh to Lemgo and Detmold, dropped off two absolutely new, unsure and apprehensive Second Lieutenants at the entrance to the Officers Mess, 1RNF, BFPO 41. It was shortly before lunchtime. The two lambs were cluttering up the hallway with suitcases and hat boxes when hungry and thirsty officers began arriving for lunch. Someone took pity upon them. They were led into the ante-room for introductions where someone told them to report to the Adjutant immediately after lunch. Even though the two newcomers hardly knew where they were, they realised that something was amiss. There was a mood of tension, concern and perhaps, even anxiety in the Mess.

To a young officer, the Adjutant is the figure of ultimate power. A source of terror. The Adjutant is not God. He directs God. His fits of pique can cause attempted suicides. When the two subalterns reported to the Adjutant they were surprised to find this terrifying person looked distinctly hunted. This Stag seemed to be at Bay. The two youths just had time to enter the office, to salute and give names before the Adjutant's thin smile of greeting was wiped off his face by telephone calls and anxious voices. The two withdrew to sit on hard chairs in the office opposite to await a restart of the interview. From there could be watched the unfolding of a drama. There was indeed a drama to be watched.

When a Regiment moves into a new posting everyone wishes, hopes, and prays that all will go well. The Fifth had just moved to Lemgo. In the space of weeks they had changed Commanding Officer, changed Adjutant and changed roles from foot to armoured infantry. 20th Armoured Brigade, its Commander and staff were having to adjust to having a new battalion in their team. This move to Germany also meant that the Fusiliers were going to have to change their beer. It was the change of beer that was proving to be the de-stabilising factor. This was what had caused the drama that now swirled about the puzzled faces of the new subalterns.

The night before, He, that was now referred to as 'The Accused' had had too much to drink in the NAAFI. This had become a boring place to drink, so 'The Accused' decided to go native. The Camp had expensive and extensive fences. These fences were patrolled by sentries. These precautions were to keep the Fusiliers in as much as to keep the Russians out. Unfortunately, the direct route to the best Gasthaus was up and over the back gate, not past the Main gate and the watchful eye of the Guard Commander.

'The Accused' made his unauthorised exit and enjoyed more beer at the Gasthaus. He drank all his money. When he wanted cigarettes, the Landlord refused. 'The Accused' swayed and weighed up the situation and then expressed his opinion that the Nazis who bombed his Granny should give him cigarettes and left.

'The Accused' now performed a sequence of impossibilities. He climbed back into the Camp, unobserved. He opened his Company's Arms Store which was heavily locked. He unshackled a rifle that had been chained and padlocked to the wall and left, again unobserved. He made his way to the Ammunition Bunkers. These were constructed like Fort Knox, guarded and heavily padlocked. He opened one, selected bullets and left, once again unobserved. Now heavily armed he broke out of Camp, once more, without triggering alarms. He loaded bullets into the magazine of the rifle, but back to front, which is said to be impossible. Then, 'The Accused' re-entered the Gasthaus. He went to the Landlord, stuck the muzzle of the rifle into the Landlord's face, dropped some bullets on to the floor before saying clearly '*Cigaretten Bitte!*'

There was a short period of awful tableau. The Bar, tables with chairs and the drinkers with glasses and bottles. A suddent total silence. All eyes fastened on the angry Geordie whose rifle was stuck firmly in the ashen face of their Landlord.

The tableau unfroze when a German struck 'The Accused' hard on the head with a bottle. 'The Accused' slumped to the ground. He was firmly stood upon and separated from his rifle while the local police were called.

The first the British knew was when the guard at the Main Gate called anxiously to the Guard Commander. 'There is something strange going on down the Street, Sarge.' Indeed, there was something strange going on down the street. A German policeman, brandishing a British rifle, was leading a stretcher party of four up the pavement. On the stretcher lay 'The Accused', who, no longer concussed, was sound asleep and snoring loudly. The Landlord, his guests and assorted townsfolk followed noisily.

Events moved swiftly. The Orderly Officer woke the Field Officer. Both woke the Adjutant. The Regimental Sergeant Major, who never slept, appeared to begin enquiries. The Commanding Officer spoke to Brigade. Army Headquarters arranged for someone to put a note in front of the British Ambassador's dinner plate. 'The Accused', still sound asleep, was joined in the cells by the sentries from the Back Gate, the sentries from the Ammunition Bunkers and the Y Company Arms Storeman.

The next day was complicated. 'The Accused' awoke to find he had a shocking hangover and bruises on his head. He was surrounded by angry people, many of whom asked him questions of an evening about which he had no memory. Men in suede shoes were asking questions about Security. The Commanding Officer had been asked by the Brigadier if he actually was in command of his battalion.

Small wonder that the Adjutant seemed to lack interest in two newly arrived subalterns.

Major Jumbo Wilson was sent on an exchange to a United States Army Regiment in the south of Germany whilst his American counterpart, Major James Curtis, took over X Company at Soltau. Captain John Masters, the temporary Company Commander and now, once again, the Second in Command of the company, was running around, with a crate of Coco Cola, in a state of nervous excitement. Jim Curtis was an excellent officer who was very popular. He and his wife Margery spent a year with the Battalion. The only mishap was when Jim decided to buy a German Shepherd dog. Unfortunately it did not understand American or English and it duly bit Mrs Curtis on the bottom. The Curtis family were last heard of in Pigeon Cove, Massachussetts, with Jim, like his erstwhile Second in Command, being in real estate.

One Christmas, during a performance by a visiting concert party, the Gym caught fire. Sadly the cause of the fire was an electrical fault under the stage exacerbated by the temporary wiring to the Christmas decorations. The Gym was soon well ablaze and, although the German Fire Brigade did its best, it was too late to stop its total destruction. The Battalion Fire Picquet had a chance to save all, arriving on the scene very quickly with the hose-carrying trailer. However, the iron key to turn on the hydrant fell off on the way to the Gym, burying itself in the deep snow which was so thick that it could not be found. W Company had to be evacuated and the kit was passed out down a line of soldiers. The Company Quartermaster Sergeant soon discovered that quite a few personal and desirable stores were missing. The helpers were all well charged with beer and there is no doubt that Geordie was not slow to replace any items deficient from his own kit.

At this time *St George's Gazette* reported the following telephone conversation:

IO: 'Can I speak to Captain Marr?'
CSM: 'I'm very sorry, sir, but he's gone for an operation.'
IO: 'Good Lord, what's happened?'
CSM: 'He's gone to have his hair cut, sir.'

(Adjutant – Please note)

Forbes Burn lived next to the British Forces Education Service headmaster. The latter, who was often late to school, had been taking a short cut across the Quartermaster's lawn to make up for lost time. Forbes Burn decided to put an obstacle in the path of the intruder by laying a strand of barbed wire across his lawn. It had an immediate result – an infuriated headmaster with torn trousers. The ensuing charge and counter-charge caused muffled ribaldry at Battalion Headquarters, however, good sense eventually prevailed and 'no further action' was agreed.

The Battalion seldom had the chance to operate as a complete unit because companies were detached to the cavalry regiments of 20th Armoured Brigade, which had the tremendous advantage of the companies getting to know both operationally and personally three very fine cavalry regiments.

Living in the confined space of a Saracen Armoured Personnel Carrier with eight others needs a certain amount of tolerance. This is particularly so if the day's rations include a generous amount of baked beans. Major John Dean, a Lancashire Fusilier commanding Z Company, used to smoke some particularly noxious small, fat German cigars, one after another when huddled in the corner of his command Saracen. Even Company Sergeant Major Butch Baker, a heavy smoker himself, would only enter the vehicle with extreme reluctance (others did say the atmosphere was not the true reason but a hatred of radios). Certainly the wireless operators said that after a shift in the Command Saracen a slice of their flesh would not be unlike smoked salmon.

However there were good moments too. Captain David Thompson, X Company Second in Command, had to go ahead to find a new hide area. This had to be done so that when the company vehicles arrived with the command and the platoon Saracens, they could be fitted in to the area with the minimum of fuss. Waiting at the rendezvous in the still of the night and in the depths of a German forest could be an eyrie experience. That is until the still night air is broken by the high-pitched whine of approaching, but still distant, Saracens.

Sometimes the sound would disappear behind a hill or into a valley. Then the Second in Command would hastily consult his map to make sure that he had got his grid reference right. However, the sound would come again and gradually get louder as the drivers used their pre-select gearboxes to keep their revolutions up. With practice, drivers could move silently and could surprise the Second in Command by suddenly arriving with no noise at all.

Captain David Thompson received one of the biggest rockets in his life at the hands of an irate Royal Electrical and Mechanical Engineer Staff Sergeant who was in charge of the company fitters. This rocket was quite justified. The only place David Thompson could find for a hide was down a narrow firebreak and before he had a chance to look elsewhere the company arrived. They drove down the track to halt one behind each other at the far end. That seemed all very well and the engines were turned off. What David Thompson had not appreciated was that the number three in the line of the Saracens, and the last but one, found it difficult to restart, which meant that they blocked everyone. Luckily the engines restarted but had to be kept running through the night, which was not the best treatment for fluid flywheels because they tended to boil their contents when they got too hot. The Staff Sergeant was not amused.

There were three St George's Days at Lemgo. The most important was when the Battalion was honoured by the attendance of the Colonel of the Regiment. Field Marshal Sir Francis Festing stayed at the Colonel's house. Captain Alan Hill was his ADC for the day. He was instructed by the Field Marshal to collect him in his staff car so that they could visit a china shop as he wanted to purchase a Meissen figure for his wife. They just managed to return to camp in time for him to change into No. 1 Dress. Having taken the salute the low-slung Jaguar staff car drove him to the parade ground. The portley Field Marshal, in getting into the staff car, knocked the top off his field marshal's baton and Alan was then instructed to recover the gold St George from the floor. On reaching the CO's house the Field Marshal passed his baton to Alan to hold and he remarked 'Alan, I hope you realize that you are now in command of all troops in BAOR.'

One more excitement occurred when the Field Marshal stood up to take the salute, and there was a terrible clatter. The large star attached to the pink ribbon of one of his orders had got caught in his chair and had fallen to the ground.

On another St George's Day Parade there was the moment when the Commanding Officer stood in front of the Battalion ready to give the command for the 'Advance in Review Order'. 'Fifth Fusiliers,' shouted the Commanding Officer. It was the special privilege of the Commanding Officer of the Fifth to call the parade to attention using that title rather than the conventional mode. He then took a deep breath to shout, 'By the centre', when a cry from the Regimental Sergeant Major rang out loud and clear.

'Slope, sir'.

Only one thing to do. 'As – you – were,' in measured and unhurried tones from the Colonel. After that all was well.

Later Brigadier Dick Ward, the Brigade Commander, waylaid the Colonel and said, 'Only you could have done that, Gerald!' Gerald Style has never been quite sure what the Brigadier meant. Had the 'friendly' remark a double meaning? Unfortunately General Ward cannot now tell as he is no longer with us.

Gerald Style's last St George's Day at Lemgo also had its ups and downs. All went well until the pudding was served at the Officers' Mess luncheon after the parade. Then Brigade ordered a 'stand-to'. Colonel Gerald had several rough phone calls to Brigade Headquarters, all to no avail, and so the Battalion had to get into top gear for the 'stand-to', all of which provided a fantastic display for the guests and old regimental comrades who attended the event.

Chapter XXII

St George's Gazette and an Undistinguished Career

Finding humour in well over one thousand copies of the monthly magazine of the Regiment was a difficult task. An example of an attempt at humour was in the June 1961 edition:

WHAT'S IN A NAME? At the Cenotaph:

The Writer (R. C. Denness): 'Good morning, sir! May I introduce myself? My name is Denness.'

Major D. Young: 'Good morning – so is mine.'

Some attempts at humour were more successful than others. From the Signals Platoon notes of 31 July 1963:

The weekly wireless day is gradually improving, and everyone seems to be getting the hang of things. When it was heard that the Commanding Officer was listening into the net all 'Seagulls' (Sergeant Majors) did a disappearing act. Fus. Oliver, being a good control operator, told all 'Seagulls' to stay by their sets. Call sign 99's (CSM Forrest) reply was, 'Talk to me like that and I'll wrap this f——g stick around your f——g neck'.

From the same edition:

CONVERSATION PIECES
Overheard at Cocktail party.

Young Officer:'Have you met my wife?'

Older Officer: 'No.'

Young Officer: (Craning neck over heads of crowd to try and locate missing spouse): 'She's a fair-haired tramp – very attractive.'

And again:

Overheard [spelt overhead!] before Dinner.

Senior Officer: 'You are very like your father.'

YO (dutifully): 'Yes Sir, but,' (firmly), 'I have more hair.'

Not up to the best of Punch but most writers and contributors to *St George's Gazette* found the monthly deadline a chore and, as a result, most listed what their particular unit had done and very little more. After all few were potential authors like the writer of *The Night Runners of Bengal*, although one was called John Masters.

The first editorial page of *St George's Gazette* was devoted to extracts from the *London Gazette*. This meant that at least in this part was set out the bones of many careers, some less distinguished than others. Thus in April 1954, in March 1956 and in March 1960 *St George's Gazette* duly reported the Commissioning of Henry John Walton Masters (433188) on 12 February 1954, his promotion to Lt on 12 February 1956 and his promotion to Captain on 12 February 1960. The final *London Gazette* notice in the October 1963 edition reported 'Capt. H. J. W. Masters (433188) retires receiving a gratuity, 1st Sept., 1963.'

However, *St George's Gazette* did more in its editorial columns. In October 1954 it reported that the Battalion welcomed 2/Lt Masters from Sandhurst, although it failed to mention the time between February and September. Had he walked all the way across Africa to reach the Battalion? In Z Company notes in November he was welcomed to Z Company and posted to 12 Platoon and in June 1955 it was reported that he played for the Battalion Rugby team against Nanyuki. Although it reported the death of his Platoon Sergeant it made no reference to the circumstances, nor did it report his SLR course in Nairobi, nor his attempted Rhino safari. Perhaps this would have been too much for *St George's Gazette* readers.

In September 1955 his posting to W Company on arrival in Northern Ireland was mentioned and in November 1955 his arrival in W Company was noted. What was he up to in the meantime? However in November he was training an NCO's cadre with Sgt Hennon. In June 1956 W Company's Order of Battle shows as Second in Command – Lt HJW Masters and in the company notes it was reported that 'Mr Masters has returned from a P.T. Course on which, though he looks no thinner, he assures us he did a lot of work'. While in October 1956 the W Company writer informed his readers that Mr Masters had moved to the Regimental Depot at Newcastle-upon-Tyne.

Of John Masters's time at the Depot little is said and that may be just as well. Some mention is made of a vicious game of indoor hockey in which he was so injured that he had to have stitches over his eye. Apart from when his platoon HQ was fired upon by the MT Platoon on an operation in Kenya, this was the only time he seemed to have been in any danger, other than from rows with his seniors. At the time of his sacking from the Depot in 1957, it was said that his memorial there would be a large-scale model he made of a regiment in battle, although he has no recollection of that at all. Perhaps he was too busy trying to resign his commission, only to be told that Sandhurst officers are, like lunatics, in the Army at Her Majesty's pleasure and it was not Her pleasure that he should leave in 1957.

In September 1957 it was reported that he, with Major Webb and 2/Lt

Byers, won a sailing race in 'Psyche', the Battalion boat. This was because 'she was so far behind on one tack that when the wind changed she sailed home an easy winner. The anchorage resounded to cheers at this unique occurrence.' Later when he was about to be married he mentioned this win, without too much detail, to his fiancée because she was a keen sailor. Although she did go on to marry him, she promptly sold her boat after he had been her crew just once.

In January 1959, in Germany, Support Company notes stated,

> For the last two months Support Company has had a small detachment at the 2 Div Winter Warfare Training Camp comprising Mr Masters, Mr Sanderson, and CSM Gardiner. Feverish work was done by all the camp, but the real laurels fall to Mr Masters who alone ran not only a most prosperous N.A.A.F.I. canteen, but also a lucrative trade in a very popular form of literature, and other items. He combined this considerable task with the jobs of Administrative Officer, M.T.O., Signals Officer, and most of the other minor appointments. In fact, so overworked was he that he has gone to hospital to recover (at least, that is where he said he was going).

(This was true but delicacy prevented *St George's Gazette* from saying that he was having an operation on his posterior).

The next entry is on 30 April 1959 where in the Order of Battle at Barnard Castle he is shown as the commander of the reinstated Machine-Gun Platoon in Support Company. No mention is made of his duties as the officer in charge of the colours which were, on his journey, used to wrap a few bottles of whisky for his father.

In August 1959, in Hong Kong, Support Company notes report that 'Lt Masters bemoans the fact that he does not have all the Battalion Motor Transport at his disposal but, nevertheless, seems to make do with his 1-ton truck and appears to spend a comfortable night even when wet!'

October 1959 reports a great triumph. The Battalion editorial relates that 'We have won the Brigade Water Polo Championship. Credit for the latter must go to Mr Masters, who by his own play and exertions produced a very fine team in a very short time.' In the Water Polo notes, which show him in the water in a picture of the team, the report states that:

> The Battalion team, led by Mr Masters, was forced unwillingly to enter the 48 Gurkha Infantry Brigade Cup Knock-Out against strong and experienced opposition . . . The Semi-final found us matched against the holders . . . After a terrific encounter the score was level at full time; extra time was played and Mr Masters forced the odd goal which put the team into the final . . . In the final the scores were level and with a prodigious effort the Battalion team rallied and once more Mr. Masters scored the winning goal.

It does not report that the team then entered the local league where Mr

Masters spent his time trying to drown tiny Chinese who nevertheless managed to defeat the larger and slower Geordies.

Support Company notes for February 1960 state that Mr Masters was expected back from his course and would be Regimental Signals Officer. In June the Signals Platoon notes give news of its move to Stanley Fort.

> Our first job was to install an intercom unit from the Commanding Officer's Office to his staff. It has been noted in some quarters that the Signals Officer does not feature in the list of extensions. This might, of course, be due to the fact that when installing it he noticed that he could be listened in to without knowing it.

July's edition notes that the RSO was redoubling his efforts to get the Colonel to cancel all radio exercises because of the Telecomms Inspection. The August 1960 *St George's Gazette* shows that Capt Masters (HQ) was second in the 66 Yards Breaststroke. Some fellow officers were annoyed to find that they were no longer considered to be the best breaststrokers in the Mess. In order to placate his colleagues he decided to enter the 100 metres butterfly in the Hong Kong Forces Championship and in October 1960 *St George's Gazette* noted he came second to Fusilier Craig. The Swimming Notes also give details of the Water Polo team's successes and failures in which Captain Masters played his full part. He may have been a rotten soldier but he was an excellent swimmer.

In September 1960 the following extract from the Signals Platoon notes was published:

> L/Cpl Ridley, much to his and the Signals Officer's surprise, had his Post Office inspected for the administrative inspection by the general. On the day itself not a soul could be seen near the Post Office except for the inspecting officer. The Signals Officer was hastily summoned and the inspecting officer and he were quickly locked in the signals office while L/Cpl Ridley was called back from his post run in Hong Kong. The grading of 'good' was obtained, but I am told that the Signals Officer has still got a sore throat.

St George's Gazette of January 1961 reported an exercise involving the Royal Marines.

> Most of the Signals Platoon had to walk considerable distances while attached to their various companies. Battalion Headquarters, under the Second-in-Command, assisted by the Signals Officer, did not have to walk a yard in doing their sterling work. There was, however, very nearly a ghastly mistake. Battalion H.Q. found themselves in the middle of the enemy lines after a Royal Marine attack. Fortunately, even though they were within 200 yards of the enemy, they were not discovered even in broad daylight until one wretched marine came to fill his water bottle at Battalion H.Q., and had to be captured. This meant that Battalion H.Q. was in danger of discovery. Here the Signals Officer

came into his own. Determined not to walk a yard further than was necessary he spied his Land Rover not more than 100 yards away. The path was, however, fully in view of the Marines. What a dreadful dilemma! Not to the determined R.S.O. Seeing that there were Chinese workmen nearby he picked up a plank and calmly walked to his Land Rover and drove away.

In June 1961 the Signals Platoon notes states that 'the platoon wishes to extend their congratulations to Capt. Masters on his recent engagement.' The full story of what happened was not reported in *St George's Gazette*; the August notes just say, 'Capt. Masters has left us. He did a very quick move, in two hours he was packed and away rejoicing. We wish him the best of luck in the future.'

The September Signals Platoon report states, 'With Capt. Masters and Sgt. Dalby away, Sgt. Robertson was reported to have been seen gliding serenely over and around the football pitch. May he soon get his pilot's licence.'

Details of the Masters wedding with a picture are in *St George's Gazette* of October 1961 together with this note from the Battalion editorial:

The Chinese Festival of Maidens coincided with the second Internal Security exercise; on this day – the seventh of the seventh month – unmarried girls make offerings to two star-gods to secure a happy marriage to a husband of their choice. Although Fusiliers were absent all night no banns have been called.

Was it at this time last year that a vision of Capt. J. W. Masters passed before the eyes of Miss Janet Mackenzie-Edwards? Whatever the cause or reason the wedding on August 19th between them both gives cause for great happiness to their friends. The Battalion joins with all their friends in wishing them every joy in this happy marriage.

The *St George's Gazette* of 28 February reported that 'L/Cpl Keddle was last seen at the all ranks' dance assuring the R.S.O. (as he gave him a mixture of brandy, rum and gin) that he would take all the blame if the R.S.O. was short of an excuse to his wife.' The 30 April edition gives details of the Battalion's last effort in Hong Kong, Exercise 'Gurkha Bluff'. In this exercise, the Battalion officers, with their signallers, were umpires. 'Apart from needing new soles to our boots nothing terrible happened except that the Signals Officer was heard to complain that curry at 0630 was not his idea of a good breakfast.'

In the August 1962 edition (in Lemgo) Captain H. J. Walton Masters was shown as X Company Second in Command. It did not report his altercation with the Colonel when he discovered that his next appointment, after Regimental Signals Officer, was to be Recce Platoon Commander. It was not the fact he thought this was a step down but the job involved months away from camp and his newly wedded wife and first daughter. The Commanding Officer acceded to his wish but, as a punishment, posted him to

X Company which not only was on detachment some distance from Lemgo but was also under the command of Major Wilson who the CO knew had had the odd set-to with Captain Masters. To give Major Wilson his due there were very few problems.

On 28 February 1963, in X Company notes, it was reported, 'What else? We have also been soldiers. Training has gone on in the snow. Even the Company 2 i/c was seen doing his P. E. tests, not as he usually does from across the "in tray" to the "out tray", and looks none the worse for his experience.'

The final entry was in X Company notes of 30 September 1963,

We must now say farewell to Capt. and Mrs Masters. Capt. Masters has been both 2 i/c and Company Commander of X Company since Major Wilson's departure. He has had some practice at this as he was doing the same job four years ago when the Battalion were last in Munster. It remains only for us to wish him every happiness and success in his new vocation as an estate agent.

No mention, of course, of one very senior officer's remarks on the lines that 'John Masters is casting off the Regiment like an old shoe' or that another senior officer told John Masters that he would be welcomed back after he had got over his wife.

Chapter XXIII

The Territorial Army

The 4/5th Battalion (TA) had its headquarters in Walker which was, at that time, a run-down inner-city area. There was much poverty and there were some unusual sights from the Drill Hall. The Battalion office watched, with a mixture of horror and fascination, a coal bill being paid in kind on the kitchen table of a house opposite.

At a party two wives were overheard discussing their ailments. 'The doctor said I had piles and gave me a box of lozenges to take "per rectum", whatever that meant. I took them for a week and they were very hard to swallow. For what good they did me I might as well have stuffed them up my bum.'

In 1954 the 43rd Royal Tank Regiment, soon to become the 6th (City) Battalion of the Fifth Fusiliers was on exercise in Wales. There was to be a night exercise and march along the coast which had very high cliffs to the west not too far away. Colonel Richard Rogers decreed that the Second in Command, Major Eb Wood, would command the exercise. The preparations during the day were intense and the air was filled with the noise of engines grinding up as each tank and Daimler scout car got extra-special attention.

At the Orders Group Eb laid it all on the line: harbour areas, start points, start lines, order of march, emergencies, strict convoy drills, even the weather, and there was to be a full moon.

Towards the end of the 'O' Group Eb said he would lead from the front. The Training Major, Terence Corkery, or perhaps the Adjutant, Mike Gollin, queried this decision but Eb was adamant and some wag was heard to say, 'I wonder if he can read a map at night?' There were to be no lights other than a very small, almost blacked-out convoy light at the rear of each tank, and *complete* wireless silence.

H Hour came and went and a long snaky, noisy, dusty column formed as each troop and squadron nosed out of its harbour area, over start lines, to join on hopefully in the correct order. The night was fine but the predicted moon did not materialize. It was cloudy and pitch black. Tanks stopped and moved on, some didn't move. Tank commanders, held up by the tank in front, jumped and stumbled forward in the dark. 'Why the hell have you stopped?' above the noise of the engine.

'The bastard in front has stopped.'

He moves forward again. No engine noise from this tank. 'What the hell's the matter?' and so it went on. The odd tank was left behind but the snake kept moving.

The hierarchy at the finishing line were waiting at the appointed time, hopefully, but heard nothing other than a very, very distant rumble.

149

Allowances would be made because of the unpredicted weather. It was still bloody dark. Soon after the ETA came the obvious noise of a tank. Hopes and excitement rose. The changing gears could be heard and a tank at last appeared through the gloom. Torches were waved about and the first tank ground to a halt. Great excitement and engine revving as a small, lean figure leapt down from the turret waving his map.

'Who said I couldn't boody map read in the dark?' demanded Eb.

The Training Major, not to be outdone, shone his torch eastwards into the gloom and silence and laconically said, 'Marvellous, Eb, where's your Regiment?'

For the record, almost every tank and scout car arrived that night. None went off the cliff.

Whilst on an exercise with the 6th (City) Battalion, Corporal Burns of B Company, having spent a cold night with his platoon on the edge of a wood, spied the Commanding Officer, Colonel Eb Wood, approaching with his retinue at 6 a.m.

'Oh hell! Haway lads, gerron yer feet, hear cooms Monty Joonyer.'

In June 1962, there was an exercise between the 6th (City) Battalion, in defence, commanded by Lieutenant Colonel Michael Van Gruisen and the 7th Battalion, who were to be the dawn attackers, commanded by Lieutenant Colonel Jim Smail. All was set for a fine battle on a fine summer morning. Even the Brigadier, 'Crackers' May, was nearly excited, although he was to become very excited later.

Everything was in the attackers' favour. There was a mist right up to and just over the start line which was down in the valley. However, after the usual TA night before, there was a stiff upward climb ahead of them. The Colonel of the 6th Battalion had sited his defensive position well and there was the usual anticipatory silence broken only by the usual Fusilier morning chorus and some accompanying lavatorial repartee. Suddenly a piper, a lone Northumbrian piper, was heard down the valley as he appeared out of the mist dressed in his piper's finery. A jig past the 6th by the 7th? More surprises; behind the piper, a long thin line emerged from the mist. It was miles wide, or so it seemed.

The 6th smirked and grinned. This was going to be a walkover. Fingers twitched but no one moved. The Colonel could already see the champagne and the Newcastle Brown Ale flowing. The piper came on, when suddenly, a bugle blew. Must be the bugler playing a long and unusual version of the charge. No, it was 'Come to the cookhouse door, boys!'

The piper turned, slowly, and so did that long, thin green line. In a few seconds every single man was enveloped in the mist. They had all gone! The bugle stopped and all that could be heard was a lament from the piper. The men of the 6th Battalion could not believe their eyes. The Brigadier was beside himself with rage. As his wireless blew up, he too vanished into the mist in his Landrover.

The battle did take place, much later in the day. At the debriefing the

Brigadier, more composed now, queried the tactics. Colonel Jim Smail, more pithy than usual said, 'You must know, Brigadier, that an army marches on its stomach; breakfast was late this morning.'

The 7th Battalion had two spies out that morning – two lovers, from the Sergeants' Mess, billing and cooing in no man's land. The lady was scantily clad in a short skirt and very hairy legs, and caused great excitement until rumbled and captured in full flight.

In St George's Drill Hall at St Mary's Place in Newcastle, there was a doorstop in the Officers' Mess. This consisted of a brass tank shell case from the 43rd Royal Tank Regiment, which had been the wartime and the early 1950s designation and role of the 6th (City) Battalion. The end of the case was badly melted, mangled and bent, and the story behind this was that a certain Troop Commander was in the habit of taking two bottles of Newcastle Brown Ale for his lunch. To keep them reasonably cool and stable he would store them in the breech of the main gun of his tank. On an exercise on Salisbury Plain, the troop was brought very quickly into action and the gunner loaded without removing the bottles so that two bottles of Newcastle Brown Ale were duly fired across Salisbury Plain. The bad news came when they tried to unload the cartridge case from the breech. It was a hard extraction and the Royal Electrical and Mechanical Engineers had to be called in to remove the shell case and repair the damage. Sales of Newcastle Brown Ale doubled. If it could do that to a thick, brass shell case, what would it do to you?

On an exercise at Otterburn the 6th Battalion was ordered to infiltrate through the 4/5th Battalion's positions during the night. Points were to be given for every officer and man who got through the lines without being captured. Captain Geoff Ridley, who had a good Northumberland accent, nipped back to camp and donned a pair of old breeks, tweed cap and jacket. He found a crummock in his car and walked through the lines at dawn asking the outposts of the 4/5th Battalion, 'Hey ya seen a blidly sheep dog?' They looked at him doubtfully but accepted he was a local. He walked right through to Battalion Headquarters, banged his crummock on the Colonel's table and declared he was from the 6th Battalion.

At a Civil Defence Camp at Devizes, the 6th Battalion was working alongside a battery of gunners from London, many of whom had originated from the West Indies. Regimental Sergeant Major Dickie Million was a regular with a good Geordie accent. The sun was beating down on the soldiers who were digging in with the gunner battery just down the hill from the 4/5th positions. Everyone was getting very hot and sticky. Eventually it was decided that shirts could be removed. The RSM yelled at the top of his voice, 'Noo every one can take ya shorts off.' The West Indian's eyes showed their whites very prominently as they started unbuttoning their trousers.

At the same camp, Second Lieutenant A. G. Rutherford had to give a character reference for some Fusiliers who were up before the local Magistrates. There were, of course, language problems. Rutherford could understand the

Fusiliers and had to spend most of his time pretending that he had stomach cramp because he was doubled up with laughter. The first case concerned two Fusiliers who were accused of stealing a bicycle during the night to ride back to camp. The defence was,

> Wed sen a lamp in tha hidge, so wed thought well thur must be something rang thur. Thur must be something the matter. So wed reached into the hidge pulls oot the lamp and, wey man, thur were a bike fastened to it. So wed thought sum one had lost tha bike. So wed take the bike back to camp and report it in the morning.

It can be imagined how that went done in translation.

The second case was of two Fusiliers who were accused of stealing a keg of Guinness and rolling it back to the camp. The keg had been taken into the billet and a monkey wrench was pressed into use. When they managed to release the stop the pressure inside the keg was so great that foam had filled the billet and was still dripping from the lamps and the rafters when the police arrived the next morning. The Fusiliers were still flat out on the bed with the monkey wrench on the floor. The evidence was damming, but the defence was equally robust. Their excuse was that they had fallen over this keg of Guinness, finding it on the way back to camp and thought that the object was very dangerous. So they had rolled it back to their billet with the intention of reporting it and returning it the next morning. However, an argument had arisen as to what it might contain and whether it might be a bomb or whether it was really a proper beer like Newcastle Brown Ale or some other southern rubbish. For that reason the monkey wrench was acquired and to settle the argument they had decided to look inside – which did not find much favour with the Magistrates. However they had a sense of humour and the fines were modest.

Army food at TA Camps was not at its best. Once, at a camp at Otterburn, Second Lieutenant Rutherford overheard the following exchange at the cookhouse:

'Bye, I like yer dumplings, Sarge.'
'Them's not dumplings, that's the gravy.'

The Brigadier was touring a defensive position at camp and the Fusiliers were in slit trenches, just as dusk was approaching. Everyone was standing to. He spoke to one of the Fusiliers, saying, 'Now tell me, Fusilier, do you know what you are doing just now?'

The reply came, 'Oh aye, sur, this is stand to.'

'Well done,' said the Brigadier, 'and what about this morning, at dawn, when you did the same thing, was that stand to as well?'

'Augh, I dinnah think see, sur, that must have been stand one.'

Some Fusiliers were being drilled by a cockney Sergeant who must have come from the Royal Fusiliers. A Fusilier from the 7th Battalion came across, very late, to the squad. His equipment was in disarray and he was buttoning up his battledress. The Sergeant bawled him out and asked him where he had been and why was he so late? The Fusilier replied, 'Wey, I'm sorry, Sergeant, but I left me galasees in the netty.' After the explanation had been delivered seven times without any glimmer of understanding, the Sergeant gave up.

Lieutenant Rutherford took a platoon from the 6th Battalion to join the 1st Battlion on exercise at Soltau Training Area in Germany. At one point in the exercise an order came from Battalion Headquarters that all pilfering of items such as eggs and potatoes from local farms must cease, unless a fair bargain or an exchange was agreed. Rutherford found a bunch of Fusiliers digging over part of a potato field, leaving the tops of the potatoes in place. Their pockets were bulging with new potatoes. He stopped them and asked if they were aware of the order against pilfering. They looked wide-eyed and innocently at Rutherford and said, 'But this is fair exchange, sur.' They scooped the soil aside and there were a number of 'Compo' tins of POM, powdered potato. Rutherford gave up.

On the same exercise, the platoon was resting in pup tents for about 48 hours. There had been continuous torrential rain. The Company Commander, from the First Battalion, decided that this was a good time to stop the issue of water so that the company could get used to drought conditions, although the order rationing water was pointless because water bottles could be filled from the rain coming off the tents. The Company Commander asked the men how they were getting on with water rationing and they duly explained how they had enough water from off their tents. The Company Commander said, 'There is a good lesson for you. You now know what to do if there is a drought.' This kept morale going in Rutherford's platoon for at least three days.

There was a very short Fusilier who must have been right on the bottom edge of the Army's height limits as he could not have been taller than five feet two inches. One day he was issued with the largest pair of denim trousers ever to be made for the Army. He had a great sense of humour and so donned the trousers, which came right up to his armpits, tucked his elbows in, pulled the trousers up to his shoulders and was able, with difficulty, to walk to the stores. He looked like a walking pair of trousers. The Regimental Quartermaster Sergeant saw him approachng and thought it was a pair of trousers with a red and white hackle on top. The Fusilier stopped, came to attention and the RQMS, stifling a grin, said, 'Yes, what can I do for you, Fusilier?'

The muffled voice inside the trousers, just behind the fly buttons, replied, 'Please, Sur, can I have a pair of three-inch braces?'

Chapter XXIV

Encounters
with Field Marshal Festing

T he title 'Colonel' has, in the Army, many meanings, and it is like
explaining cricket to an American. This English sport, at which the
Scots, the Welsh and the Irish are not real proponents, is one that well suits
the phlegmatic Englishman, and is best illustrated by a marvellous picture
taken in Hong Kong during the Red Guard riots in the late 1960s. The
local Chinese communists were rioting in Queens Road and Des Voeux
Road, encouraged by the loud speakers set up on the Bank of China building
and were confronted by a large force of police, with a Gurkha Battalion
standing by. Just at the end of Queens Road and Des Voeux Road, some
50 yards from the Bank of China was the Hong Kong Cricket Club ground.
Here 24 Englishmen were playing cricket, seemingly oblivious to the racket
no distance from them, which does not explain cricket but demonstrates its
flavour.

The title 'Colonel' must be explained. Each infantry regiment, except the
Fifth before the 1960s, had three Colonels. A Colonel-in-Chief, an honorary
figure like the present Colonel-in-Chief of the Royal Regiment of Fusiliers,
the Duke of Kent. There is then the Colonel of the Regiment. This is usually
a very senior officer, often a General, who has served with the Regiment.
Once you reach the rank of full Colonel you cease to be on the Regimental
list but are transferred to the staff list. Finally there is the Colonel commanding the First Battalion, who is a serving officer and a Lieutenant
Colonel.

The Royal Northumberland Fusiliers did not have a Colonel-in-Chief for
many years because the appointment is made via a tortuous route and is all
veiled in secrecy between Buckingham Palace and the War Office. Eventually
a letter is sent to the Colonel of the Regiment suggesting that if he writes
to a certain Royal personage, he or she, might well be willing to serve as
Colonel-in-Chief of the Regiment. Before the war the Colonel of the Royal
Northumberland Fusiliers received such a letter, but for some reason failed
to respond to it. When the error was discovered, it was too late. A faux pas
had been made and for many years the Royal Northumberland Fusiliers had
no Colonel-in-Chief.

When General Herbert decided that the time had come to retire as
Colonel of the Regiment, a new Colonel had to be found. However, there
was no suitable Fifth Fusilier General around. It was then discovered that
General Festing's father had been a Fifth Fusilier, although he himself was

a Green Jacket. However, he lived in Northumberland and so he was asked to become Colonel of the Regiment. To some it seemed strange that this genuine Northumberland officer should preside over the Fifth Fusiliers who at the time were largely led by non-Northumberland officers. Such are the contradictions of life.

Lindsay Stemp had several encounters with Field Marshal Festing, all of them thoroughly difficult, and on reflection it is not surprising that his career stopped short at the lowly rank of Major. His first one was, as has already been described, in the Camberley branch of Woolworths, where he was to receive his vetting as a suitable officer for the Regiment, ably sponsored by no less a figure than the flamboyant Robert Ferguson.

Lindsay Stemp's second encounter was what he has since regarded as one of the worst days of his life. It was one of those days when everything goes wrong, but is now quite funny in retrospect. He had been appointed ADC to the Field Marshal for the presentation of new colours to the 7th Battalion (TA) at Alnwick Castle. He reported to the Castle at the appointed hour to be greeted by 'the Duke' and the Field Marshal, who were taking the morning air in the inner bailey after breakfast, where he was informed that his sash was on the wrong way round and that his ADC's aiguillette (borrowed from a local RAF ADC) was of the wrong type. There was nothing he could do about the latter.

They were then taken off into the Castle where he was left with these two very awesome people to await the start of the parade. He had had no briefing, no rehearsal and no idea as to what he was required to do. After an agonizing wait, during which he was wondering what on earth he was expected to do, and with the Field Marshal becoming more and more impatient, there were at last footsteps on the stairs and a 7th Battalion officer arrived to escort them to the parade ground. (He does not know to this day whether this was planned or not, but does remember wondering if he dared tell the Field Marshal that he had dandruff all over the back of his uniform.)

The parade seemed to go without incident, and mercifully he was required to do nothing except follow the Field Marshal around. After the parade he had about five hours to kill because there was to be a ball at Pallinsburn that evening and there was no point in going all the way back to Newcastle; anyway, Patrick Robinson had his car and was to drive up in it and pick him later. Lindsay was kindly given a room in the porter's lodge in the Castle to change in and, at the appointed hour, left to meet up with Patrick. He remembers creeping out of the Castle hoping that he would not be seen by anyone because they would wonder what on earth he was doing so long after the parade. The inevitable happened and who should drive in through the outer bailey but the Duke and the Field Marshal. He felt two inches high. The ball went off without incident, and the next day he received a phone call from the Duke telling him that he had left his sword behind and that he would send someone down with it for Lindsay. The Duke was an incredibly kind and sensitive person who should long be remembered in the

Regiment. Lindsay Stemp is afraid that the Field Marshal did not find him a very good ADC, and he is sure letters were exchanged, but only rumours came to his ears for which he has to thank his Commanding Officer, Andrew Scott.

Lindsay Stemp's next encounter with the Field Marshal was on King's Cross Station from where, with his newly engaged fiancée, he was travelling on the night sleeper to Newcastle. Although their engagement had been in the paper, he does not remember whether he had asked permission of the Field Marshal, but he seemed to know who they were, especially when he observed the passenger list as 'Captain and Mrs G. L. Stemp'. Anyway, he gave them rather an odd look next morning as they left the train at Newcastle. David Welch and Sam Phillips were on the same train, and seemed to have no illusions about the arrangement. After 30 years of happily married life Lindsay and Robin Stemp can now look back and laugh at what at the time seemed a fearfully embarrassing incident. Why do your friends always turn up, at just the moment when you wish they were 100 miles away?

His final encounter was at St George's Barracks, Sutton Coldfield, where his platoon was to provide the Guard of Honour for the Field Marshal on the official opening of the barracks – indeed, there is a large plaque there commemorating the event to this day. Festing had driven all the way down from Northumberland in his rather antiquated Rolls Royce. Rumour had it that he drove at a maximum of 30 m.p.h. in the middle of the road, stopping to blow his horn at every crossroads. No wonder he was nearly an hour late. Lindsay Stemp's Platoon Sergeant, who had seemingly inherited his accident proneness, stepped forward and in doing so fell flat on his face in front of the Field Marshal, who was clearly in a thoroughly bad mood and did not see the funny side of it at all. Instead, he stomped off, giving Lindsay Stemp a thunderous look in the process. It was the final straw and the last time Lindsay Stemp met him.

The Field Marshal had a fairly cavalier attitude to uniform. He was not the most smartly dressed Field Marshal at the best of times. As mentioned earlier, when visiting a regiment, he would drive down from his home wearing jodhpurs and a well-worn tweed coat. On arrival at an engagement he would discard the coat and don his Field Marshal's service dress top. Appearing at one guardroom he reported his presence to the Guard Commander who rang up the Commanding Officer saying, 'There's a chap here who says he is Field Marshal Festing.'

Chapter XXV

Kirton-in-Lindsey

Major David Thompson was serving as a Company Commander with the First Battalion of the Royal Fusiliers under the command of another Fifth Fusilier, Lieutenant Colonel C. M. Barrett OBE. It was decided that there would be a battalion exercise at Otterburn, although everyone was sure that the decision was not coloured in any way by the fact that the Commanding Officer had a house near Alnwick. There was little time for briefing and making final arrangements before the deployment into the training area.

The Advance Party, 'O' Group and Rear Echelon would motor north and break the journey from Shorncliffe with the First Battalion of the Fifth Fusiliers at Kirton-in-Lindsey. To celebrate the occasion a guest night was called at short notice, and it was quite a night.

David Thompson spent a very convivial evening with many colleagues and an old friend, Major Adam Hope. He was the Officer Commanding Headquarter Company and had made a brilliant job of organizing the transit arrangements. The officers of the two battalions had had an excellent evening and many ended up at the bar in the early hours of the morning, swapping stories as officers do on such occasions. David Thompson and Adam Hope were the last at the bar, David cannot think why, when Adam let out an expletive like a grunt. He grabbed for his side hat and leapt for the front door with David Thompson following, wishing to say 'Goodbye' and join him relieving himself in the rose bed. However, the last David Thompson saw of him was a figure bounding for the barracks at the other side of the road, and heard later that the rush out of the Mess was in order for Adam Hope to organize the departure of the Advance Party of the First Battalion of the Royal Fusiliers. He was next seen in the middle of the square, in his mess kit, directing traffic at 3 a.m., seemingly oblivious to the penetrating drizzle and staying until everyone had left.

Chapter XXVI

Promotion Examinations

For junior officers, promotion examinations are both a hazard and a lottery. Officers need to remember that war experience counts for nothing and it's the book that counts.

Captain Humphrey Walker learnt this to his cost after his return from Korea. His Lieutenant to Captain Exam was going to be a doddle for he had, after all, been an active service Platoon Commander. When the first question was about medical evacuation he knew he was going to pass, and in answer to the question on what happened to a soldier wounded on the battlefield, he described what had happened to him when he was wounded. A helicopter picked him up from the forward positions to a field hospital and then he was sent back to Japan for further treatment. Quite wrong. The book said you were given a field dressing, then you were taken back to the Regimental Aid Post and then . . . as per the good book.

John Masters made a similar mistake. He viewed the examining officer, with his lack of campaign medals, with an air of superiority, his own lonely medal proclaiming his veteran status. He was asked to lay out a mortar platoon defensive fire plan and knowing from Sergeant Pilcher that in wartime conditions a good mortarman like Sergeant Pilcher could bring a mortar bomb down to within 100 yards of his own lines, and allowing a 100 per cent moron factor, he laid on DF within 200 yards of his own lines. Wrong again, it was not as per the book. In this case the examining officer had the superior hand even if he lacked the medals. Lesson: you can never be too clever in the Army.

Robert Parsons's military skills rose and fell according to his employment. Straight from his Platoon Commander's Course he could have handled an Armoured Division with dash and elan. After commanding an Army Youth Team, marketing the Army career rather than recruiting, he was not so sure. The timing of his Lieutenant to Captain exam was not only awkward but a potential fiasco. Hardly 'match fit' might have been a good description. A day's pre-exam training with his old friends, the Queen's Own Hussars, at Catterick gave him an appalling hangover, but little help with an integrated fire plan. A high and very exposed hill near Harrogate was to be the setting for this career disaster.

The examination took the form of numerous officers scattered around the hillside. These officers were numbered. Candidates were given a piece of paper giving them the order in which to report to their examiners. The Signals question; the Map Reading question; the Encoding question. Ten minutes for this; Twenty minutes for that. Right on the top of the hill was the Big One – thirty minutes for the Tactical Appreciation and Orders.

At the top of this hill, numbered and holding his millboard, was a portly officer. A Major, wearing battledress, a garment that was almost extinct by then, but which allowed the display of a sign on his shoulder, 'Hallamshires'. Having been with the Army all his life, and in the Army for five years, Robert was confused. He had never heard of Hallamshire, or their distinguished regiment. Salutes and greetings.

'Parsons, sir.'

'Ah! You're a Fifth Fusilier.'

'Yes, sir.' Nervously.

'Do you know Paddy Baxter?'

'Yes, sir. I believe he's in Germany at the moment.'

'Oh, give him my regards. You see . . .'

To cut a long story short, his examiner had been wounded at the same time as Paddy in Korea. Paddy had been shot in the lungs and Robert's examiner in the guts. They were in beds beside each other in a hospital in Japan and Paddy had made the examiner laugh so much that, literally, he had split his stitches. Not once, but several times. Eventually he had to be moved to another ward to stop the stitches from being split again. Paddy and the examiner had other adventures, such hilarious adventures that tears were coursing down his cheeks at the memories as they stood high on a hill near Harrogate. This took time. At last the examiner looked at his watch.

'Oh Lord, only five minutes for your question and orders. Look, enemy are there, there and there. Your battalion is here, guns there, tanks behind the hill. You are to attack that.' All shown with wide sweeps of his arms. 'Would you make a two- or three-phase attack? Three phases usually cause a balls-up.'

'Two-phase, sir,' rather tentatively.

'Quite right. Good. Would you use an Artillery Fire Plan? Help you across that open ground? Smoke, perhaps?'

'Oh yes, sir. Lots of smoke, and I'd ask the Mortars to join in.'

'Excellent answer. I liked the bit about the Mortars. How would you lay out your Orders? Headings and things?'

'Situation, Mission, Execution . . .'

'That seems fairly comprehensive. I'll pass you. Give my regards to Paddy.'

Paddy was probably a thousand miles away at the time, but he could still get a Fifth Fusilier out of the mud!

Chapter XXVII

A Brother Officer

Robert Parsons's brother was about five years older than Robert and, therefore, better known to his brother officers. They had, after all, five more years experience of playing and working with him. When Robert joined the First Battalion in Germany his brother had been posted to remotest Arabia. Remotest Arabia was so awful in those days that after nine months in the desert an officer was flown home for two months' leave and his brother's two months' leave included the month of March – skiing time.

In those days, making or receiving calls between England and Germany was almost unheard of because it was both difficult and expensive, and so Robert was surprised to be called to the Mess telephone to speak to his brother who had had a wonderful idea – he, Robert, must get three weeks' leave beginning in two weeks' time, and his brother would find a resort and accommodation for them, using discounts and the good offices of the Army Ski Association. He would telephone again with full instructions in four days' time.

Robert returned to the ante-room full of excitement; colleagues eagerly waited for his news.

'How is he?'

'What is he doing?'

When Robert told them what was planned, their eager faces became anxious. A solemn voice broke the atmosphere. 'Watch that bugger. He will have you halfway up the Brenner Pass in a tent. Worse, he will not even organize the dog to call with the brandy in its barrel.'

'Oh no! I'm sure my brother is organizing an hotel.'

'Beware when he rings back.'

Four days later Robert's brother telephoned again: 'Hotels are an awful waste of money. We're going skiing, not poncing about in an hotel. You know those little tents in the stores for Arctic Warfare? Well, ask Forbes Burn if you can borrow one.'

With his other brother officers' advice in mind, Robert stoutly refused, so after much muttering about wasting money, Robert's brother agreed to find an hotel.

In fact they stayed in the chalet of the remarkable Billy Patterson in Alpbach. There, Robert's brother met a lady called Jane, who he married and from then on they stayed in hotels or chalets whenever they went on holiday, that was except when they went yachting.

Now wind and sail was created by God for the sole purpose of moving yachts through water. Engines and propellers are a noisy, smelly, heavy, space-consuming and expensive way of making soda water at the back of the boat. Well, that was Robert's brother's considered opinion.

After their tour of duty in Aden, Robert and his brother had been lent a lovely big yacht. They set off westwards from the Solent with not a cloud in the sky. In fact, the weather was so good that crew members who had not been to Aden covered themselves with sun protection cream, while intrepid, tough officers, seasoned in the tropics, regarded this as a form of 'nancy behaviour' and were duly sunburnt, whereas the 'ninnies' escaped unharmed.

It was Britain at its very best in July. On a light but steady breeze they cleared the tidal nightmare of Portland Bill, but about ten miles beyond the Bill the wind dropped and they were becalmed. On a foul tide, and this has other meanings when you know that the Weymouth sewer outlet is nearby, they drifted back towards the Bill, however, all was not lost as the wind got up again and the tide turned. Once again they cleared Portland Bill and headed across Lyme Bay. The prospect of several pints in Brixham that evening had much appeal, but sailing is never predictable and once again Portland Bill loomed closer. The wind had dropped and the tide had turned again, so the yacht was going backwards.

To Robert's brother sailing meant sailing. If the misfortunes of wind and tide meant going backwards and forwards for a few days, then so be it. To the rest of the crew, sailing was now a way of getting to Brixham as soon as possible to have a pint, but by now the drinking of a pint had moved from being a future pleasure to a more immediate need and this need had to be passionately fought for. The only hope was to use the engine. Predictably Robert's brother viewed the use of the engine in the same way as a gentleman views a pump-action shotgun – with extreme distaste. The crew dropped hints, pointed conversations about the taste of a pint were held within earshot of Robert's brother. When this was to no avail, the crew went below and composed a 'humble petition'. Still the 'Captain' said 'No', no use of the engine.

Then Jane put down her sketching, looked at the enlarged Portland Bill and suggested to her husband that he use the engine to get her to Brixham as she wished to have a good bath. The Captain, and Adjutant of the First Battalion of the Fifth Fusiliers, complied. The engine rumbled, Portland Bill disappeared, a certain person had a bath in Brixham and the crew had a pint or two or more.

(Lt Col Anthony Parsons MBE died as a result of a wound he received in Northern Ireland.)

Chapter XXVIII

Aden

A den was once described by a sunstruck warrior thus: 'if Basra is the arsehole of the British Empire, then Aden is that Empire's bloody armpit.' It was a grim station, made even grimmer by a small war being fought in 1966 and 1967. Britain was trying to disentangle itself from the chaos of post-colonial wrangling between local factions. It was not a lovely place. The Fifth Fusiliers' part in the demise of the British Empire was hardly glamorous. It was sometimes frightening, sometimes painful, seldom internationally newsworthy – that was until a United Nations delegation from the Committee on Decolonisation paid a visit.

That produced a mild flurry of interest, a sharp rise in terrorist activity and the appearance of some real combat veterans, the Press. Actually some of them had been covering the Americans in Vietnam for some years and so they understood 'Crack and Thump' as well as any soldier.

There were several disagreeable aspects of Fusilier life in Aden, not least of which was the total absence of women, or at least women they could get their hands on. When it was discovered that the correspondent for *Paris Match* was a woman, the Fusiliers' gallantry knew no bounds. Not only was she a woman, she was a very pretty one and inclined to wear the latest fashion, the miniskirt. She was actually a French Canadian with considerable experience of trouble spots.

Of course, it was far too dangerous to allow journalists into the operational area. The Battalion's was Crater, and quite a sight to see, reminiscent of a film set for an old Arab town, but very dangerous. Journalists are journalists, so it wasn't long before a section patrol set out from the Chartered Bank towards the Armed Police barracks, with a very pretty French Canadian lady in the middle of it. How can a woman look sexy in a sweat-stained shirt and short skirt? She did.

The route for the patrol was up a sort of boulevard, the road was dual carriageway, with trees and shrubs in the middle. To the patrol's right were high-rise apartments; to the left was a wide pavement bounded on the left by a wall, about knee high, which dropped straight down to the bottom of a wadi, and with gaps at intervals in the wall for steps down to the wadi. Across the wadi the ground rose to about the same height as the road to be used by the patrol and was a mass of Kucha huts, dwellings made out of any old packing case or cardboard box.

The patrol moved in fairly open order up the pavement to the left of the boulevard. Recent experiences indicated that the high-rise flats were very hostile, so the patrol commander was giving the flats as wide a berth as possible. It was not that Corporal's lucky day as terrorists (Gollies) opened fire with a machine-gun from the Kucha huts to the left. The initial burst missed and everybody dived for the nearest cover, which meant being pressed up against the low wall. The patrol commander was now in a very awkward position. The weapon being used was a heavy machine-gun, and any attempt to put up a head to return fire was greeted by heavy fire. The Gollies seemed to have plenty of ammunition and were preparing to wear down the wall as big chunks of masonry flew off the top. The whole patrol, plus lady journalist, was cowering behind the same bit of wall as any attempt to put down covering fire was countered by the enemy. They couldn't go forward across a gap in the wall, nor could they go back, and they couldn't cross the street in the face of that machine-gun. Nor could they go left over the wall towards the enemy. They were well and truly stuck. Even the security of the wall was getting less as the heavy machine-gun chipped away at it. The Corporal was shouting orders; the radio operator was calling for help; a Fusilier had just told the Corporal to 'Put your own f——ing head up to have a look 'cos I'm not so f——ing daft.'

Things were not going well.

There was a moment of silence, then a very broad Geordie-accented voice was heard from the back of the patrol. 'Gor, I can see right up her skirt.'

Help came. The enemy packed up their gun and departed. Order was restored. The patrol moved on. One Fusilier had just had the most satisfying experience of his last six months, and there would be nothing like it for the next three.

Two Fusiliers were in a lookout post on a very hot summer's day in June. One turned to the other and said, 'It's the first Saturday in June, Harry. It be Northumberland Plate day'.

Fusilier 'Harry' thought for a while and turned back to his mate. 'Aye well, they've got a grand day for it.'

There was a detachment on a roof. A curfew had been declared for 6 p.m. Anyone seen out in the area of the building was in a prohibited zone after curfew and curfew breakers were liable to be shot. At 5.55 p.m., a shot rang out from the roof and an Arab was shot dead. The Company Sergeant Major galloped up the stairs shouting, 'Who the f— fired that shot?'

'I did, Sergeant Major.'

'What the hell are you playing at, Thompson, it's only five to six?'

'I naw that, Sergeant Major, but I naw the Arab as weel, and there was nee chance of him getting yem afore six.' Probably not true, but some wished it was at the time.

A large crowd had gathered in Crater and the Armed Police were sent to disperse them. The crowd and the police were eyeing each other up, when a Landrover pulled up between them and out jumped Sgt Mills and two Fusiliers. The crowd fled down the street. Sgt Mills felt quite proud of this and turned to the Armed Police only to see them disappearing in the opposite direction. Later, some wags in the Battalion asked him if he should use 'Amplex'.

The Battalion sent the Band to Addis Ababa in November 1966. The Second in Command and Band President, Major Paddy Baxter, went with the Band because he had been at school with Emperor Haile Selassie's youngest son. The highlight of the visit was the Band's performance outside the Jubilee Palace in front of the Emperor. Paddy Baxter and the Band were presented to the Emperor prior to the performance. St George was also the patron saint of Ethiopia, so it was particularly appropriate that the emblazoned bass drum and the side drums showed the crest clearly when the march 'Standard of St George' was played. Paddy Baxter was very proud that the 'Hackle' was never more upright nor the honour of the Regiment in safer hands. The Band played for about 20 minutes before the hardest part came when the Band Sergeant Major had to line up the Band in fives so that it could march out backwards, and whilst marching, bow to the Emperor three times. It was not in the book, but this movement was carried out with all the dignity required and expected of a Fifth Fusilier. Major Baxter was so proud to be a Fifth Fusilier in the company of that very imperial old man. He was prouder still when the Band was invited into the Palace to take their champagne and cigars and conducted themselves in the presence of the Emperor as though they were to the manner born.

Swimming was the main leisure activity when off duty. This took place either at the Khormaksar Club or at one of the many rock-covered and boulder-strewn beaches which skirted yet another of the 'Empire's Barren Rocks'.

Major John Campbell, who commanded Headquarter Company, initiated several leisure pursuits. One of these was snorkel diving and minor marine exploration. Major Ronnie Cowe accompanied John Campbell with a party of Fusiliers on one of his trips to a rocky promontory where the group disported themselves in the relentless heat. Even the pea-green water was barely cooling. John Campbell spent long periods well out from the shore bobbing up and down with his snorkel and eventually waved to Ronnie Cowe to join him. When Ronnie Cowe reached him, John Campbell pulled out his mouthpiece and shouted, 'Fantastic sight down here. Come and see.'

Having made his dive, Ronnie Cowe waited for the bubbles to clear and started to peer through the green murk. He could see John Campbell ahead of him, pointing down excitedly at something beneath him, and to his amazement and horror, about 20 feet below him, he caught sight of the motionless outline of a large basking shark. He made a rapid ascent to the surface and completed a record-breaking flipper-assisted return to the shore. John Campbell eventually followed at a leisurely pace.

'What's the matter?' he panted, 'Why did you shoot up like that?'

'There's a whacking great shark down there!' Ronnie Cowe protested.

'But it was fast asleep.'

Ronnie Cowe had no wish to be around when it woke up.

Jack Stacey was the Battalion's Padre in Aden. He quickly became a popular member of the Battalion and a frequent visitor to all the companies when they were both on and off duty. He was a truly integrated Fifth Fusilier, wearing his uniform with flair if not with great accuracy. Long putties were a great trial to him, often looking like great disks round his ankles and he wore his peaked cap at a debonair angle, but he was an unmistakable figure. Like many men of the cloth, he showed his trust in his Maker in ways which might appear naive but nevertheless he was courageous and compassionate.

Strikes were frequent in the steaming urban sprawl of Crater, the Battalion's zone of operations, one of which caused a severe shortage of bread. The Padre was concerned for the families living in quarters close by the barracks, for although the Battalion did not have its own families with them, the Padre had taken all service families living locally under his wing. He was determined that they should have bread.

So he contrived to get himself into Crater to pay a visit to a baker's shop. When he was on his way, another frequent Aden phenomenon arose in the form of a marching and rioting crowd in support of the strike.

The company on internal security duty was quickly on the scene. One platoon formed up to confront the mob in the time-honoured fashion at the end of the long street where the crowd was milling. As they approached, the Platoon Commander was amazed to see the Padre in the front rank of the crowd, struggling with an armful of bread which he had persuaded the baker to sell him. He was extricated without incident as the crowd dispersed but from then on the Battalion kept a closer eye on his movements. It was considered later that the Padre merely thought that the streets were busier and noisier than usual.

The Battalion was fortunate to have Admiral Sir Michael Le Fanu as Commander-in-Chief during the difficult closing days in Aden. He had an impish sense of humour and there were many stories of his exploits.

On St George's Day 1967, the Battalion was operationally deployed and so it was not possible to lay on the traditional programme of events. However, there was a church service and a special meal for the Fusiliers, supplemented by a liberal supply of Newcastle Brown Ale for those off duty. It was decided that the officers should hold an informal lunch in the Mess with no official guest list, but a few close friends of the Battalion were invited. A very happy party was in full swing when a worried President of the Mess Committee relayed to Lieutenant Colonel Dick Blenkinsop, the Commanding Officer, that the Admiral had arrived.

The Commanding Officer went into the hall to greet the Admiral who was dressed in bermuda shorts, a beach shirt and plimsoles, pushing his invalid wife in her wheelchair. 'Heard you were having a bit of a party, so we thought we'd come incognito and wish you a happy time.'

They stayed for a while, with a word for everyone. The Fifth Fusiliers greatly appreciated this gesture by a thoughtful and well-briefed commander.

St Georges Gazette reported on some correspondence on 31 May 1967:

FROM ADEN.

The Editor has received the following correspondence arising out of a bet between Admiral Sir Michael Le Fanu, Commander-in-Chief Middle East Land Command, and Lieutenant Colonel Dick Blenkinsop, Commanding First Battalion The Royal Northumberland Fusiliers, Aden.

From Admiral Le Fanu.

Dear Dick,

I suppose you are so busy hoggin it round Crater on your plaffs, or, if you have a tailled wing, sitting in the upper ky clamming and thinking about ganging yem that you've forgotten to send me my 125 fills.

From Colonel Blenkinsop.

Sor

Ah would like ti hev yi naa that plaffs is not proper geordie, ah hev been telt tho that plaffs is the things yi byuts tie on te.

No, as plaffs was niver geordie tark ah reckon ah divent ow yi a meg. Anyway ah nev nen ti gi yi as ah will need ah hev cos ah's ganning yem soon an ah heor tell Broon Ale's gone up.

Yours ever,
Dick.

Colonel Blenkinsop maintains 'Plaffs' is Morpedian or pit language.

St Georges Gazette of 31 August 1967 gives a glimpse into the strains of life in Aden:

Heard at a road block where an Arab insisted on reversing his car instead of driving it forward:
'You write backwards, you read backwards and you even f——g well drive backwards.'

Although Korea was a serious war, Aden was also no picnic for the First Battalion of the Royal Northumberland Fusiliers. Two officers, a company sergeant major and six other ranks were killed in action. Two officers, a company sergeant major, three sergeants and thirty other ranks were wounded or injured in action. Those killed died in the last few days of the Battalion's time in Aden when they and their relieving counterparts of the Argyll and Sutherland Highlanders were ambushed in Crater.
St Georges Gazette of 31 July 1967 summed up the situation:

ADEN

By now the story of triumph and disaster played out in Aden during the tour of duty there of our 1st Battalion is familiar to all.

The pages of *St George's Gazette* during the past nine months have carried cheerful accounts in story and picture of an extremely onerous duty, well, truly professionally, and comparatively safely, done. With the Battalion due home within the week and all preparations for a thankful and triumphant home-coming well forward, the blow fell.

It remains for us to record in these pages, possibly not immediately in this edition, the accounts, the obituaries, the tributes, the messages of condolence and congratulation which follow from this final scene of Greek-like tragedy enacted on 20th June.

For an editor of *St Georges Gazette* it is an all too familiar task. Once more we must be reminded that truth is stranger than fiction. Was it that the Gods slept, or jealous of such success, withheld momentarily their shield, whilst treachery took over to wreak such damage in so short a time? To look for an explanation is futile. Providence? Fate? All the ages have sought an answer. '*Quo Fata Vocant*' is still a Motto for a soldier and for a Regiment which has seen so much of triumph and of tragedy. If the Fifth must now close its long history, let it stand on this.

It would not be inappropriate. How came the news of Bunkers Hill to the Colonel's tenantry bereaved at Alnwick, or the letter to the Kinsale mother of a Colour-bearing Ensign struck down at Salamanca? Was the news from Cawnpore and Lucknow more terrible in its impact? Did messages from Afghanistan, Khartoum or South Africa mean the same? What about the endless lists from the fifty-two Battalions of Fifth Fusiliers from France, Italy and the East in 1914/18? How many have been reminded of Tobruk and the Desert, France, Italy, Singapore, The Imjin and Korea.

One thing is sure, the personal tragedy and loss are the same and are shared now, as always, by the whole family which is The Regiment.

Postscript from the *Daily Telegraph* of 19 July 1967:

HACKLE RAISERS

The First Queen's Dragoon Guards formed the vanguard for the reoccupation of Crater by the Argyll and Sutherland Highlanders, commanded by Lt Col Colin Mitchell, this month, arriving with the red and white hackles of the Royal Northumberland Fusiliers on their radio aerials.

The Dragoons sent a message to the Fusiliers – 'Your hackles fly again in Crater.'

Chapter XXIX

Kirton and Curtains

S*t George's Gazette* of 31 May 1968 reported the following extract from
the *London Gazette*:

THE ROYAL REGIMENT OF FUSILIERS

By virtue of the provisions of the Royal Warrant dated 5th April,
1968 (published in Army Order 18 of 1968) all officers of the Land
Forces belonging to The Royal Northumberland Fusiliers (5th), The
Royal Warwickshire Fusiliers (6th), The Royal Fusiliers (City of London
Regiment) (7th), and The Lancashire Fusiliers (20th) are transferred to
the Royal Regiment of Fusiliers with effect from 23rd April, 1968.

Thus the Fifth Fusiliers of The Royal Northumberland Fusiliers, founded
in 1674, ceased to be a regiment in its own right.

St Georges Gazette of 29 February 1964 gives a flavour of what was lost:

Eleven years from now and The Fifth Fusiliers will have completed
three hundred years of non-stop soldiering all over the world. Just about
two hundred years ago The Fifth, under Marlborough, were battling
with the French in the very lands where we manoeuvre to-day. No
doubt the soldier who stood on sentry in those days used the same
epithets to curse the chilly dawn and surreptitiously pulled his hands
out of his greatcoat pockets as the reliefs came round. He thought of
his girl friend or wife at home and puzzled out his private problem
regarding the friendly fraulein at the farm yonder. When a guard of
honour was required for some old Herzog or Graf to pay a call on the
Commanding Officer, he put just that extra bit of effort into producing
a turn-out just that much better than the one provided by the Loamshires
a few weeks previously. He noted with satisfaction if not mild disdain
that his officers upheld the honour of The Fifth by beating the Lancers
in a midnight steeplechase which some nut laid on after Wilhemstahl.

He was a member of The Fifth, not the Fourth nor the Sixth (a
tolerable bunch), but the Fifth Regiment of Foot.

The spirit has been burning pretty brightly in 1963 and being in a
Cavalry mob we have heard our unofficial name bandied about rather
more than ever before in the last decade. Even some of the ranks on
the sidelines at football matches have been heard to cry 'Come on the
Fifth' – a grand but desolate cry normally emanating rather lonesomelike
from the director's box. Let no one think that we are not equally proud
of our Northumberland name; it is, after all, the men of Northumberland
who have made the Regiment all through its history, though they have

undoubtedly been greatly helped by the many who flocked to the Gosling Green from far afield in order to have the honour of serving the The Northumberland Regiment. But the old 'Fifth' name goes right back into history and really recalls the spirit of the last two hundred and ninety years whenever it is mentioned.

So we should be grateful to our cavalry friends for giving us a shot in the arm and helping quite inadvertently to remind us of our great past, which is the basis of our present good name.

Retrospecting on this last day of the old year, I say 'Let the name "Fifth Fusiliers" come once and for all out of the sheltered halls of the Officers' Mess and be heard loud and clear in all Messes, Clubs, Canteens, Pubs and places where military men and Fifth Fusiliers in particular gather together.'

Chapter XXX

Epilogue

by Major General R. E. T. St John CB MC
(Former Colonel of the Regiment)

I do not have any amusing anecdotes of my time as Colonel of the Regiment because it was short and very much fraught by the trauma of the impending amalgamation into the Royal Regiment of Fusiliers (RRF), all of which I found most distasteful and depressing. The whole grisly affair has rankled with me ever since.

At that time I could not understand why we couldn't have carried on as the Fusilier Brigade, retaining our titles and cross-posting all ranks, as required, and face up to the disbanding of one of our regiments. As we were approaching our Tercentenary Year, this seemed logical.

When that ghastly Ministry of Defence questionnaire asked regiments to state whether they would opt to amalgamate with another regiment, or opt to convert to a large regiment or opt to be disbanded, the Regiment was undergoing an emotive time in Aden and voted to opt for Disbandment. When I announced this to the Council of Colonels as a straightforward answer to the hypothetical MOD questions, I was accused of gamesmanship, i.e. relying on the MOD refusing on account of our recruiting potential, etc. I insisted that the views of the Regiment were placed on record.

I was then sent for by the Vice Chief of Staff and given a good dressing down for rocking the boat. Disbandment was out of the question and we were strongly advised to accept the large regiment voluntarily rather than be ordered to do so in three years' time along with the rest of the non-volunteers. It is galling to me today that his own regiment still retains its identity!

The ground was further swept from under my feet by the fact that the late Field Marshal Frankie Festing, my predecessor, had, during my absence in the USA, agreed to accept the large regiment should the situation arise. I also lost the battle to retain our titles in brackets, i.e. 1 RRF (RNF). And so the Royal Regiment of Fusiliers came into being and the Fifth Fusiliers ceased to be, except as loyal Old Comrades. I maintain that the RRF had no right to celebrate our Tercentenary as our identity was completely eliminated and our existence broken off when the RRF was born. But all this is so much water under the bridge and a new generation has taken over who have only known the RRF and are equally proud of it.

First Battalion Orders of Battle

St George's Day 1945, Greece
Second Battalion

Commanding Officer: Lieutenant Colonel F. H. Butterfield.
Second in Command: Major J. A. Dewhurst.
Adjutant: Captain L. F. Hay.
Regimental
Sergeant Major: WOI C. V. Caborn.

No. 1 Company	No. 2 Company
Major A. E. Richards.	Major H. R. M. Wilkin.
Captain R. R. Gibson MC.	Captain J. J. Hinson.
Captain R. V. Luther-Smith.	Lieut F. W. Little.
Lieut G. H. Hulme.	Lieut D. S. Dumbreck.

No. 3 Company	No. 4 Company
Major R. D. Brook.	Major E. H. Parkhurst.
Lieut L. C. G. Gilling.	Captain E. R. Coutts-Deacon.
Lieut C. W. Brierley.	Lieut A. D. Wood.
Lieut J. C. Brown.	Lieut A. H. Hobson.

October 1946
First Battalion

Commanding Officer:	Lieutenant Colonel P. H. Earle.
Second in Command:	Major R. F. Forbes Watson.
Adjutants:	Captain M. H. Lassetter.
	Captain R. N. Jacobson.
PRI:	Captain A. R. Kerr.
Intelligence Offr:	Lieutenant R. Sharpe.
Quartermaster:	Captain (QM) P. W. Bell MM.
RMO:	Captain J. F. Mawe RAMC.
RSM:	WOII F. Bingham (Acting).
RQMS:	WOII J. Bottoms.

W Company

OC: Major C. H. Mitchell.
2 i/c: Capt. J. A. K. Harbron.
Platoon Commanders:
Lieut D. W. B. Jarvis.
Lieut E. S. Overy.
Lieut T. E. Oakley.
CSM: WOII O. Smith.
CQMS: C/Sgt R. Hetherington

Y Company

OC: Major R. M. Pratt.
2 i/c: Capt. S. Brew.
Platoon Commanders:
Lieut G. L. R. Hill.

CSM: WOII J. Kelly.
CQMS: C/Sgt S. A. Senior.

Z Company

OC: Major S. Brown.
2 i/c: Capt P. Cheston.
Platoon Commanders:
Lieut E. F. Hunt.
Lieut E. W. Parr.
CSM: WOII T. Boniface.
CQMS: C/Sgt S. J. Ebdon MM.

Support Company

OC: Capt E. J. Ransley MC.
2 i/c: Lieut G. R. Rickman.

CSM: H. E. Hellis.
CQMS: C/Sgt T. Harton.

Headquarter Company

OC: Major C. C. G. Milward.

RSO: Lieut M. G. Quinton.
MTO: Lieut C. M. Barrett.
CSM: WOII P. Reynolds.
CQMS: C/Sgt L. W. Taylor.

St George's Day 1947, Gibraltar
First Battalion

Commanding Officer:	Lieutenant Colonel J. A. Sperling DSO.
Second in Command:	Major T. F. C. Hamilton MC.
Adjutant:	Captain A. W. J. Such.
King's Colour:	Lieutenant T. B. Ashton.
Regimental Colour:	Second Lieutenant P. M. Woodroffe.
RSM:	WOI Johnson.

No. 1 Company	No. 2 Company
Captain G. W. Buttle.	Lieutenant C. J. Rundle.
No. 3 Company	No. 4 Company
Captain C. H. Hedley.	Captain J. J. Doyle.

St George's Day 1949, Gibraltar
First Battalion

Commanding Officer:	Lieutenant Colonel B. J. Leech DSO.
Second in Command:	Major P. M. G. Anley.
King's Colour:	Lieutenant J. W. Amos.
Regimental Colour:	Second Lieutenant J. Clarke-Turner.

No. 1 Company

Major R. F. B. Hensman.
Lieut J. W. Wilson.
2/Lt P. B. Spark.

No. 2 Company

Capt R. Leith-MacGregor DFC.
Capt R. M. Kershaw.
Lieut C. M. Barrett.

No. 3 Company

Capt R. S. Ferguson
Capt M. A. S. Grose.
Lieut R. E. Blenkinsop.

No. 4 Company

Major H. R. M. Wilkin.
Capt W. H. Ellery.
2 Lt S. A. S. Phillips.

October 1950, On embarkation to Korea
First Battalion

Commanding Officer: | Lieutenant Colonel K. O. N. Foster OBE.
Second in Command: | Major M. C. Spear.
Adjutant: | Major R. D. Brook.
A/Adjutant: | Lieutenant G. H. McEwan.
Intelligence Offr: | Lieutenant A. R. D. Perrins.
Quartermaster: | Major(QM) J. W. M. Purcell MBE.
RMO: | Captain C. W. Bowen RAMC.
Padre: | Captain R. G. Knox Wylie MBE, RAChD.
RSM: | WOI G. E. Richardson.
RQMS: | WOII Brown.
Drill CSM: | WOII Blower.

W Company

OC: Major C. H. Mitchell.
2 i/c: Capt A. M. H. Scott.
Platoon Commanders:
Lieut J. P. Lindsay.
Lieut J. Schofield.
Lieut W. S. Cooper.
CSM: WOII A. Tong.
CQMS: C/Sgt G. Connolly.

X Company

OC: Major R. M. Pratt.
2 i/c: Capt J. E. V. Butterfield.
Platoon Commanders:
Lieut J. M. Cubiss.
Lieut S. D. Draper.
2/Lt M. D. Young.
CSM: WOII P. J. Reynolds.
CQMS: C/Sgt T. Connolly.

Y Company

OC: Major R. Leith-
    MacGregor DFC.
2 i/c: Capt M. H. Lassetter.
Platoon Commanders:
Lieut A. Macnamara.
2/Lt S. A. S. Phillips.
2/Lt L. S. Adams-Acton.
CSM: WOII A. J. Hardisty.
CQMS: C/Sgt C. Chambers.

Z Company

OC: Major H. J. Winn MC.

2 i/c: Capt J. A. H. Pearson.
Platoon Commanders:
Lieut J. P. Baxter.
2/Lt H. D. Walker.

CSM: WOII E. J. Radcliffe.
CQMS: C/Sgt C. H. C. Lyons.

Support Company	Headquarter Company
OC: Major C. C. G. Milward.	OC: Major R. M. Kershaw
Platoon Commanders:	Platoon Commanders:
Capt. F. W. Chester (MMG).	Capt. M. A. S. Grose (RSO).
Lt. P. B. Williams (MMG).	Lt. M. N. Kearney (A/RSO).
Capt. R. E. Blenkinsop (Mor).	Lt. J. W. Wilson (MTO).
Lt. A. M. P. Dillon (Mor).	
Capt. J. W. Amos (A/Tk).	
Lt M. Parker.	
2/Lt G. M. Fitz-Gibbon (Pioneer).	
CSM: WOII S. Ambury.	CSM: WOII M. Blanchard.
CQMS: C/Sgt S. W. Baily.	CQMS: C/Sgt F. H. Burn.

May 1951, Korea
First Battalion

Commanding Officer:	Lieutenant Colonel M. C. Spear.
Second in Command:	Major R. M. Pratt DSO.
Adjutant:	Major R. D. Brook.
A/Adjutant:	Capt J. P. Lindsay.
Intelligence Offr:	Lieut M. N. Kearney.
Quartermaster:	Major(QM) J. W. M. Purcell MBE.
RMO:	Captain C. W. Bowen MC, RAMC.
RSM:	WOI G. E. Richardson.
RQMS:	WOII Brown.

W Company

OC: Capt A. M. H. Scott.
2 i/c: Lieut J. A. Yeo.
Platoon Commanders:
Lieut L. J. Beavis.
Lieut R. Price.
Lieut W. Doyle.
CSM: WOII A. Tong.
CQMS: C/Sgt G. Connolly.

X Company

OC: Major R. M. Kershaw.
2 i/c: Capt P. B. Williams.
Platoon Commanders:
Lieut J. M. Cubiss MC.
Lieut R. R. F. Cowe.
Lieut A. N. Jordan.
CSM: WOII P. J. Reynolds.
CQMS: C/Sgt T. Connolly.

Y Company

OC: Major R. Leith-MacGregor DFC.
2 i/c: Capt J. H. G. Deighton MC.
Platoon Commanders:
Lieut S. A. S. Phillips.
Lieut D. A. White.
Lieut M. M. G. Beach.
Lieut M. H. Haggard.
CSM: WOII A. J. Hardisty.
CQMS: C/Sgt C. Chambers.

Z Company

OC: Major J. H. A. Pearson.
2 i/c: Capt J. W. Amos.
Platoon Commanders:
Lieut J. P. Baxter.
2/Lt W. J. Sheppard MC.
2/Lt H. D. Walker.
2/Lt R. Hurlstone-Horton.
CSM: WOII E. J. Radcliffe.
CQMS: C/Sgt C. H. C. Lyons.

Support Company

OC: Maj. J. E. V. Butterfield.
Platoon Commanders:
Capt F. W. Chester (MMG).
Capt R. E. Blenkinsop (Mor).
Lieut P. L. Martin.
2/Lt J. Marshall.
CSM: WOII S. Ambury
CQMS: C/Sgt S. W. Baily.

Headquarter Company

OC: Capt M. H. Lassetter.
Platoon Commanders:
Capt M. A. S. Grose (RSO).
Capt J. W. Wilson (MTO).
Lieut M. D. Young.
Capt J. Schofield.
CSM: WOII M. Blanchard.
CQMS: C/Sgt F. H. Burn.

September 1951, Korea
First Battalion

Commanding Officer:	Lieutenant Colonel M. C. Spear.
Second in Command:	Major R. M. Pratt DSO.
Adjutant:	Captain M. H. Lassetter.
A/Adjutant:	Capt J. P. Lindsay.
RMO:	Lieutenant G. E. Langley RAMC.
Intelligence Offr:	Lieut M. N. Kearney.
Quartermaster:	Major(QM) J. W. M. Purcell MBE.

W Company

OC: Major R. D. Brook.
2 i/c: Capt J. L. Baume.
Platoon Commanders:
Lieut D. White.
Lieut J. A. Yeo.
Liut J. T. Beavis.

X Company

OC: Major R. M. Kershaw.
2 i/c: Capt M. A. S. Grose.
Platoon Commanders:
Lieut S. D. Draper.
Lieut R. R. F. Cowe.
Lieut A. N. Jordan.

Y Company

OC: Major J. E. V. Butterfield.
2 i/c: Capt J. H. G. Deighton. MC.

Platoon Commanders:
Lieut S. A. S. Phillips.
Lieut M. H. Haggard.
Lieut M. M. G. Beach.

Z Company

OC: Major H. J. Winn DSO MC.
2 i/c: Lieut. J. P. Baxter.

Platoon Commanders:
Lieut H. D. Walker.
Lieut W. P. Sheppard.
Lieut R. Hurlestone-Horton.

Support Company

OC: Major J. H. A. Pearson.

Platoon Commanders:
Capt F. W. Chester (MMG).
Capt R. E. Blenkinsop (Mor).
Capt P. B. Williams (MMG).

Headquarters Company

OC: Major R. Leith-MacGregor MC DFC.

Platoon Commanders:
Lieut A. J. Chaplin.
Capt J. W. Wilson (MTO).
Lieut M. D. Young (RSO).

180

Lieut R. M. H. Weeks (A/TK).
Lieut P. L. Martin (Pioneer).

October 1953, Kenya
First Battalion

Commanding Officer:	Lt Col R. E. T. St John MC.
Second in Command:	Major J. D. Buckle.
Adjutant:	Major R. D. Wilson MBE MC.
IO:	Lt D. Holmes.
A/Adjutant:	Lt E. P. Adams.
RMO:	Capt A. C. White RAMC.
Chaplain:	Rev. D. V. S. Asher CF.
RSM:	WOI G. E. Richardson.

X Company

OC: Major H. J. Winn DSO MC.
2 i/c: Capt J. P. Baxter.
Platoon Commanders:
2/Lt D. E. Corbett.
2/Lt R. Cobham.
2/Lt R. H. L. Althaus.

CSM: WOII F. Bingham.

Y Company

OC: Major G. W. Thornton.

2 i/c: Capt I. J. R. Bennett.
Platoon Commanders:
2/Lt D. E. H. Buckingham.
2/Lt R. St L. Gordon-Steward.
2/Lt A. L. Hutchinson.
2/Lt C. Yeoman.
CSM: WOII A. Stubbs.

Z Company

OC: Major P. Bulman.
2 i/c: Capt H. D. Walker.
Platoon Commanders:
2/Lt D. H. Welch.
2/Lt A. J. R. Fairclough.
2/Lt J. H. Baty.
CSM: WOII F. H. Burn.

Support Company

OC: Major R. F. B. Hensman.
2 i/c: Capt P. T. Ward.
Platoon Commanders:
Lt R. R. F. Cowe.
2/Lt T. Charlesworth.
2/Lt J. D. G. Wagstaffe.
CSM: WOII R. E. Harrison.

Headquarter Company

OC:	Major G. Rickman.
QM:	Capt (QM) P. W. Bell MBE MM.

PRI:	Capt J. M. Webb.
RSO:	Capt. A. M. H. Scott.
	Lt A. K. C. Hill.
	2/Lt G. G. Campbell.
RQMS:	WOII M. D. Blanchard.
CSM:	WOII C. A. D. Bailey.
CQMS:	C/Sgt H. Hobbs.
Supernumerary:	WOII T. Connolly.

September 1954, Kenya
First Battalion

Commanding Officer: Lt Col R. E. T. St John MC.
Second in Command: Major R. F. B. Hensman.
Adjutant: Capt R. G. Style.
IO: 2/Lt J. S. Baty.
RMO: Capt S. J. Rogers RAMC.
Chaplain: Rev. D. V. S. Asher CF.
RSM: WOI F. Bingham.

X Company

OC: Major H. J. Winn DSO MC.
2i/c: Capt J. P. Baxter.
Platoon Commanders:
2/Lt D. E. Corbett.
2/Lt R. Cobham.
2/Lt M. R. C. V. Browne.
2/Lt R. K. Middlemas.
CSM: WOII C. Riley.
CQMS: C/Sgt H. Hobbs.

Y Company

OC: Major D. F. T. Colbeck.
2 i/c: Lt E. P. Adams.
Platoon Commanders:
Lt D. E. H. Buckingham.
2/Lt A. E. Hutchinson.
2/Lt W. D. H. Smith.
2/Lt C. K. Smith.
CSM: WOII J. D. Bailey.
CQMS: C/Sgt I. A. Hepton.

Z Company

OC: Capt H. D. Walker.
2 i/c: Lt J. W. Moncur.
Platoon Commanders:
Lt D. H. Welch.
2/Lt A. J. R. Fairclough.
2/Lt C. Yeoman.

CSM: WOII F. H. Burn.
CQMS: C/Sgt H. Thorpe.

Support Company

OC: Major P. S. Ward.
2 i/c: Capt R. R. F. Cowe.
Platoon Commanders:
Lt D. Holmes.
Lt A. K. C. Hill.
2/Lt J. D. G. Wagstaffe.
2/Lt J. A. Yewall.
CSM: WOII K. E. M. Baker.
CQMS: C/Sgt H. C. H. Weatherdon.

Headquarter Company

OC:	Major P. Bulman.
QM:	Major (QM) P. W. Bell MBE MM.
RSO:	Capt A. M. H. Scott.
	2/Lt G. S. Crawshaw.
	2/Lt G. G. Campbell.
RQMS:	WOII M. D. Blanchard.
CSM:	WOII T. Connolly.
CQMS:	C/Sgt H. Hobbs.

St George's Day 1957, Northern Ireland
First Battalion

Commanding Officer:	Lieutenant Colonel W. A. C. Collingwood MBE.
Second in Command:	Major P. V. Cowley.
Adjutant:	Captain C. M. Barrett.
Queen's Colour:	Lieutenant D. M. Thompson.
Regimental Colour:	Second Lieutenant D. M. B. Yorke.
Drummers' Colour:	Boy Duke.

No. 1 Company

Captain E. P. Adams.

No. 2 Company

Lieutenant A. K. C. Hill.

No. 3 Company

Lt R. St L. Gordon-Steward.

No. 4 Company

Lieutenant J. B. Oakley.

St George's Day 1958, Munster
First Battalion

Commanding Officer:	Lieutenant Colonel R. F. B. Hensman OBE.
Second in Command:	Major R. D. Brook MC.
Adjutant:	Captain M. D. Young MC.
Queen's Colour:	Second Lieutenant A. F. A. Parsons.
Regimental Colour:	Second Lieutenant I. L. Cummin.
Drummers' Colour:	Fusilier R. Thompson.
RSM:	WOI P. J. Reynolds.

No. 1 Company

Captain E. P. Adams.

No. 2 Company

Lieutenant J. B. Oakley.

No. 3 Company

Lieutenant D. R. G. Seidl.

No. 4 Company

Lieutenant J. A. H. Sanderson.

March 1959, Hong Kong
First Battalion

Commanding Officer: Lt Col R. F. B. Hensman OBE.
Second in Command: Major R. G. Style.
Adjutant: Capt M. D. Young MC.
A/Adjutant & IO: 2/Lt J. E. M. Kitching.
Quartermaster: Capt (QM) F. Bingham.
Tech QM: Lt (QM) F. H. Burn.
RMO: Lt J. Porter RAMC.
Paymaster: Major B. G. Griffiths RAPC.

W Company

OC: Capt M. R. Dixon.
2 i/c: 2/Lt I. L. Cummin.

X Company

OC: Major A. M. H. Scott.
2 i/c: Lt D. M. Thompson.
Platoon Commanders:
2/Lt A. I A. Parsons.
2/Lt E. S. Colson.

Y Company

OC: Capt R. R. F. Cowe.
2 i/c: Capt A. K. C. Hill.
Platoon Commanders:
2/Lt P. H. D. Marr.
2/Lt D. W. Thompson.

Z Company

OC: Major J. P. Baxter.
2 i/c: Lt A. C. Hope.
Platoon Commanders:
2/Lt M. Dobson.
2/Lt R. P. T. Earle.
2/Lt G. Bodin.

Support Company

OC: Major F. W. Chester
RSO: Lt D. R. G. Seidl.
A/TK Pl: Lt J. A. Sanderson.
MMG Pl: Lt H. J. W. Masters.
Mor PL: Lt J. B. Oakley

Headquarter Company

OC: Major J. W. Amos.
PRI: Capt P. T. Ward.
MTO: Capt E. P. Adams.

July 1962, Lemgo
First Battalion

Commanding Officer:	Lieutenant Colonel R. Leith-MacGregor MC DFC.
Second in Command:	Major F. Ward MC.
Adjutant:	Captain D. H. Welch.
Intelligence Officer:	Lieutenant R. Luxton-Jones.
Quartermaster:	Lieutenant (QM) F. H. Burn.
Tech QM:	Lieutenant (QM) A. F. J. Alley.
RMO:	Captain A. Taylor RAMC.
Paymaster:	Major B. G. Griffiths RAPC.
Station Staff Officer:	Captain D. E. H. Buckingham.
Padre:	Rev. W. J. Williams RAChD.

W Company

OC: Capt A. F. A. Parsons

X Company

OC: Major J. W. Wilson
2 i/c: Capt J. B. Oakley
Platoon Commanders:
Lt P. C. Le Mesurier.
Lt E. S. Colson.
2Lt N. G. D. Robinson.
2Lt H. F. C. Woodburn.

Y Company

OC: Major C. M. Barrett
2 i/c: Capt R. St L. Gordon-Steward.
Platoon Commanders:
Lt C. R. W. Wysock-Wright.
2Lt P. Bucknall.
2Lt T. J. de C. Brown.
2Lt P. Robinson.

Z Company

OC: Major J. W. Deane.
2 i/c: Capt D. M. Thompson.

Platoon Commanders:
Lt I. C. Dobson.
2Lt C. D. Robertson.
2Lt C. F. Jackson.
2Lt M. P. Aiken.

Headquarter Company

OC:	Major J. S. Baty.
2 i/c:	Captain J. A. H. Sanderson.
RSO:	Captain J. E. M. Kitching.
Recce:	Captain H. J. W. Masters.
Edn Offr:	Lieutenant J. Rainsford RAEC.

February 1963, Lemgo
First Battalion

Commanding Officer: Lieutenant Colonel R. G. Style.
Second in Command: Major R. E. Blenkinsop.
Adjutant: Captain J. B. Oakley.
A/Adjutant: Lt E. S. Colson.
Intelligence Officer: Lt R. Luxton-Jones.
RSM: WOI G. Connolly.
Chief Clerk: Sgt. J. Charlton.

W Company

OC: Major J. S. Baty.

Edn Offr: Lt J. Rainsford.

X Company

OC: Major J. W. Wilson.
2 i/c: Capt H. J. W. Masters.
Platoon Commanders:
Lt P. C. Le Mesurier.
Lt P. J. C. Robinson.
Lt C. H. F. C. Woodburn.
2/Lt R. G. Buckton.

Y Company

OC: Major C. M. Barrett.
2 i/c: Capt D. H. Welch.
Platoon Commanders:
Lt T. J. de C. Brown.
Lt C. R. Wysock-Wright.
2/Lt P. C. Bucknall.
2/Lt S. Milne.

Z Company

OC: Major J. W. Deane.
2 i/c: Capt D. M. Thompson.
Platoon Commanders:
Lt C. F. Jackson.
Lt I. C. Dobson.
2/Lt M. P. Aiken.
2/Lt R. G. Parsons.

Headquarter Company.

OC: Major A. M. H. Scott.
2 i/c: Capt J. A. H. Sanderson.
RSO: Capt J. E. M. Kitching.
Recce: Capt R. St L. Gordon-Steward.
Quartermaster: Lt (QM) F. H. Burn.

RMO:	Capt A. J. Taylor RAMC.
Paymaster:	Major B. G. Griffiths RAPC.
MTO:	Lt (QM) A. F. J. Alley.
SSO:	Capt D. E. H. Buckingham.
Padre:	Rev. J. Williams RAChD.

December 1964, Lemgo
First Battalion

Commanding Officer:	Lieutenant Colonel R. G. Style.
Second in Command:	Major J. P. Baxter.
Adjutant:	Captain D. M. Thompson.
IO:	Lt T. J. de C. Brown.
RSM:	WOI R. V. Whitaker.
Chief Clerk:	Sgt. J. Charlton.

W Company

OC: Capt C. F. Jackson.

CSM: WOII P. M. Hoare.
CQMS: C/Sgt B. Malthouse.

X Company

OC: Major N. H. Leadsom.
2 i/c: Capt A. C. Hope.
Platoon Commanders:
2/Lt A. S. H. Thompson.
2/Lt M. A. K. Forster.
CSM: WOII W. P. Pringle.
CQMS: C/Sgt W. T. Spiers.

Y Company

OC: Major M. D. Young MC.
2 i/c: Capt P. H. D. Marr.
Platoon Commanders:
2/Lt D. Cruickshank.
2/Lt D. W. G. Riddick.
Lt C. F. Woodburn.

CSM: WOII D. Gardiner.
CQMS: C/Sgt R. Revell.

Z Company

OC: Major A. K. C. Hill
2 i/c: Capt C. R. W. Wysock-Wright.
Platoon Commanders:
Lt W. Hughes Jones RMP.
2/Lt C. N. B. Wellwood.
2/Lt R. P. D. Brook.
2/Lt J. M. Youll.
CSM: WOII J. A. Hennon.
CQMS: C/Sgt A. Willis.

Headquarter Company.

OC:	Major T. Tarmey.
2 i/c:	Lt G. Hayes.
RSO:	Lt A. C. Stutchbury R Sigs.
Quartermaster:	Lt (QM) F. H. Burn.

RMO:	Capt C. Boland RAMC.
Paymaster:	Major A. E. C. Elliott RAPC.
MTO:	Capt (QM) A. P. Elliott.
SSO:	Lt G. Hayes.
Padre:	Rev. P. H. F. Scott RAChD.
RQMS:	WOII D. D. Brown.
TQMS:	WOII C. Brown.
CSM:	WOII L. J. Lamb BEM.
CQMS:	C/Sgt G. Prior.
LAD	
OC:	Capt B. Marsden REME.
ASM:	WOI I. B. Tinsley REME.
AQMS:	WOII D. J. Turner REME.

May 1967, Aden
First Battalion

Commanding Officer:	Lieutenant Colonel R. E. Blenkinsop OBE.
Second in Command:	Major J. P. Baxter.
Adjutant:	Captain A. F. A. Parsons.
A/Adjutant and Intelligence Officer:	Captain N. G. D. Robinson.
Quartermaster(1):	Captain (QM) F. Burn.
Quartermaster(2):	Captain (QM) A. P. Elliott.
RMO:	Captain A. D. McNeal RAMC.
Paymaster:	Major A. C. E. Elliott RAPC.
RSM:	WOI R. Forrest.
Chief Clerk:	WOII H. Thorpe.

W Company

OC: Major A. C. Hope.

Bandmaster: WOI J. Pope.
Drum Major: S/Sgt T. Hood.

CSM: WOII D. J. Gardiner.

X Company

OC: Major C. E. Welch.
2 i/c: Capt T. J. de C. Brown.

Platoon Commanders:
Lt J. Price.
2/Lt M. M. Rushton.
2/Lt S. J. T. Colbeck.
Lt P. Bucknall.
CSM: WOII W. Pringle.

Y Company

OC: Major J. Moncur.

Platoon Commanders:
Lt D. W. G. Riddick.
2/Lt D. J. M. Daniels.
2/Lt J. R. Shaw.
Lt D. Cruickshank.
2/Lt J. Davies.
CSM: WOII Hoare.

Z Company

OC: Major R. R. F. Cowe.
2i/c: Captain C. Jackson.

Platoon Commanders:
Lt R. P. D. Brook.
Lt G. H. Millar.
Lt D. E. Green.
2/Lt R. V. C. Brown.
2/Lt D. M. Kershaw.
CSM: WOII Hennon.

Headquarter Company

OC: Captain J. A. Campbell.

RSO: Captain G. L. Stemp.

Recce: Lieutenant R. G. Parsons.

Edn Offr: Lieutenant G. Smith RAEC.

Padre: Captain Stacy RAChD.

MTO: Captain P. H. D. Marr.

OC Air Platoon: Captain P. T. Jones R Sigs.

       Lt J. R. Hordern.

Special Branch Officer: Captain P. J. C. Robinson.

CSM: WOII V. G. Wear.

Mukeiras Detachment

Capt R. P. T. Earle.

October 1967, Kirton-in-Lindsey
First Battalion

Commanding Officer:	Lieutenant Colonel R. E. Blenkinsop OBE.
Second in Command:	Major R. R. F. Cowe.
Adjutant:	Captain N. G. D. Robinson.
A/Adjutant and	
Intelligence Officer:	Lieutenant G. M. Youll.
Quartermaster(1):	Captain (QM) A. P. Elliott.
Quartermaster(2):	Captain (QM) J. Adamson.
RMO:	Captain A. P. O'Connor.
Paymaster:	Major A. C. E. Elliott RAPC.
RSM:	WOI R. Forrest.
Chief Clerk:	WOII H. Thorpe.

W Company

OC: Capt R. P. T. Earle.

Bandmaster:
WOI J. Pope.
Drum Major:
S/Sgt T. Hood.

CSM: WOII D. J. Gardiner.

X Company

OC: Major C. E. Welch.
2 i/c: Capt T. J. de C. Brown.

Platoon Commanders:
Lt R. Buckton.
2Lt M. M. Rushton.
2Lt S. J. T. Colbeck.
2Lt R. Baron.

CSM: WOII W. Pringle.

Y Company

OC: Capt. N. C. Brown.
Platoon Commanders:
Lt D. W. G. Riddick.
2Lt D. J. M. Daniels.
2Lt J. R. Shaw.

CSM: WOII Tomenson.

Z Company

OC: Major J. B. Oakley.
Platoon Commanders:
Lt R. P. D. Brook.
Lt G. H. Millar.
Lt D. E. Green MBE.
2Lt R. V. C. Brown.
2Lt D. M. Kershaw.

CSM: WOII M. Goodger.

Headquarter Company.

OC:	Major A. K. C. Hill.
2 i/c:	Captain P. H. D. Marr.
RSO:	Captain G. L. Stemp.
Recce:	Lieutenant R. G. Parsons.
Edn Offr:	Lieutenant G. Smith RAEC.
Padre:	Captain W. B. Mitchell RAChD.
PRI:	Captain J. A. Campbell.
Families Officer:	Lieutenant J. Hoare.
CSM: WOII V. G. Wear.	
RQMS:	WOII J. A. Hennon.
Buildings WO:	WOII G. C. Prior.
Cook WO:	WOII Atherton, ACC.

St George's Day, 1968
First Battalion

Commanding Officer:	Lt Col R. E. Blenkinsop OBE.
Second in Command:	Major R. R. F. Cowe.
Adjutant:	Capt N. G. D. Robinson.
IO:	Lt G. M. Youll.
Quartermaster:	Capt (QM) J. Adamson.
Tech QM:	Capt (QM) A. P. Elliott.
RMO:	Capt A. P. O. O'Connor RAMC.
Paymaster:	Major A. C. E. Elliott RAPC.
RSM:	WOI R. Forrest.
Padre:	Rev W. B. Mitchell RAChD.

X Company

OC: Major J. H. C. Hordern.
2 i/c: Capt T. J. de C Brown.
Platoon Commanders:
Lt S. J. T. Colbeck.
2/Lt M. M. Rushton.
2/Lt R. Baron.

CSM: WOII N. Ward.
CQMS: C/Sgt H. A. Lofthouse.

Y Company

OC: Major D. R. G. Seidl.
2 i/c: Lt G. H. Millar.
Platoon Commanders:
2/Lt D. J. M. Daniels.
2/Lt J. R. Shaw.
2/Lt W. J. Blower.
2/Lt T. V. Merritt.

CSM: WOII S. Tomenson
CQMS: C/Sgt J. J. Spencer.

Sergeants

Oliver, Kirby, Orchard & Stevenson.

Law, Doyle, Heslop & Hall.

Z Company

OC: Major J. B. Oakley
2 i/c: Capt R. P. T. Earle.
Platoon Commanders:
Lt D. E. Green MBE.
2/Lt R. V. C. Brown.
2/Lt D. M. Kershaw.

Support Company

OC: Major N. C. Brown.

Platoon Commanders:
Lt R. P. D. Brook.
Bandmaster J. Pope.
Band WO P. G. Hutchings.

CSM: WOII M. Goodger.

CQMS: C/Sgt P. O'Toole.

CSM: WOII D. J. Gardiner.

CQMS: C/Sgt B. Malthouse.

D/Maj T. Hood.

S/Sgt L. Buckley.

Sergeants

Bell, Clough, Hayman & Hellens.

McDonald, O'Brien, Stenhouse, Lowes, Moss, Rowlands, Cappleman, Lafferty, Brown & Hebden.

Headquarter Company

OC: Major N. C. Brown.

2 i/c: Capt G. L. Stemp.

RSO: Lt D. Strong R Sigs.

A/RSO: Lt R. G. Buckton.

OC Air Pl: Capt J. R. Hordern.

LAD: Capt R. H. Unwin REME.

MTO: Lt D. D. Brown.

MQAS: Lt J. Hoare.

Recce: Lt R. G. Parsons.

UEO: Lt G. Smith REME.

CSM: WOII V. Wear.

RQMS: WOII J. Hennon.

TQMS: WOII W. Pringle.

Accom. WO: WOII C. Prior.

ASM: WOI J. L. Barnes.

LAD WO: WOII C. Vickers.

ACC WO: WOII H. Atherton.

W (Training) Company

OC: Capt P. H. D. Marr.

Training Sergeants:

Pick and Armstrong.

Colour and Staff Sergeants: J. Charlton, D. Shields.

Sergeants: Armstrong, Brownlie, Christy, Douglas, Duke, Gilmore, Goodlet, Hempshall, Holliday, Howell, Langan, Robertson, and Whyte.

St George's Day Parade, 1968

Commanding Officer:	Lieutenant Colonel R. E. Blenkinsop OBE.
Second in Command:	Major R. R. F. Cowe.
Adjutant:	Captain N. G. D. Robinson.
RSM:	WOI R. Forrest.
Bandmaster:	WOI A. Pope

No. 1 (Colour) Company

Captain P. H. D. Marr.
CSM: WOII Goodger.

No. 2 Company

Lieutenant R. P. D. Brook.
CSM: WOII Tomenson.

No. 3 Company

Lieutenant D. E. Green MBE.
CSM: WOII Gardiner.

No. 4 Company

Second Lieutenant R. Baron.
CSM: WOII Ward.
CSM: WOII Wear.

Queen's Colour:	Lieutenant S. J. T. Colbeck.
Regimental Colour:	Second Lieutenant D. M. Kershaw.
Drums Colour:	Fusilier W. D. Robson.
Padre:	Rev. W. B. Mitchell RAChD.

TA Battalions Orders of Battle
December 1963

Newcastle-upon-Tyne, 4th/5th Battalion of the Royal Northumberland Fusiliers, Territorial Army

Commanding Officer:	Lieutenant Colonel F. Ward MC.
Second in Command:	Major J. M. Webb.
Adjutant/Training Officer:	Major D. R. G. Seidl.
Intelligence Officer:	Lieutenant T. J. Buchanan.
RMO:	Major E. D. Mackie RAMC.
RSM:	WOI J. Gidman LF.
ORQMS:	WOII F. W. Fenwick.
Chaplain:	Rev J. F. Gunning.

Headquarter Company (Walker)

OC:	Major L. Harking.
2 i/c:	Captain D. Beattie.
QM:	Captain(QM) F. E. Stevens.
Recce Platoon:	Captain G. M. Youll.
RSO:	Captain R. O. Matthews.
MTO:	Captain(QM) J. W. Sanderson.
Paymaster:	Second Lieutenant G. C. Nicholls RAPC.
Bandmaster:	WOI S. B. Milburn.
RQMS:	WOII R. W. Allen.
CSM:	WOII D. R. Jones.
Assault Pioneers:	WOII Robinson.

W Company (Prudhoe and Hexham)

OC:	Major D. A. Ridley.
2 i/c:	Captain I. F. Davidson.
Platoon Commanders:	Lieutenant P. J. McWhirter.
	Second Lieutenant J. Toulmin.
CSM:	WOII N. Roberts.

X Company (Newburn)

OC:	Major B. J. Elliott.
2 i/c:	Captain H. L. Bullen.
CSM:	WOII A. E. W. Black.
PSI:	WOII J. D. Bailey.

Y Company (Walker)

OC:	Major P. W. D. Vaughan.
2 i/c:	Captain T. Johnston.
Platoon Commanders:	Second Lieutenant D. S. Miller.
	Second Lieutenant A. J. Oliver.
CSM:	WOII W. E. Davidson MBE.

Z Company (Walker)

OC:	Major R. W. Mordue.
2 i/c:	Lieutenant P. H. Shaw.
Platoon Commander:	Second Lieutenant M. M. Davis.
CSM:	WOII D. Walsham.

Newcastle-upon-Tyne
6th (City) Territorial Battalion

Commanding Officer:	Lieutenant Colonel M. H. Van Gruisen TD.
Second in Command:	Major R. E. O. Waddell TD.
Training Major:	Major E. P. Adams.
Admin Officer:	Captain R. H. Herbertson.
Adjutant:	Captain R. M. Mullens.
RSM:	WOI D. Million.

A Company

OC:	Captain D. W. Horne.
Platoon Commanders:	Lieutenant J. A. Cooper.
	Second Lieutenant S. A. Robinson.
PSI:	Sergeant P. J. M. Cosgrave.

B Company

OC:	Major C. S. Todd TD.
2 i/c:	Captain M. A. Swallow.
Platoon Commanders:	Lieutenant S. D. Rutherford.
	Second Lieutenant A. G. Rutherford.

C Company

OC:	Major G. C. Wilkinson TD.
2 i/c:	Captain J. R. Kirkup.
Platoon Commanders:	Lieutenant J. Muir.
	Lieutenant H. R. Mould.
	Second Lieutenant D. G. Leslie.
PSI:	Sergeant G. Heslop.
Recruit Cadre	
OC:	Lieutenant G. W. Ridley.
PSI:	WOII K. Dalby.

Headquarter Company

OC:	Major T. T. Ritson.
RSO:	Captain T. H. Ogle.
Recce:	Lieutenant G. W. Meikle.
	Second Lieutenant B. I. Charsley.
Quartermaster:	Lieutenant (QM) J. Barlow.
RMO:	Major M. L. Fisher RAMC.
Paymaster:	Captain R. E. Young RAPC.
Padre:	Rev. A. C. Beniams RAChD.
PSI:	WOII R. A. Wade.
Supernumerary:	Captain J. D Kirkham.
	Captain J. L. Smith.
	Captain A. W. A. Oliver.
	Lieutenant G. M. Walker.
	Second Lieutenant D. Scott Phillips.

Alnwick
7th Territorial Battalion

Commanding Officer:	Lieutenant Colonel W. C. H. Sanderson.
Second in Command:	Major F. L. Potts.
Training Major:	Major J. S. Baty.
Adjutant:	Captain F. A. Calvert.
RMO:	Major K. A. Stone RAMC.
Padre:	Rev. A. J. Meakin RAChD.
PSO:	Captain R. Campbell.
RSM:	WOI J. Hoare.

A Company (Morpeth)

OC:	Captain S. M. Calvert.
2 i/c:	Second Lieutenant T. D. Stirk.
Platoon Commanders:	Second Lieutenant G. R. Proudlock.
	Second Lieutenant P. N. Q. Swales.
PSI:	Sergeant R. Armstrong.

B Company (Ashington)

OC:	Captain R. Scott.
Platoon Commanders:	Lieutenant C. A. Streets.
	Second Lieutenant J. R. Mackenzie.
	Second Lieutenant A. C. Robson.
CSM:	WOII G. Hamilton.
PSI:	WOII H. Wilson.

C Company (Amble)

OC:	Major P. O. R. Bridgeman.
2 i/c:	Lieutenant D. M. B. Yorke.
Platoon Commanders:	Lieutenant the Hon. C. E. Baring.
	Lieutenant R. Fryer.
	Lieutenant J. P. Bell.
	Second Lieutenant M. J. McHugh.
CSM:	WOII W. F. Guy.

PSI: Sergeant A. Davenport.

D Company (Berwick-on-Tweed)

OC: Major C. A. F. Baker-Creswell.
Platoon Commanders: Second Lieutenant J. J. M. Edwards.
                              Second Lieutenant D. R. McCreath.
CSM: WOII A. T. Mackenzie.
PSI: WOII E. J. Delay.

Headquarter Company (Alnwick)

OC: Captain J. M. W. Burn.
2i/c: Captain J. S. Calvert.
RSO: Lieutenant R. G. Turnbull.
Recce: Second Lieutenant P. N. Roberts.
Quartermaster: Captain (QM) A. P. Elliott.
CSM: WOII G. R. Henderson.
PSI: Sergeant W. J. Howe.

List of Contributors

Baxter, Lieutenant Colonel Paddy.

Bland, Arthur.

Bowen, Colonel Cecil, MC RAMC.

Buckingham, Major D. E. H.

Carr, Ian (His contribution was extracted from the book *All Bull* with his kind permission).

Chester, Major Charles.

Cowe, Lieutenant Colonel Ronnie.

Deighton, Colonel John, OBE MC.

Garner, Sergeant George.

Hazeldine, George.

Hemsley, Fusilier David.

Hill, Major Alan, JP.

Hordern, Major John.

Hulme, J.

Laing, Gerald.

Leith-MacGregor, Lieutenant Colonel Robert, MC DFC.

Little, Preston.

Miller, Fusilier Gilbert.

Mills, Corporal.

Neeson, A.

Oakley, Major John.

Parsons, Robert.

Prout, Dennis H.

Rutherford, Colonel A. G., OBE.

St John, Major General Roger, CB MC.

Seidl, Colonel Danny, OBE.

Stemp, Major Lindsay.

Style, Colonel Gerald.

Symons, John.

Thompson, J. J.

Thompson, Major David.

Turner, Fusilier Ray.

Waddell, Lieutenant Colonel R. E. O., TD.

Walker, R.

Walton Masters, Captain John.

Wilson, Major General Dare, CBE MC DL.

Webb, Lieutenant Colonel John, DL.

White, Sergeant A.

Wysock-Wright, Major Christopher.

Appendix D

Abbreviations and Army Ranks

Abbreviations

BEM: British Empire Medal.

Cpl: Corporal.

CQMS: Company Quartermaster Sergeant.

C/Sgt: Colour Sergeant.

CSM: Company Sergeant Major (WOII).

DFC: Distinguished Flying Cross.

DL: Deputy Lieutenant (of a County).

DSO: Distinguished Service Order.

GC: George Cross.

LCpl: Lance Corporal.

LF: Lancashire Fusiliers (The Twentieth).

Lt: Lieutenant.

2nd Lt: Second Lieutenant.

Lt Col: Lieutenant Colonel.

MBE: Member of the British Empire.

MC: Military Cross.

MM: Military Medal.

NCOs: Non-commissioned Officers.

OBE: Order of the British Empire.

ORQMS: Orderly Room Quartermaster Sergeant (WOII).

QM: Quartermaster.

RAChD.   Royal Army Chaplains' Department.

RAPC: Royal Army Pay Corps.

REME: Royal Electrical and Mechanical Engineers.

RQMS: Regimental Quartermaster Sergeant (WOII.).

RSM: Regimental Sergeant Major (WOI.)

R Sigs: Royal Signals.

S/Sgt: Staff Sergeant.

TD: Territorial Decoration.

VC: Victoria Cross.

WOI: Warrant Officer Class One.

WOII: Warrant Officer Class Two.

Army Ranks

Officers

Field Marshal.

General.

Lieutenant General.

Major General.

Brigadier.

Colonel.

Lieutenant Colonel.

Major.

Captain.

Lieutenant.

Second Lieutenant.

Non-Commissioned Officers and Other Ranks.

Regimental Sergeant Major (WOI).

Regimental Quartermaster Sergeant. (WOII).

Orderly Regimental Quartermaster Sergeant (WOII).

Company Sergeant Major (WOII).

Company Quartermaster Sergeant.

Colour Sergeant

Staff Sergeant.

Sergeant.

Corporal.

Lance Corporal.

Fusilier (Private).

Index